25 YEARS OF LIMESTONE COLLEGE MEN'S LACROSSE

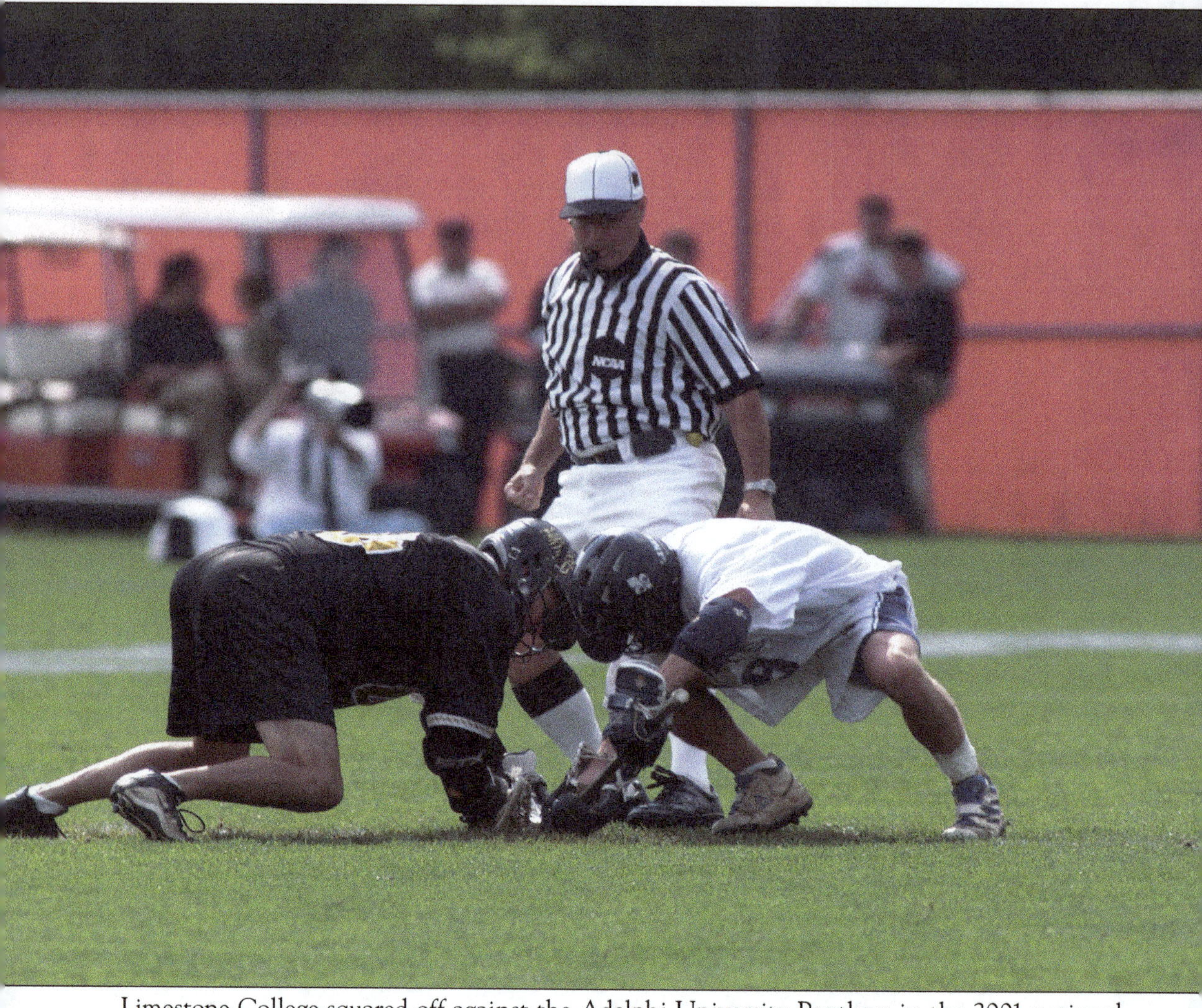

Limestone College squared off against the Adelphi University Panthers in the 2001 national championship game, hoping to bring home a second straight title. (Courtesy of Sports Information Department archives.)

Front Cover: The 2014 NCAA Division II national championship game (courtesy of Stacey Wylie; see page 82).

Upper Back Cover: First team picture in 1990 (author's collection; see page 11).

Lower Back Cover: From left to right: Pregame huddle (author's collection; see page 12), drawing up a play (author's collection; see page 13), pregame prayer (courtesy of Stacey Wylie; see page 87).

25 YEARS OF LIMESTONE COLLEGE MEN'S LACROSSE

Ben Price
Introduction by Dr. Walt Griffin

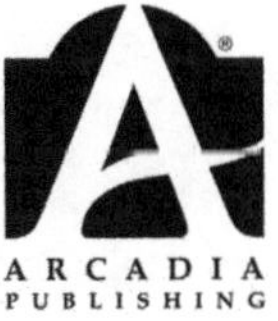

ISBN 9781540214270

Published by Arcadia Publishing
Charleston, South Carolina

Library of Congress Control Number: 2016945431

For all general information, please contact Arcadia Publishing:
Telephone 843-853-2070
Fax 843-853-0044
E-mail sales@arcadiapublishing.com
For customer service and orders:
Toll-Free 1-888-313-2665

Visit us on the Internet at www.arcadiapublishing.com

To each and every person who has supported Limestone lacrosse and helped make it what it is today.

Contents

Acknowledgments

For over 25 years, men's lacrosse at Limestone College has been a staple of the Gaffney, South Carolina, community. Hundreds of young men have made their way to this town to pursue an education and play lacrosse for one of the most dominant teams in all of college sports, and we have these men to thank for producing the materials in this book.

The completion of this book would not have been possible without fact-checking help and knowledge of the program from several who have spent much of their lives working with Limestone lacrosse. A special thank-you goes to Mike Cerino and Chris Phenicie for taking the time to identify countless players, locations, years, and dates.

It would be impossible to not mention the Limestone Sports Information Department, which has stored these images and thousands more over the years. The majority of these pictures were captured by various members of the sports information office, often by student assistants and volunteers. This book is a testament to their hard work and the many tough hours put in on the job. More thanks to those former players who were able and kind enough to send in pictures of their own from their respective playing days, many of which made it into this book. Additionally, thank you to media outlets *The Gaffney Ledger*, *The Cherokee Chronicle*, and Spartanburg *Herald-Journal* for all of your coverage of Limestone lacrosse and Limestone athletics and for so often providing an easy information database when other records were not kept.

On a final note, an effort was made to include as many various players and coaches who have made a special impact on Limestone lacrosse while still keeping to the relevancy and limits of this book. We extend our sincerest apologies that we were unable to identify and include each individual who has played his or her own role in building this legacy.

All images not credited to a specific photographer belong to the Sports Information Department archives.

INTRODUCTION

The year was 1989.

The cost of a first-class stamp was 25¢. A gallon of regular unleaded gasoline was just under a dollar. The price of a movie ticket was $3.99.

George H. Bush succeeded Ronald Regan as the 41st president of the United States. *Batman*, starring Michael Keaton, was dominating the box office. The San Francisco 49ers defeated the Cincinnati Bengals 20-16 in Super Bowl XXIII. Artists such as Chicago, Janet Jackson, Paula Abdul, and Milli Vanilli were burning up the radio airwaves.

And a small college in Gaffney, South Carolina, with fewer than 300 students and many deteriorating buildings, announced a somewhat curious decision that would end up altering the future of the school.

Limestone was adding a men's lacrosse team.

Lacrosse? In the heart of the South, where football was king, the college was bringing on a sport largely played in the Northeast. The first college lacrosse team in the state of South Carolina was going to reside in Cherokee County, situated on Interstate 85 between Greenville and Charlotte.

Many wondered why.

But Dave Rilling, Limestone's vice president for financial affairs at the time, knew that for the college's enrollment numbers to move upward, intercollegiate athletics was the answer. And lacrosse would start the reawakening for Saints athletics and Limestone as a whole.

At Pfeiffer College in Misenheimer, North Carolina, Rilling was instrumental in bringing lacrosse to that campus. One of the players on Pfeiffer's inaugural team was Mike Cerino. Five years later, Rilling, who had joined the administrative staff at Limestone in 1986, helped establish Saints lacrosse and Cerino was hired as the first coach.

Many of the doubters still loomed when Cerino, a young, largely unproven New York native, was brought in to construct the lacrosse program from scratch. But Cerino quieted the critics as he quickly started building a recruiting pipeline to Limestone, thanks to his ties to the Northeast and his knowledge of the South. He assembled a team of youngsters who would join him in an area where lacrosse was still largely an unfamiliar sport.

It was certainly a leap of faith for those players who traveled hundreds of miles from home to play for an upstart team with no history at a school that had only modest athletic success, save for an NAIA men's golf championship in 1984.

And as expected, growing pains were constant in the beginning. The often unbearable South Carolina heat was a new adversary for the natives of Long Island and New Jersey who experienced their first summer at Limestone. And the team rookies would have a rough go of it against much older, stronger, and quicker teams on a weekly basis.

The Saints went through grueling workouts heading into the fall of 1989, when they surprised many in exhibition games against club teams in the region. The competition during the 1990 spring season, however, would be much different.

Limestone traveled to the Virginia Military Institute for the program's first official men's lacrosse game, but the outcome was one to forget for the Blue & Gold. VMI rolled to an 18-5 victory, and Limestone's next three outings were not much better.

Sitting at 0-4 to start the inaugural season, Limestone traveled to Vanderbilt University to face the Commodores' club team—and the season took a drastic turn in Nashville. The Saints surprised Vanderbilt 13-12 to claim the program's first win, and the squad showed steady improvement the rest of the year. The win against Vanderbilt was the first of three straight, including a 29-0 thumping of the Furman University club team. Limestone went on to win six of its final eight games to finish the season at 6-6—an almost unthinkable achievement for a first-year program cutting its collective teeth south of the Mason-Dixon line.

While the 1990 schedule featured several club teams that were not quite up to the standards of NCAA squads, things got tougher in 1991 with a schedule featuring some of the nation's best. After going 1-9 that year, the next several years saw Limestone take significant steps forward. In 1993, Limestone played its first year as an official member of NCAA Division II, and the Saints achieved the program's first winning season at 7-4 overall. A signature victory over Lynchburg College and a narrow one-goal loss to New York Tech signaled that the Saints were becoming serious competitors.

That momentum seemed to stall in 1996 and 1997, as Limestone finished with records of 6-6 and 7-6, respectively. Although the Saints proved they were capable of beating many quality teams and making it tough on others, the team just couldn't seem to get over the hump and into the national spotlight. But that was about to change.

The Saints won a record nine games in 1998, including a 5-0 mark in the Deep South Conference, and took the season finale in overtime against VMI. Something special was in the air.

In 1999, the Blue & Gold reached even greater heights with 10 wins and the program's first conference tournament championship with a 16-7 victory over Wingate University.

Then the unthinkable happened in 2000. Ten years after their first season, the Saints brought home a national championship trophy.

Limestone College started the year 5-0 before dropping consecutive one-goal games to Radford University and Washington College. However, eight straight victories to end the regular season placed the Saints in the national title game against perennial power C.W. Post, the 1996 national champions who were appearing in their third straight title game and their fifth in eight years. The Pioneers had also enjoyed recent success against Limestone with four straight wins, including a 12-4 victory the previous season. Hardly anyone was giving Cernio's Saints much of a chance in the showdown between North and South. But on May 28, 2000, at the University of Maryland's Ludwig Field, Limestone All-Americans Chris Campbell and Rick Matthews powered the Saints to a shocking 10-9 victory and the college's first NCAA team championship. Maybe even more impressive, Limestone became the smallest co-ed school to ever win a team NCAA title.

The Saints would go on to play for the national championship in each of the next five seasons, including 2002, when a T.W. Johnson–coached squad gave Limestone its second national championship, this time over New York Tech 11-9.

Now considered one of the finest men's lacrosse programs in Division II, the Saints are a constant in the national championship conversation. With J.B. Clarke at the helm, Limestone advanced to the title game four times between 2012 and 2016, winning back-to-back championships in 2014 and 2015.

Entering the 2017 campaign, Limestone has won four national titles and appeared in 10 championship games, making the Saints one of the more improbable dynasties in all of college athletics.

Since its lacrosse team's meager beginnings in 1989, Limestone's athletics department has swelled to 25 teams with nearly 900 student-athletes, making it one of the largest in Division II. The college has flourished over the years and is now enjoying an era of growth, stability, and renewal.

The evolution of Limestone and its campus has been nothing short of remarkable—just like its men's lacrosse team that started it all.

—Dr. Walt Griffin
President, Limestone College

One

Building a Tradition from the Ground Up

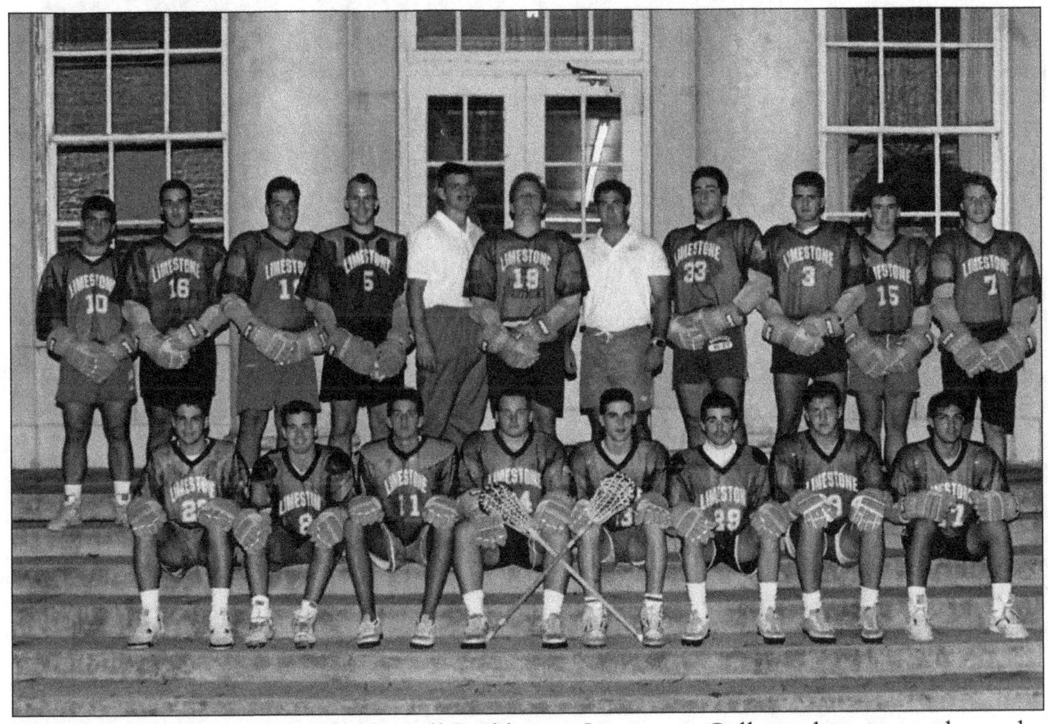

Taken on the front steps of the Carroll Building at Limestone College, this picture shows the first men's lacrosse team ever fielded at "The Rock," back in 1990. A team consisting mostly of freshmen, the Saints dropped their opening game against the Virginia Military Institute, but finished the inaugural season with a 6-6 record.

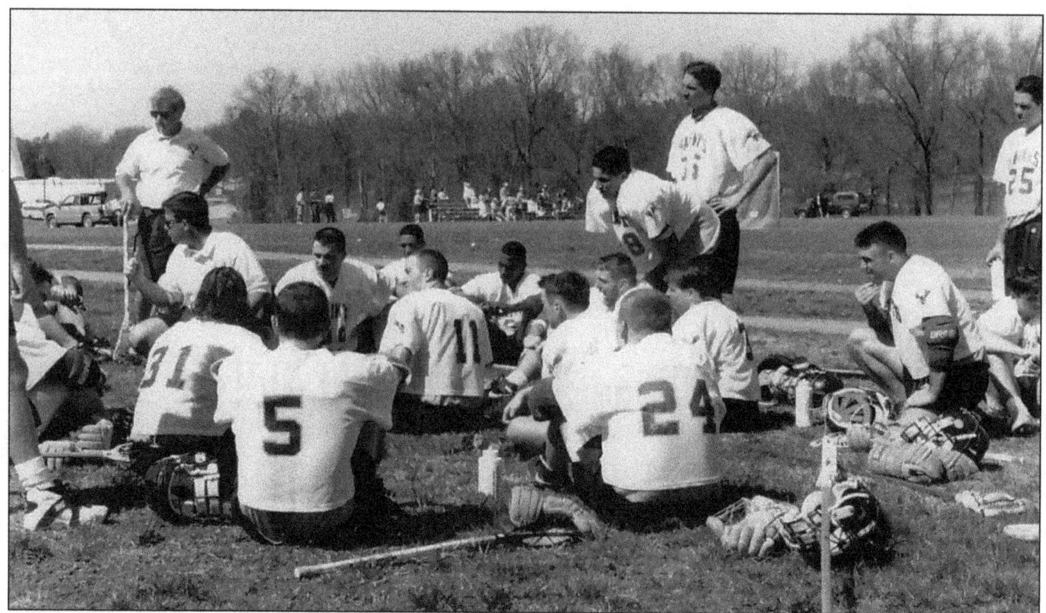

Coach Mike Cerino addresses his team at halftime of a game in the early 1990s.

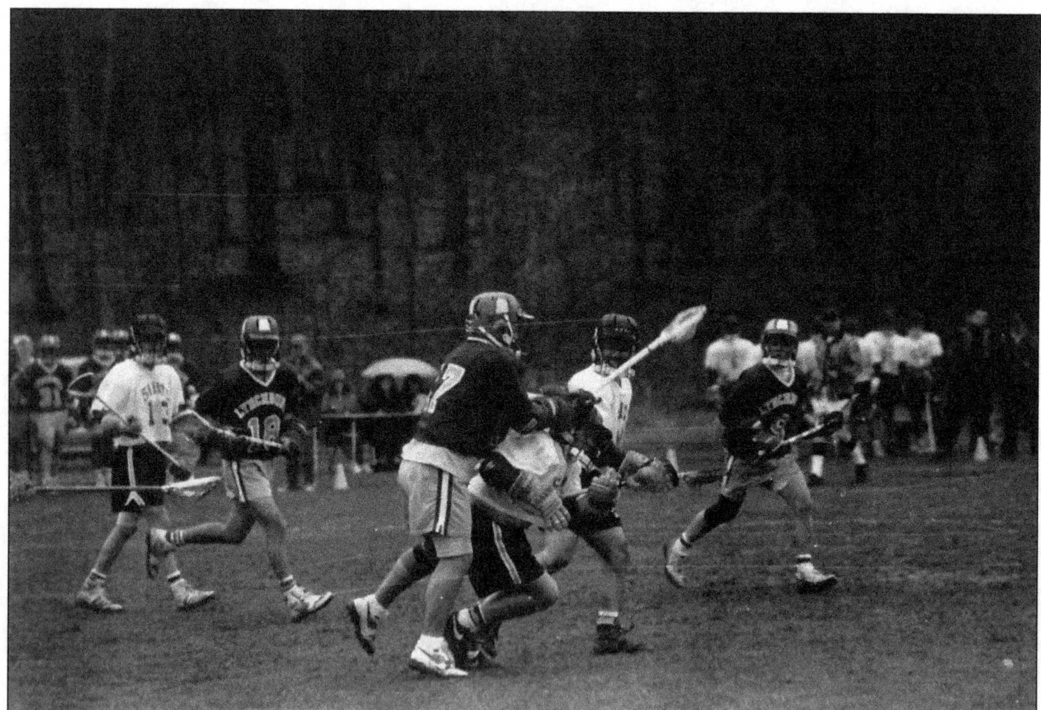

In 1991, Limestone traveled to play perennial powerhouse Lynchburg College in Lynchburg, Virginia, and took a 24-5 thumping. Things quickly improved, however. The 1992 matchup shown here was physical with a youthful Blue & Gold squad falling just short of an upset in a 14-13 defeat. Ken Thornby (No. 13, far left) and Vinnie Grazidei (right) watch as an unidentified Saint takes a high shot from a Lynchburg player. The Blue & Gold eventually avenged these two losses in 1993 with a 10-7 win over the Hornets in a victory that sent a message across the country.

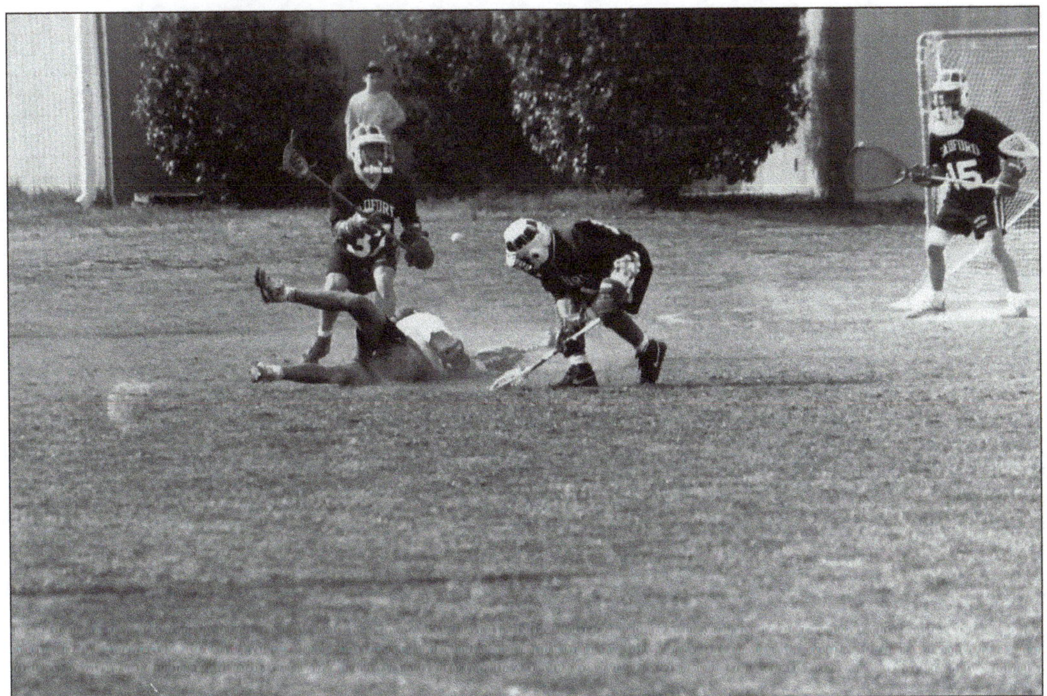

Hosting another tough opponent in Radford University during the same season resulted in another one-goal loss for the Saints, but much like the series with Lynchburg College, Limestone bounced back in the ensuing season with a 14-11 win.

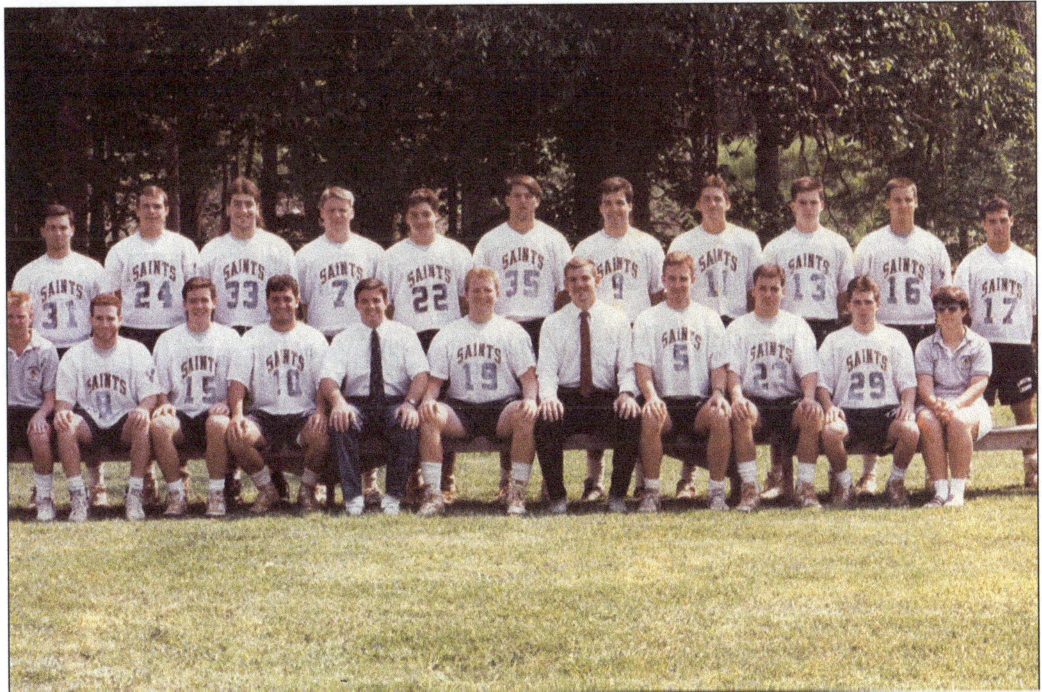

Exploring unknown territory as a college lacrosse program in South Carolina, the 1990 team is shown here in the spring before beginning preparation for their first season.

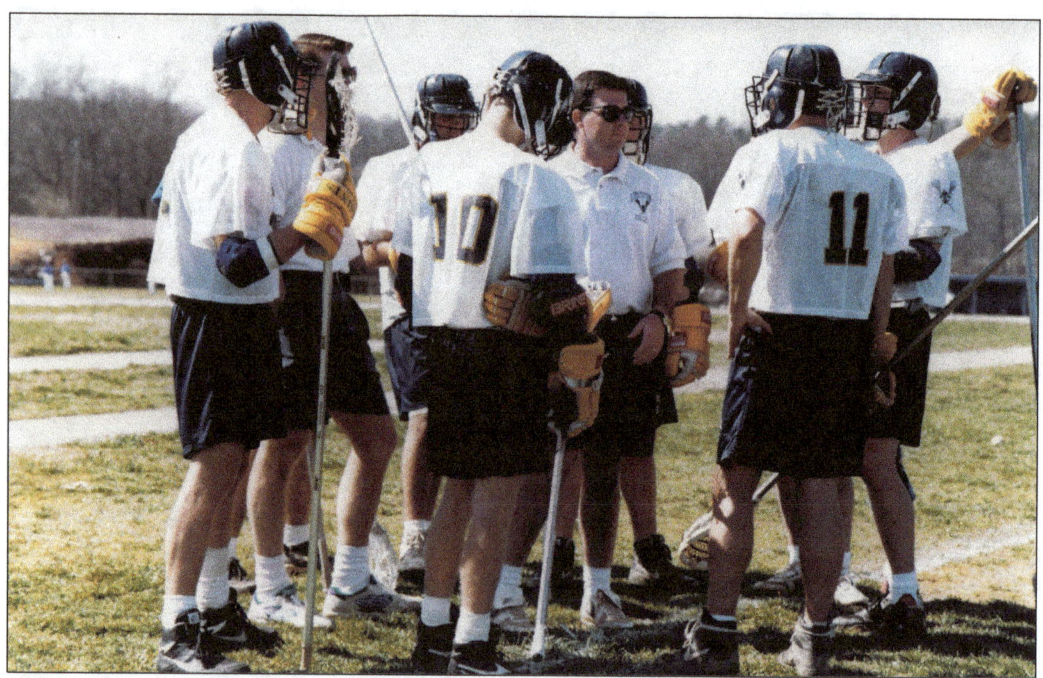

Head coach Mike Cerino addresses team members John Smith (No. 11), Keith Nyberg (No. 10), and others during a time-out. While the majority of lacrosse games were played adjacent to the field house on what is now known as Saints Field, this team huddle took place elsewhere, as Limestone's Bob Prevatte Baseball Field and baseball players can be seen in the background.

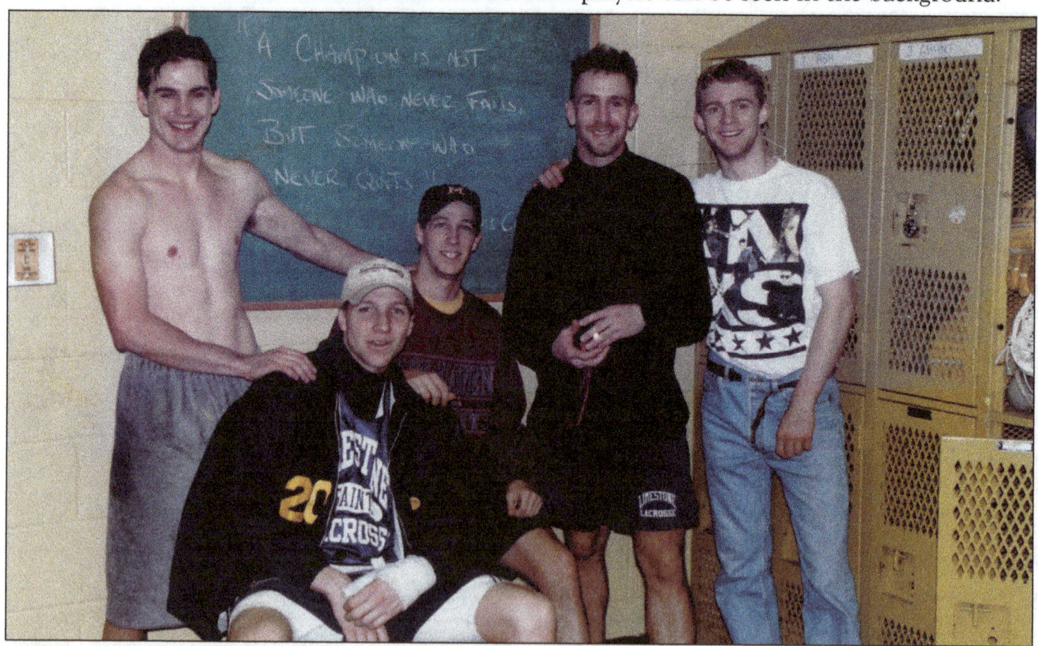

Taken in the original men's lacrosse locker room in the Timken Center, this 1994 photograph shows, from left to right, Ken Thornby, Jeremy Shek, Nick Pitruzella, Will Doyle, and Keith Nyberg. Head coach Mike Cerino's messages on the blackboard were written daily before the players came in for practice.

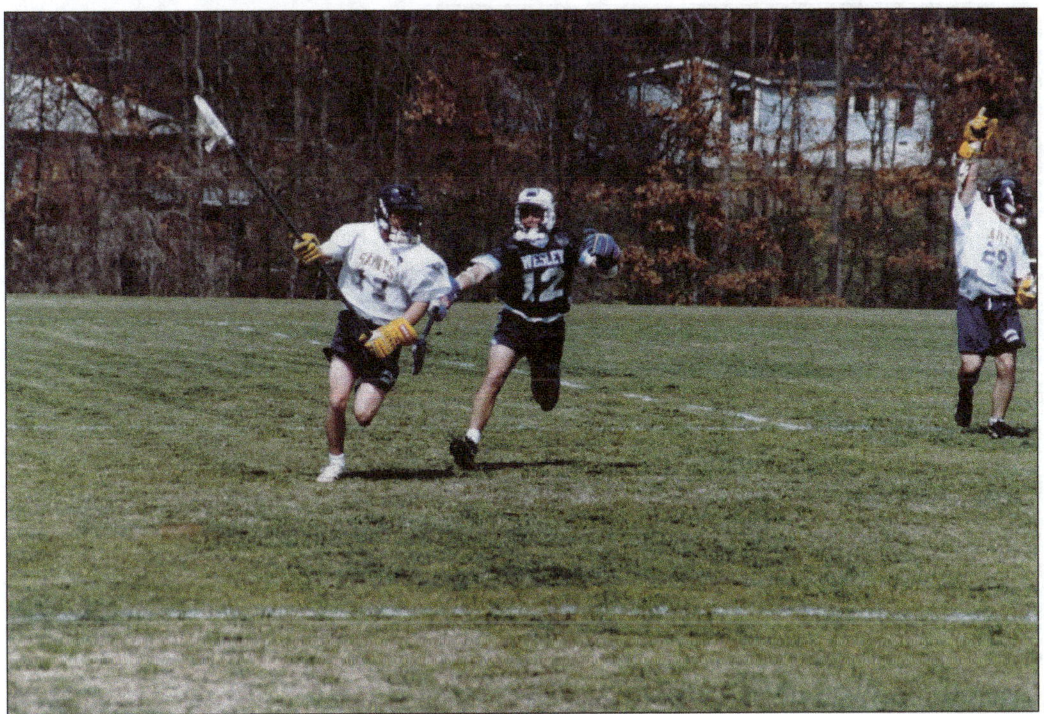

Ken Thornby and the Saints breezed by the Wesley College Wolverines in the early-season 1994 matchup seen here. Limestone College tallied an easy 19-4 home win while Thornby and crew racked up huge numbers. The team finished the 1994 season with an 8-5 mark for the most wins in a single season during the program's young lifetime.

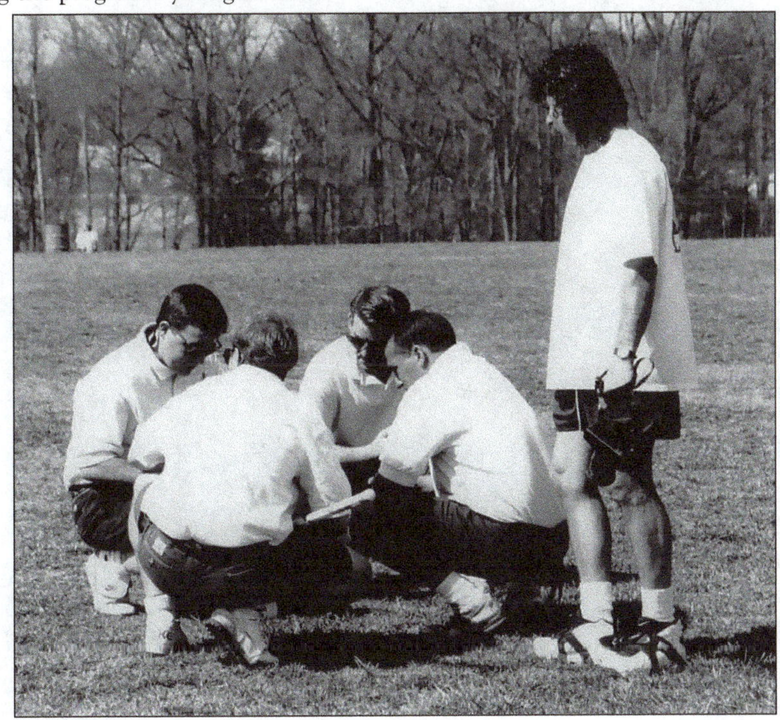

Pictured kneeling from left to right, head coach Mike Cerino along with assistant coaches Chris Phenicie (back turned), Will Gillis, and Mike Sessa huddle closely to draw up a play during a game. Australian native and longtime friend of Limestone Paul Mollison stands to the side and observes as the coaches try to brainstorm a winning formula.

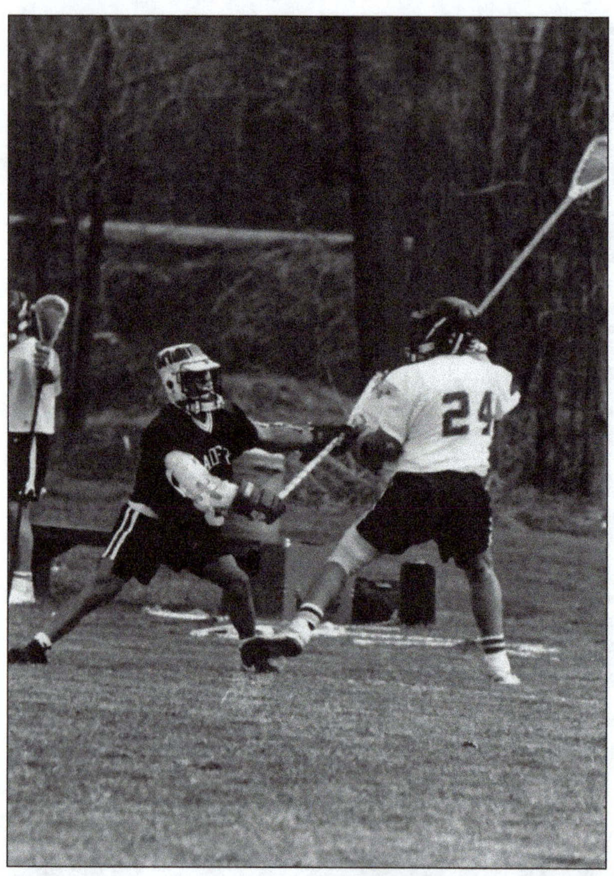

Jimmy White (No. 24) of Limestone College tries to make a move against a Radford University defender in an early 1990s matchup.

In a fall tournament at Guilford College in 1991, head coach Mike Cerino delivers a message to Tom Cerino (No. 15), Mike Sessa (No. 17), Peter Hauhuth (No. 11) and the rest of the Blue & Gold squad.

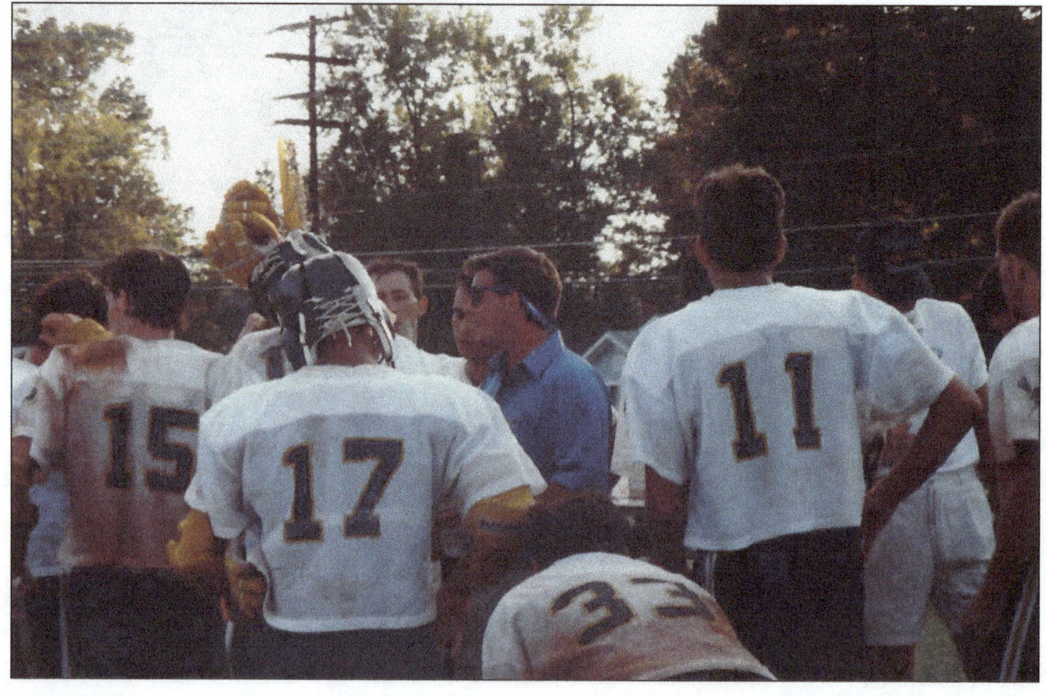

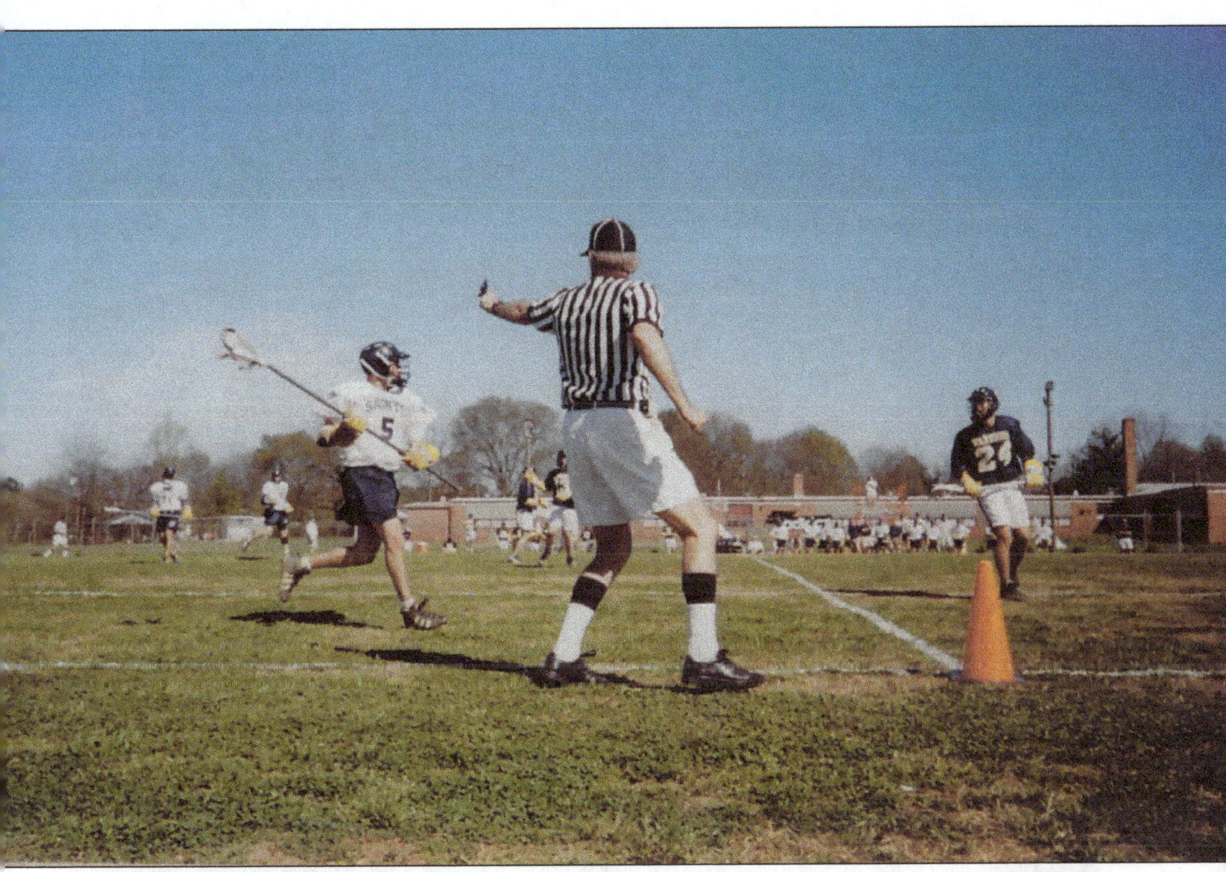

Two-time All-American Ryan Lanigan attacks the Merrimack College Warriors in a 1997 clash in Gaffney. The Saints won 21-7 for their second consecutive blowout of the Warriors, giving the team a 6-1 record through the first half of the year. However, Limestone College struggled through the latter half of the schedule and ended the season at 7-6 after a loss in the Deep South Conference Tournament. (Courtesy of Chris Ruben.)

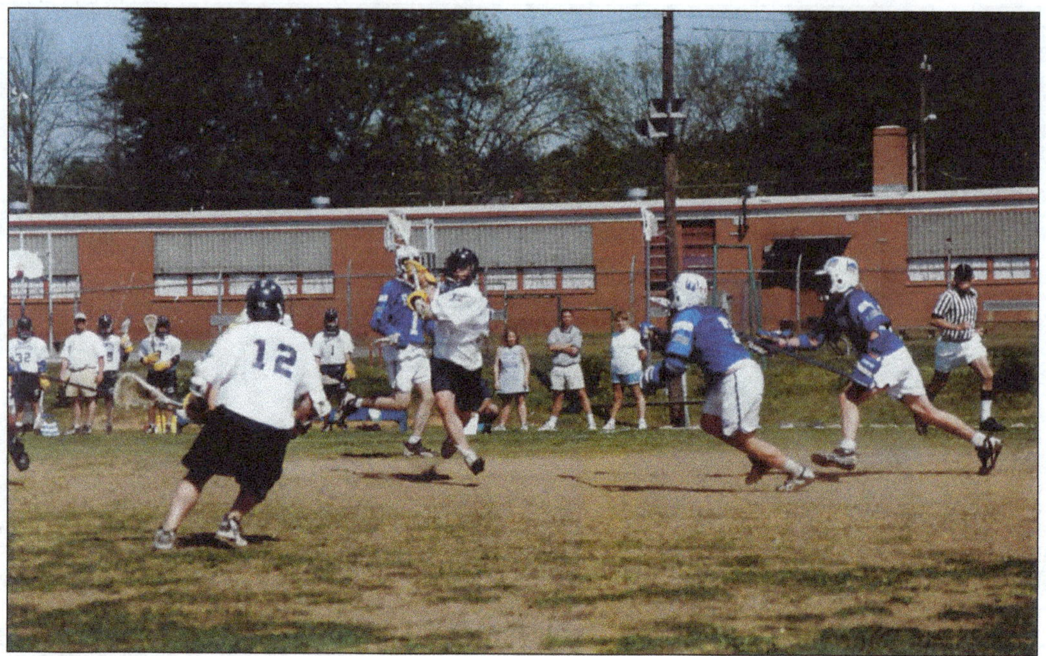

Matt Collins (No. 12) sets up to receive a pass from a teammate against St. Andrews College in the 1998 Deep South Conference Tournament Semifinals at Limestone College. (Courtesy of Chris Ruben.)

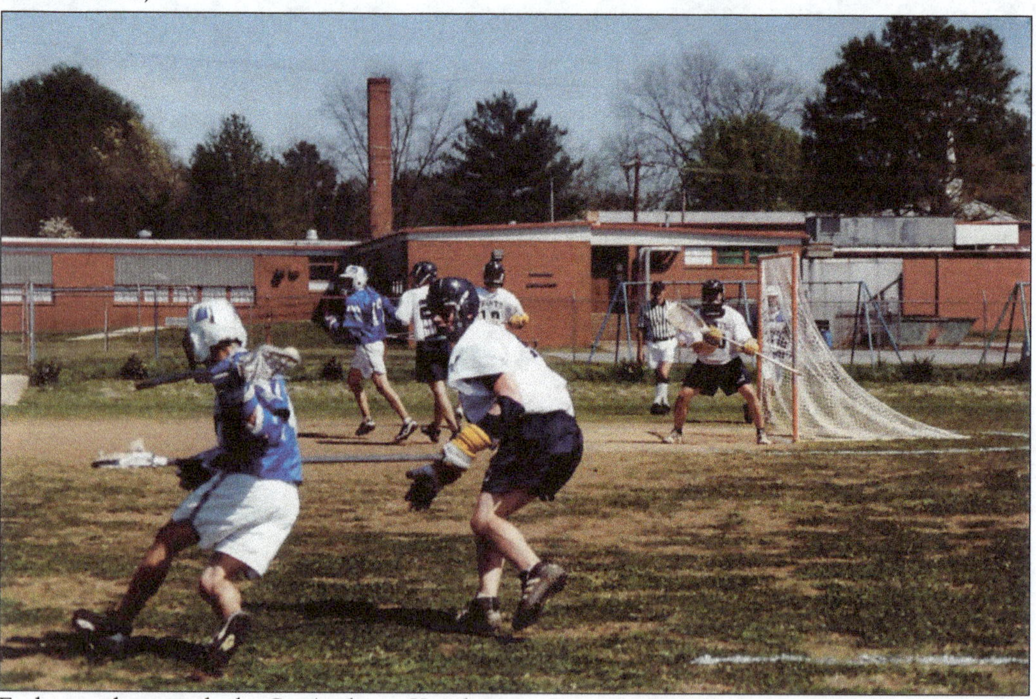

Early matchups with the St. Andrews Knights saw Limestone College drop four of the first five in the series, but the Saints have won 22 straight matches dating back to 1999. Pictured here, Joe Bender patrols the pipes in a patch of worn-out field while the defense keeps the pressure away. (Courtesy of Chris Ruben.)

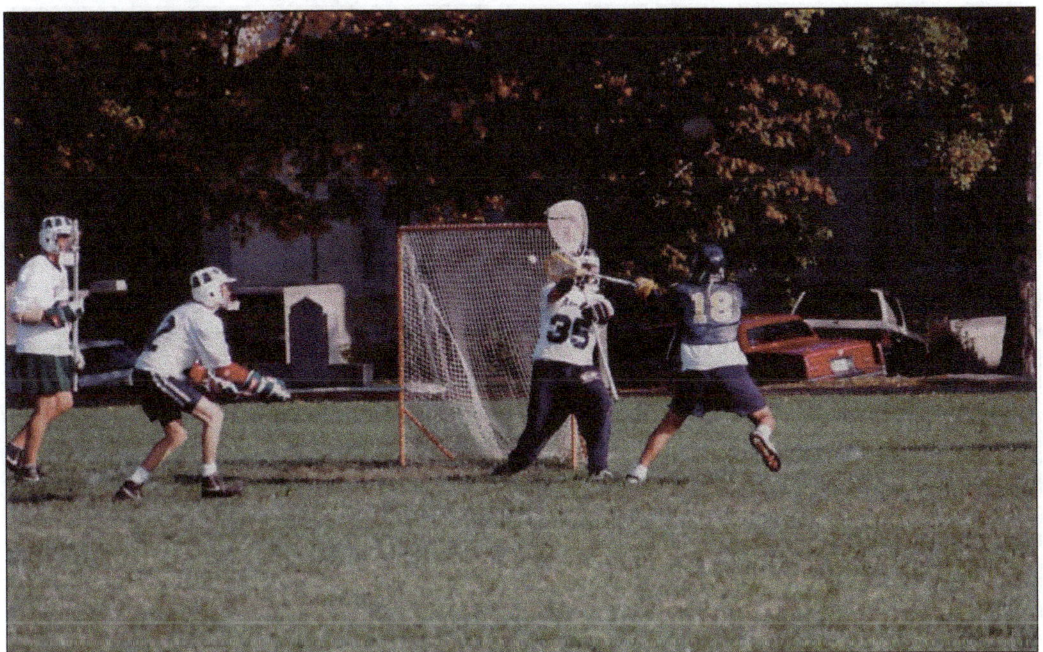

Limestone traveled to the Virginia Military Institute in 1993 for a neutral site matchup with Radford University. One of Limestone College's all-time greats, Paul Casey, is seen here making a move past the goalie's right side to sneak between the posts for one of Limestone's goals in the 14-11 victory.

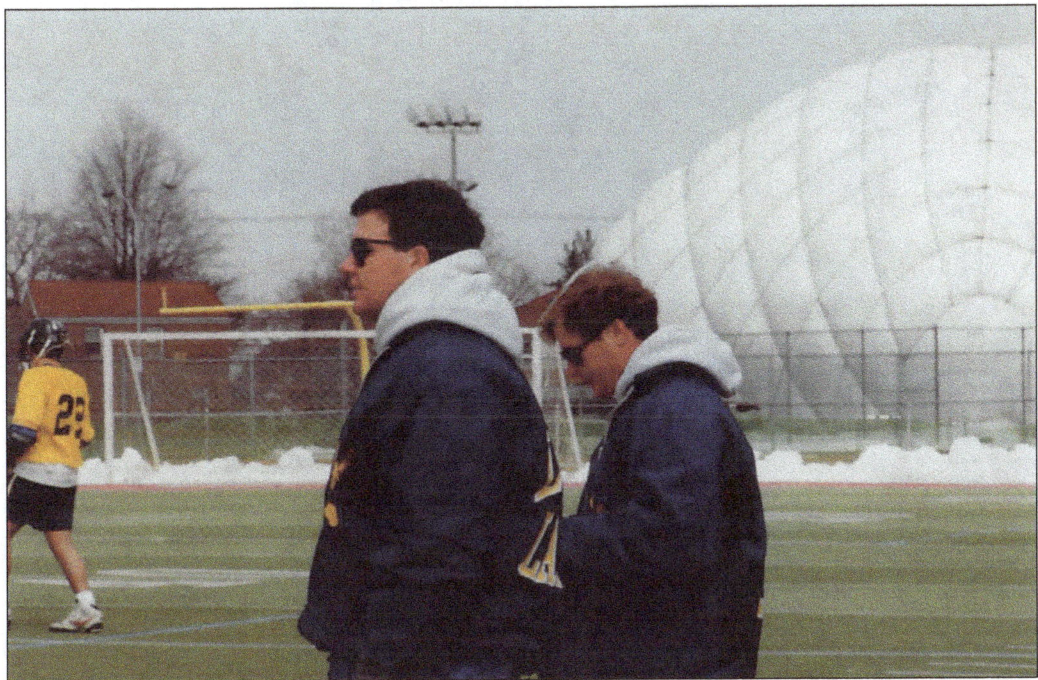

Limestone College and New York Institute of Technology faced off at St. John's University in 1993 in a matchup that saw the Saints earn some respect from one of the more established programs. The Blue & Gold took things to overtime but eventually fell 12-11.

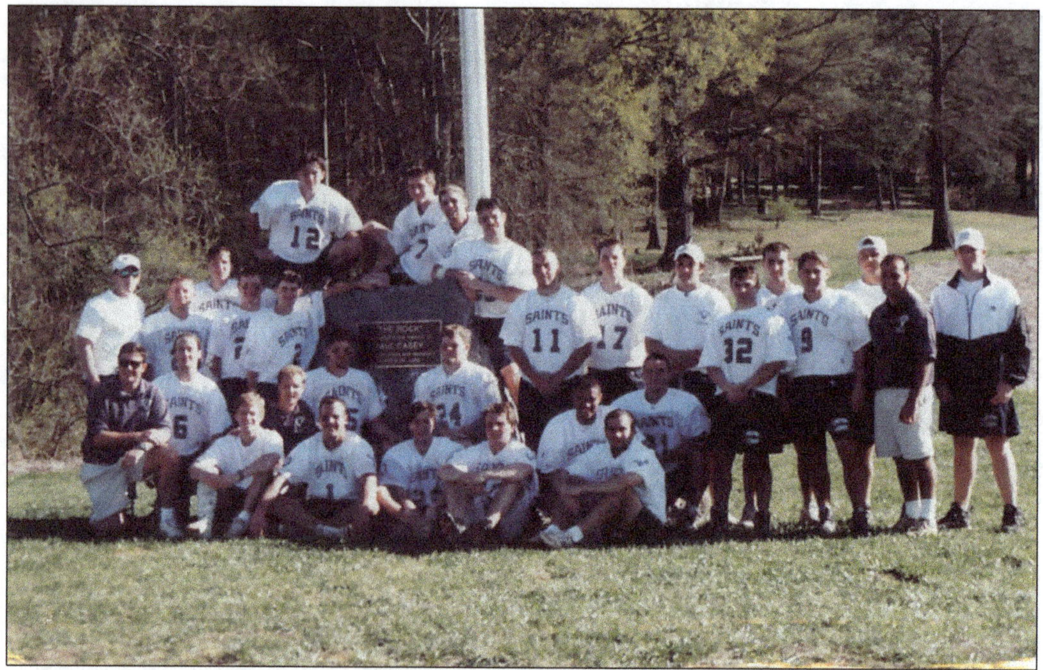

Pictured here with the 1995 team, The Rock was dedicated on March 25, 1995, to the memory of Paul Casey, a Limestone lacrosse player in the early 1990s who lost his life in a hiking accident. Today, more than 20 years later, The Rock still firmly sits alongside the field, where players march together before each game to gather and remember a former teammate.

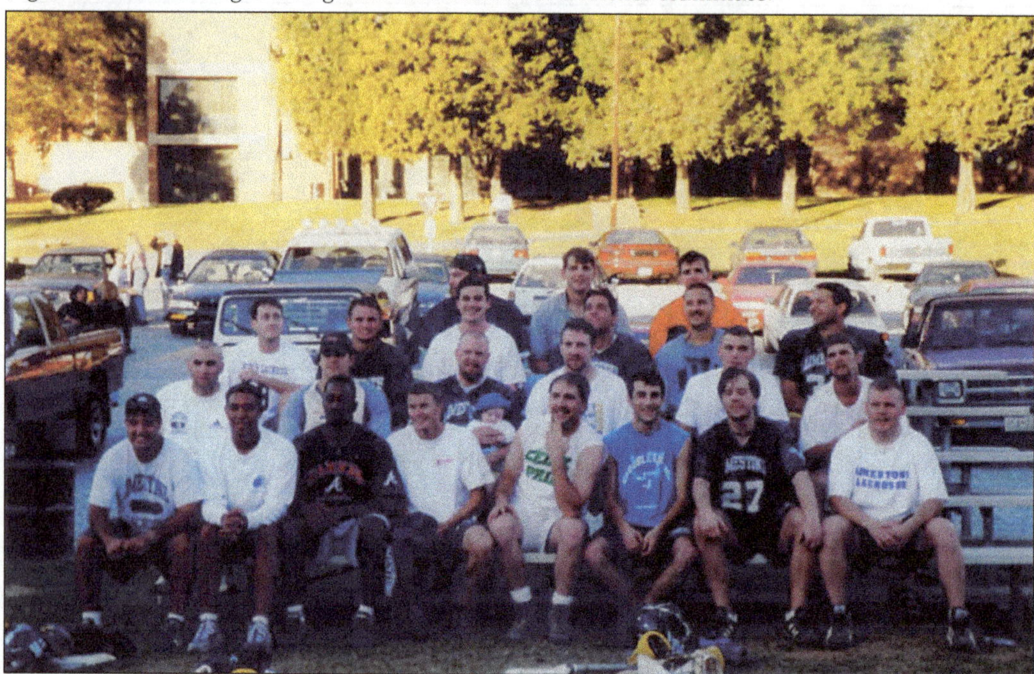

In what is thought to be the first ever Limestone College men's lacrosse alumni game, former players gather on campus in the mid-1990s at the original lacrosse field for a quick game and meal afterwards.

Still trying to make a name for themselves, Keith Nyberg and the Saints traveled to Adelphi University for a mid-season game against the Panthers in 1997. Limestone took a loss here but eventually wrapped up the campaign with a winning record.

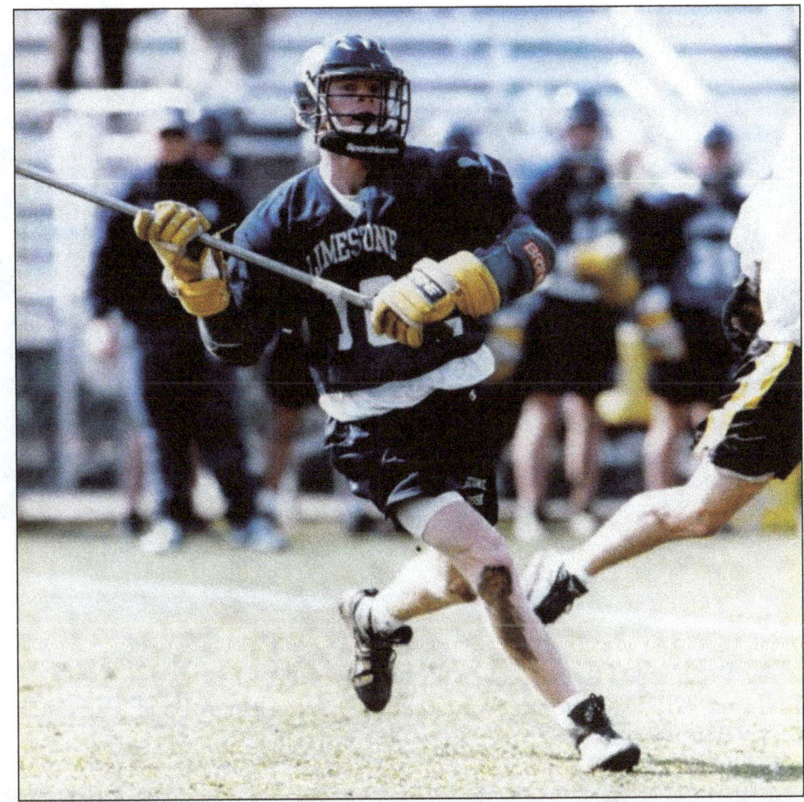

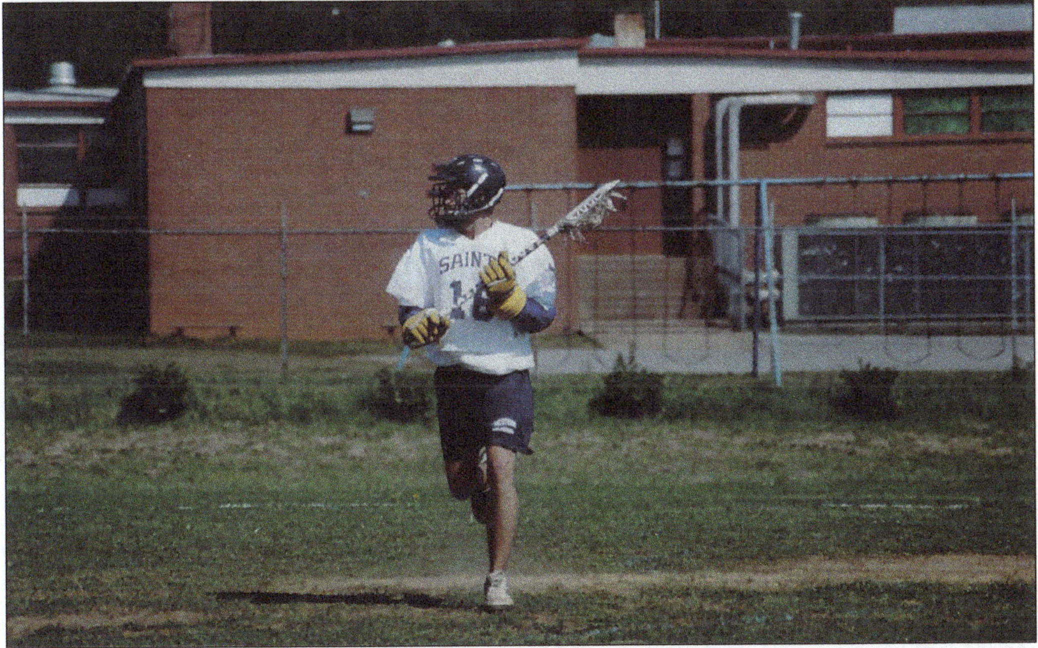

Brendan Spilker stands unguarded with the ball during a game in the late 1990s. In the background is the Limestone Elementary School, which has recently been converted into the Bob Campbell Fieldhouse.

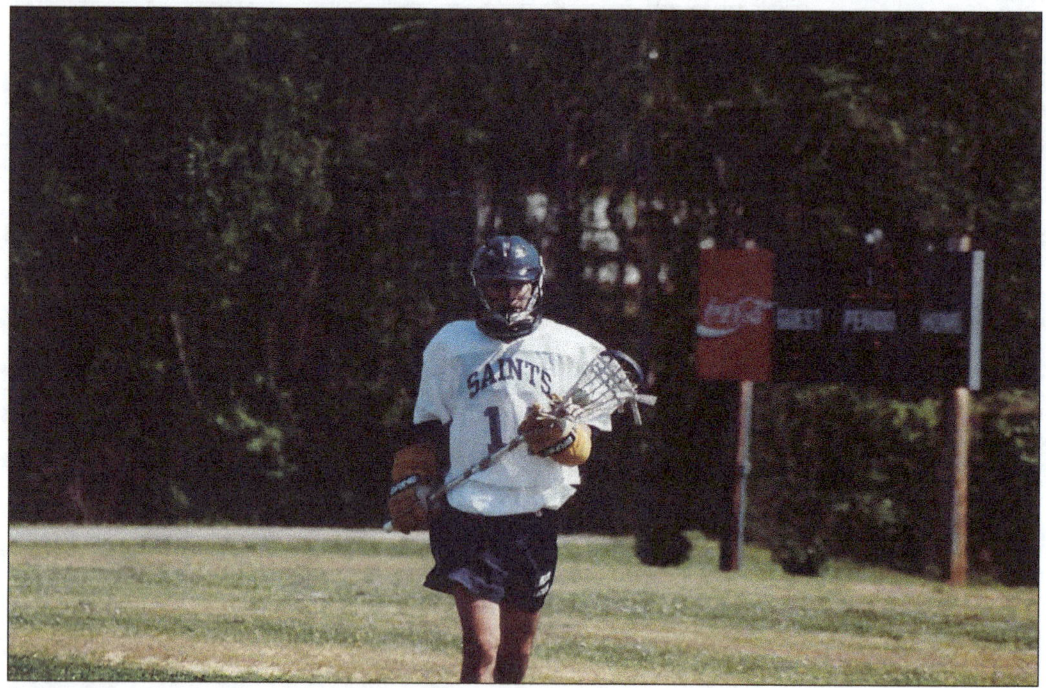

Two-time All–Deep South Conference selection Brian Bauer carries the ball during the first period of a 1997 game.

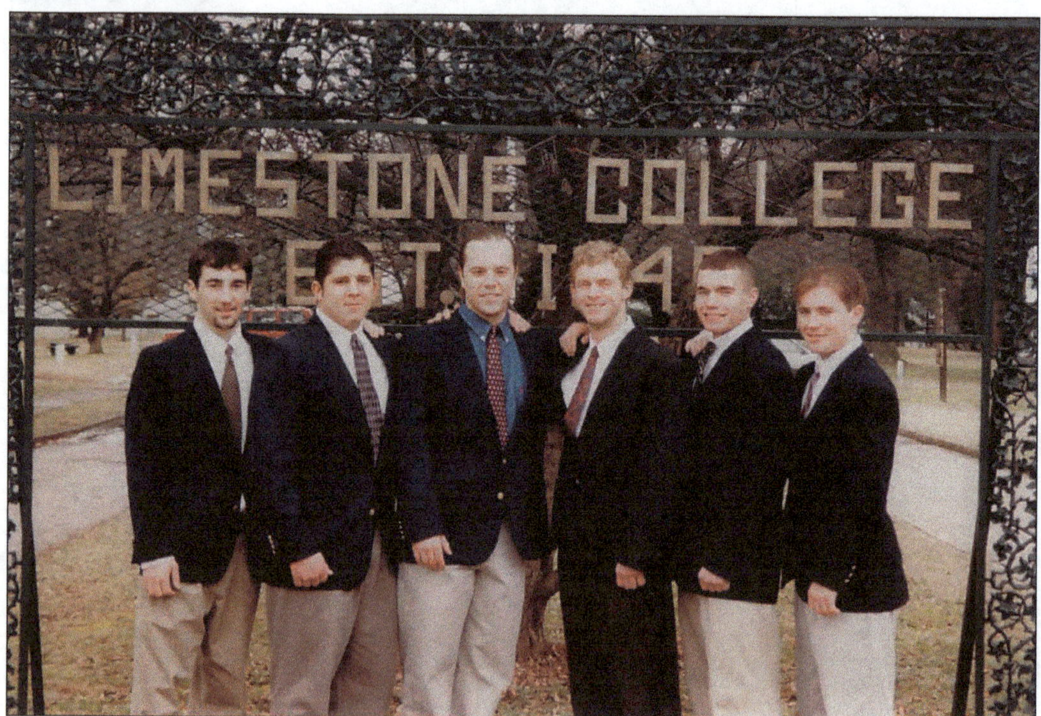

This photograph was taken at the front entrance to Limestone College's campus in 1997. From left to right are Brian Bauer, Joe Bender, John Farr, Keith Nyberg, Jason Caulder, and Gavin Higgins.

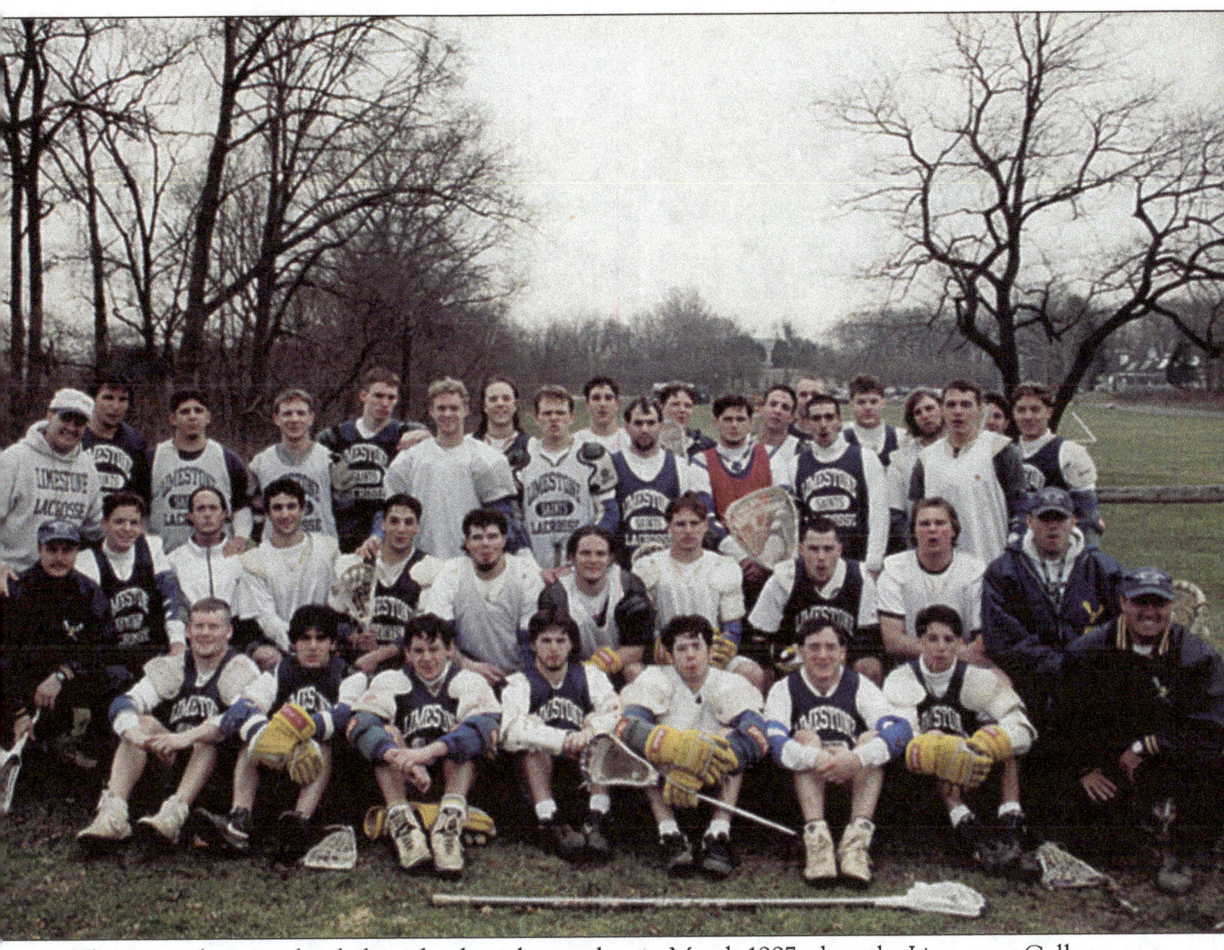

This team photograph is believed to have been taken in March 1997 when the Limestone College lacrosse team made a trip to Maryland to play a neutral site game against C.W. Post. (Courtesy of Ron Cerino.)

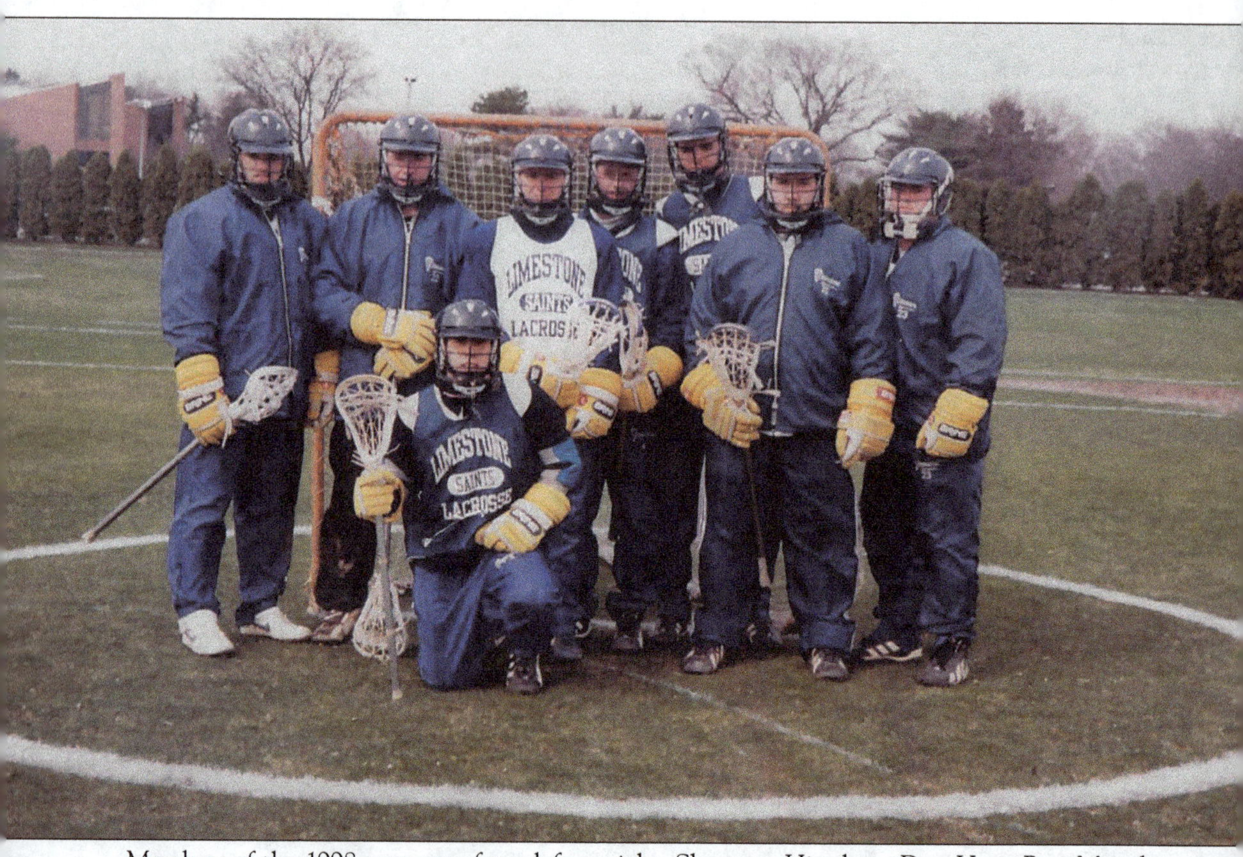

Members of the 1998 team are, from left to right, Shannon Hiteshew, Dan Hart, Pete Murzda (kneeling), Ken Handy, Kevin Krause, Matt Haynes, Joe Hayes, and Mark Collins.

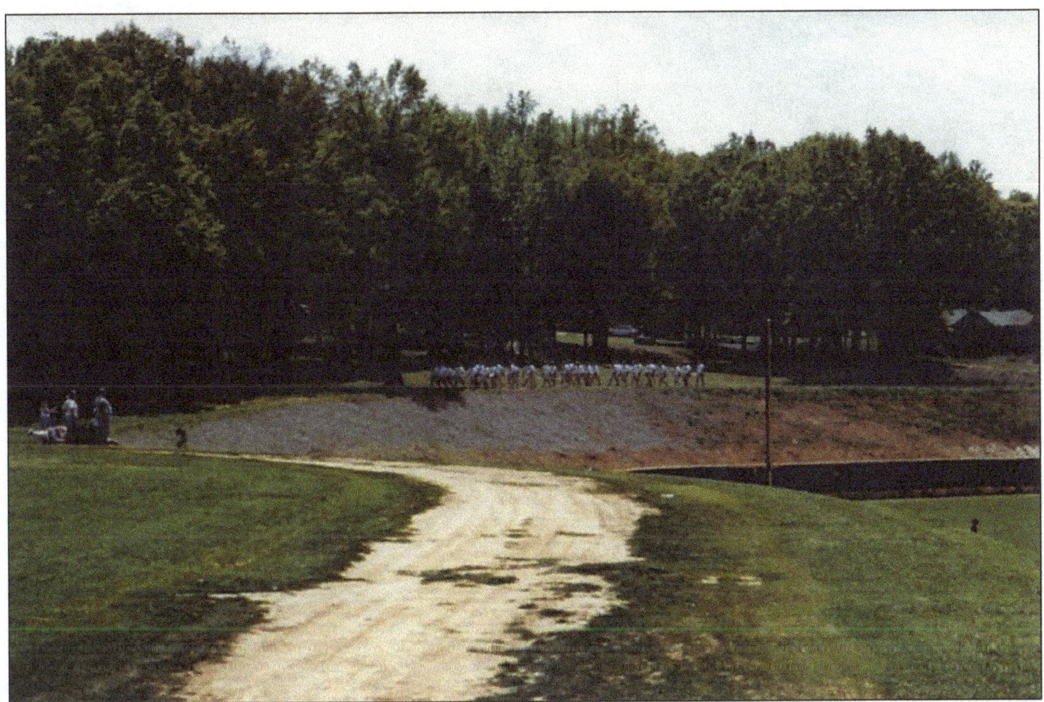

A tradition that began when the games were moved to a new field, Limestone marched from the locker room on campus, around the quarry, and up to the athletic complex for each game. The tradition was discontinued, however, when locker rooms were built in the Bob Campbell Field House next to the lacrosse field. (Courtesy of Lynn Murzda.)

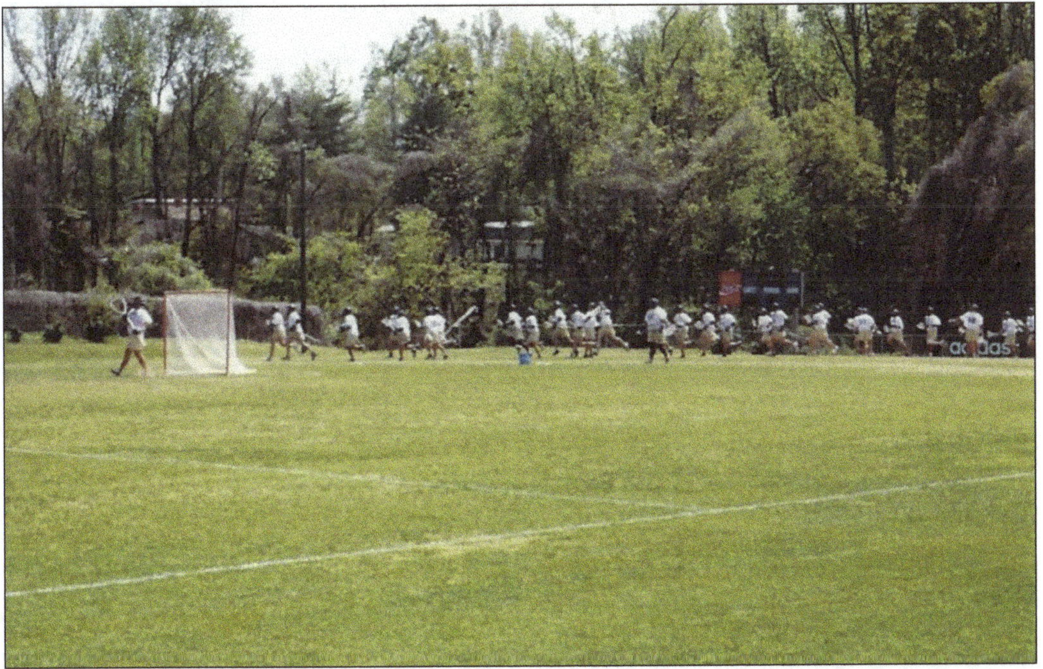

In this 1998 photograph, Saints Field is a much different sight with all grass as the team comes across and prepares to begin warm-ups. (Courtesy of Lynn Murzda.)

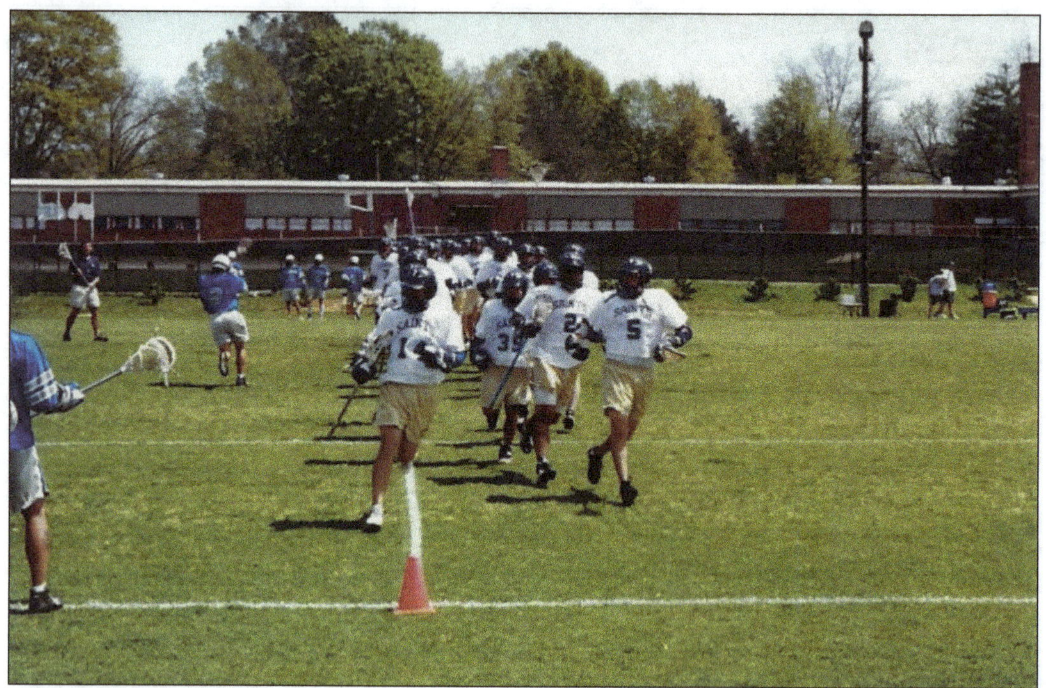

The team continues its trip around the field before making its way over toward Paul Casey's Rock to start warm-ups. This 1998 game against St. Andrews went against the Saints, unfortunately, with the Knights taking a two-goal win. (Courtesy of Lynn Murzda.)

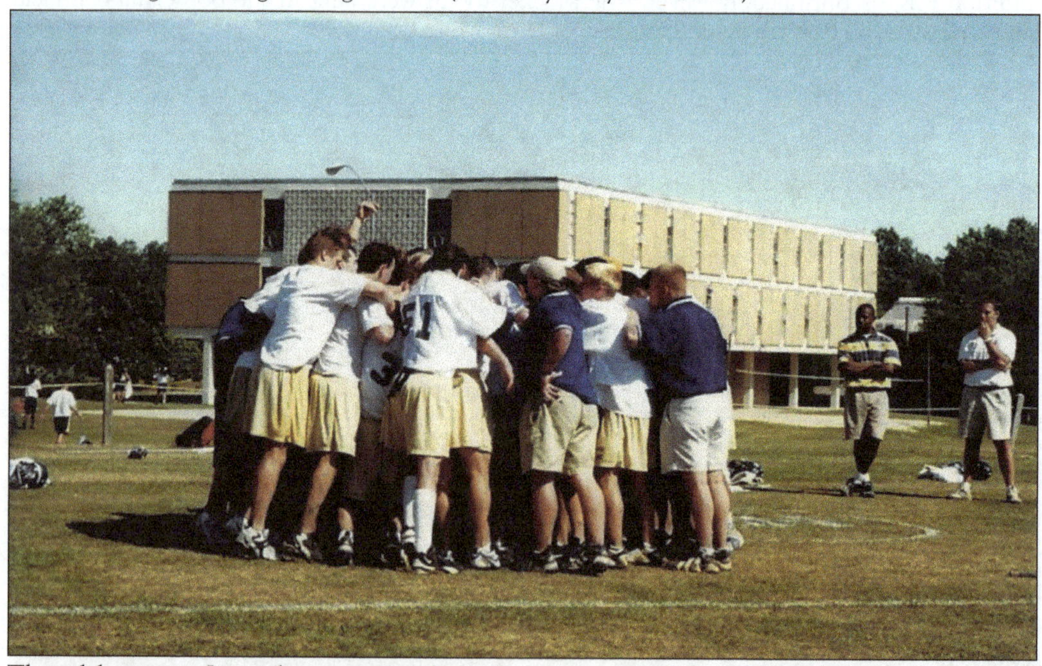

The celebration in Laurinburg continued after Limestone won the program's first ever Deep South Conference Tournament. The Saints had been beaten by St. Andrews Presbyterian College in 1998 and Pfeiffer University in 1997, but knocked off St. Andrews in the 1999 semifinals and cruised against the Wingate University Bulldogs in the finals.

Two

Making a Name for the Saints

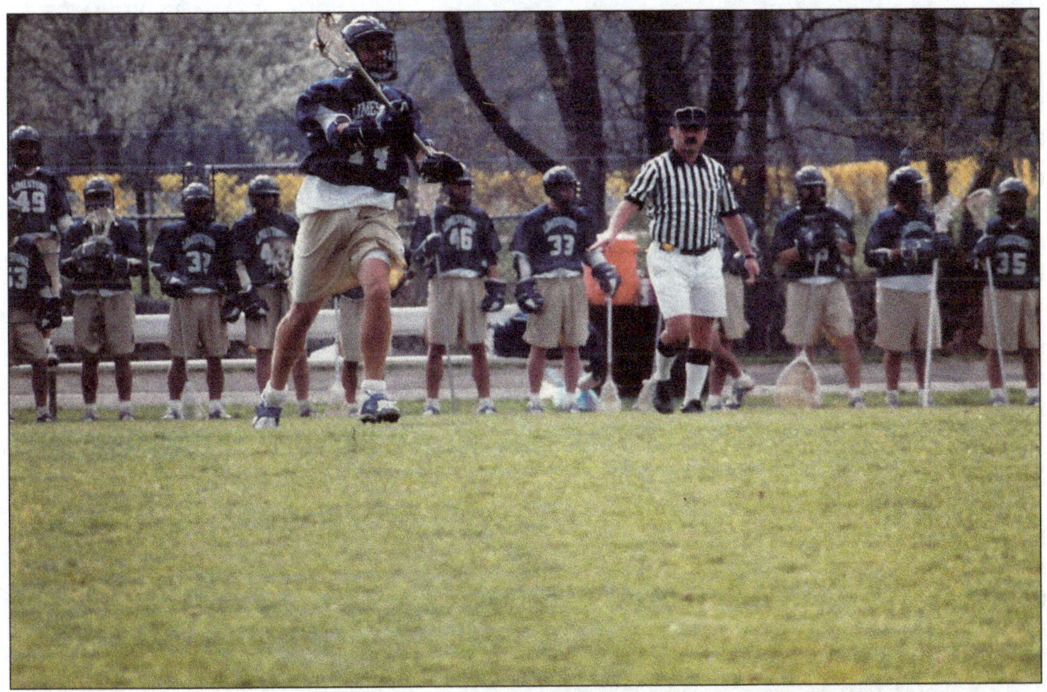

Although the Saints hoisted the trophy at the end of the year, the middle of the season saw two speed bumps slow things down for Jake Lawson and crew. A road trip to Washington College on March 25 resulted in Limestone's second straight one-goal loss but would prove to be the final defeat in the Saints' championship season.

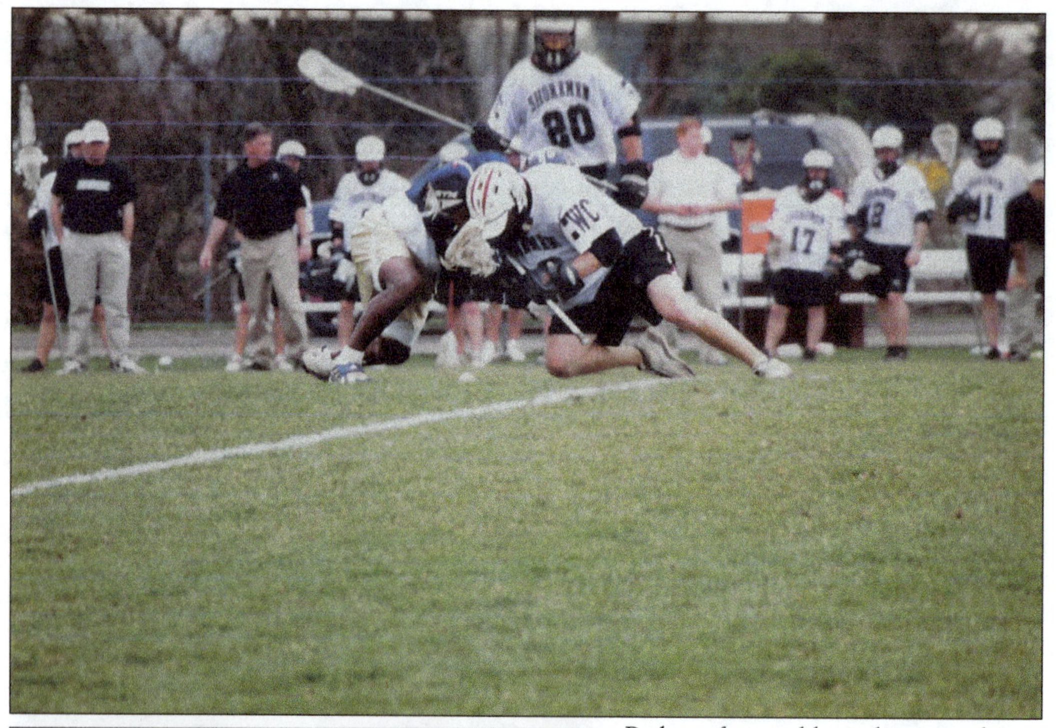

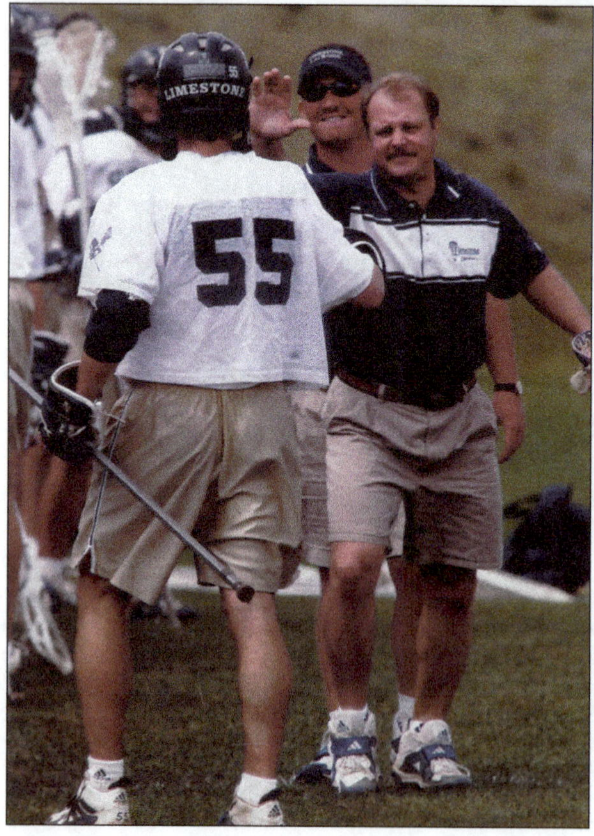

Perhaps forgettable at the time, this picture, taken during the March 25 matchup at Washington College (WC), includes a special element. Shoremen head coach J.B. Clarke can be seen in the background as two players face off at midfield. Clarke spent 12 seasons at WC before making his way to Limestone College in 2010, where he has cemented his place as one of the greats in the game and still coaches today.

All-American Greg Hiltz high fives assistant coaches Chris Phenicie and Bill Milone before a 2000 conference tournament game against Wingate.

Two-time All-American Ricky Matthews and the Saints cruised by the Wingate Bulldogs 16-5 and eventually earned a spot in the national championship game, where they would take on C.W. Post.

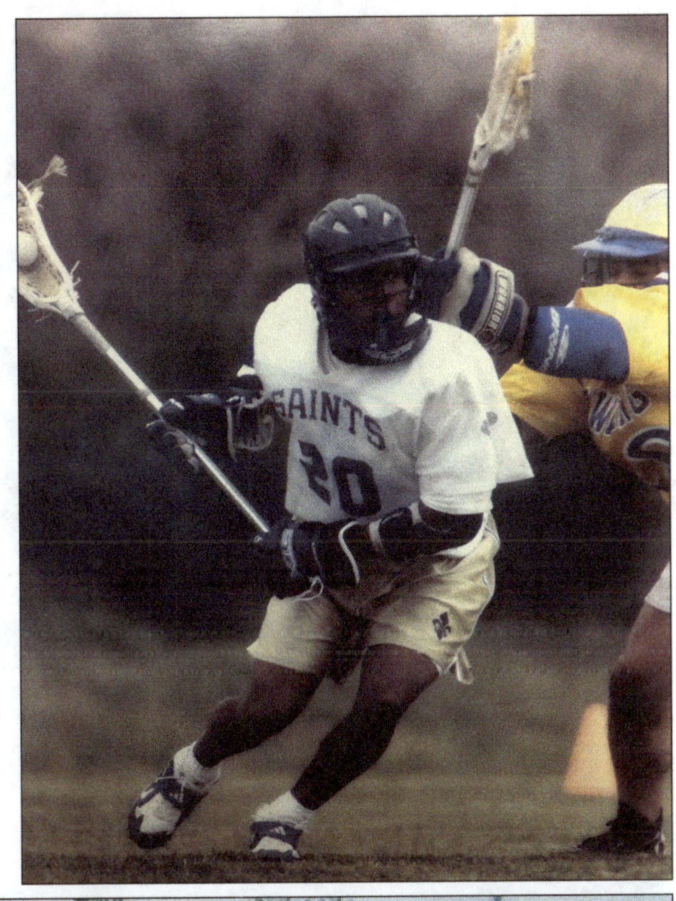

Appearing in their first ever NCAA national championship game, the Limestone Saints go through normal warm-ups at Ludwig Field as they get set to face C.W. Post. Visible in the background behind the fence is a tailgating scene where thousands gathered before the game, including a mass of Limestone College fans and former players hoping to witness history.

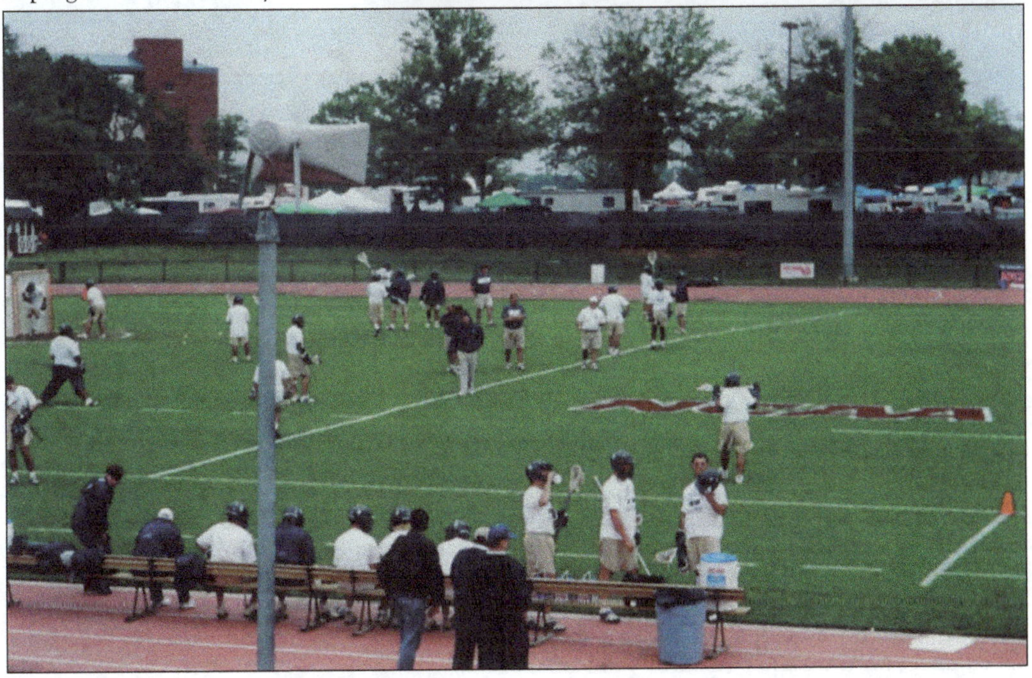

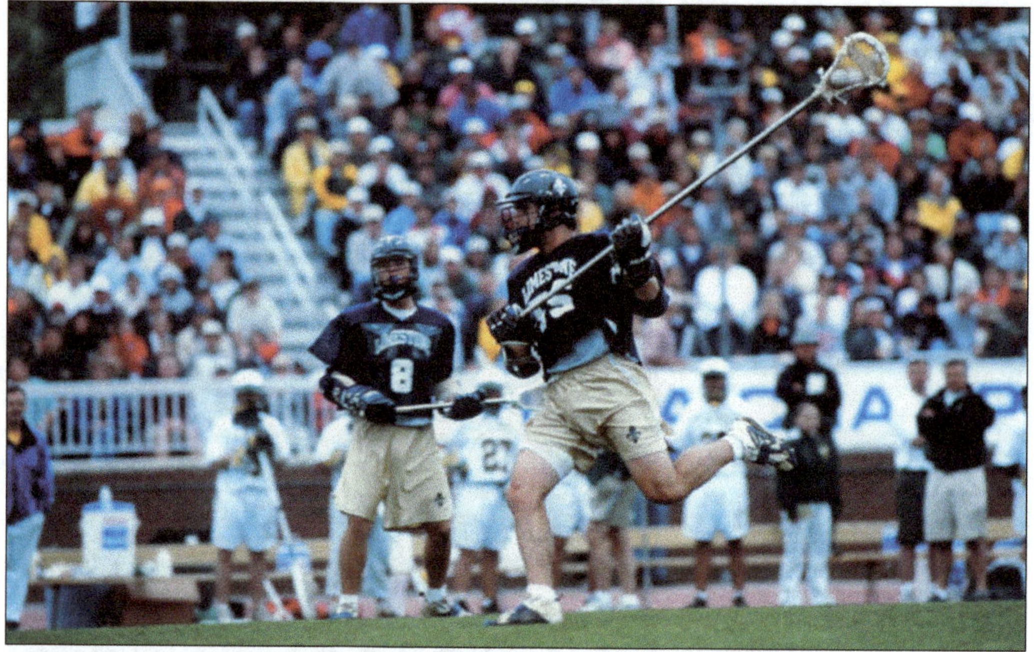

All-American Greg Hiltz runs alongside fellow All-American Nick Carlson during the 2000 NCAA Division II national championship game against C.W. Post. This photograph shows one of the more monumental moments in the history of Division II men's lacrosse, as no southern team had ever won a national title before this game.

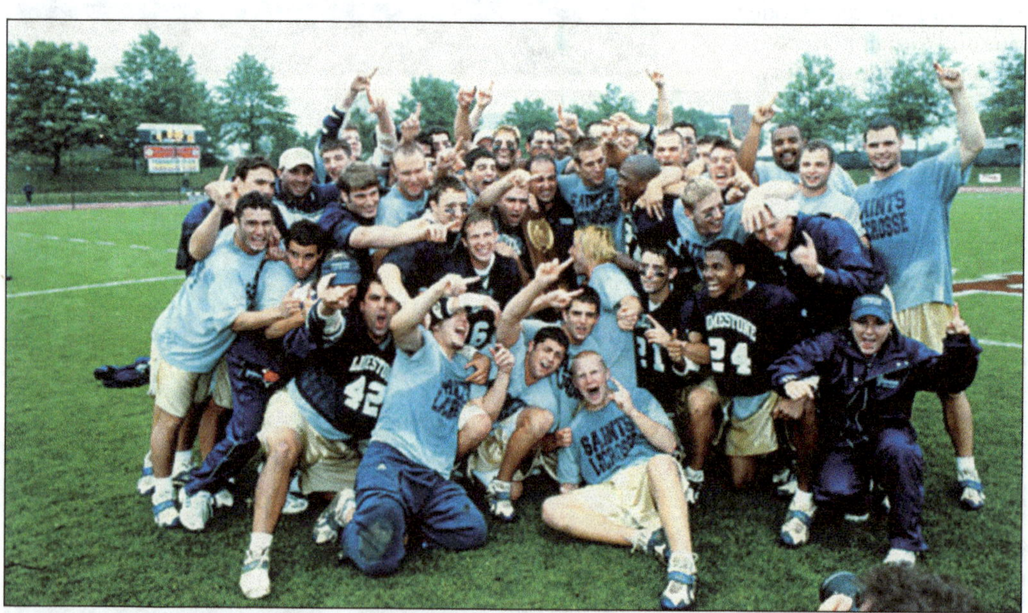

Just 10 years removed from their inaugural season, the 2000 Limestone Saints brought home the school's first ever NCAA national championship by knocking off traditional power C.W. Post, 10-9. This title brought legitimacy to a southern lacrosse program, which many felt could not compete with the more-established northern programs, and began a run of six straight title game appearances for the Saints. (Courtesy of Ron Cerino.)

Todd Shanesy, writer for the Spartanburg *Herald-Journal*, highlighted Limestone College's 10-9 national championship win over C.W. Post in 2000 with a feature story on the college's minuscule enrollment.

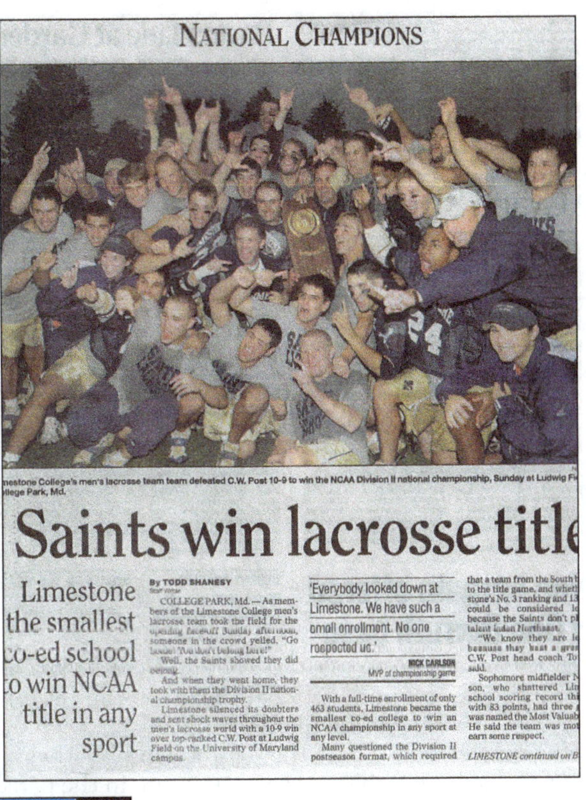

NATIONAL CHAMPIONS

nestone College's men's lacrosse team team defeated C.W. Post 10-9 to win the NCAA Division II national championship, Sunday at Ludwig Fi llege Park, Md.

Saints win lacrosse title

Limestone the smallest co-ed school to win NCAA title in any sport

By TODD SHANESY

COLLEGE PARK, Md. — As members of the Limestone College men's lacrosse team took the field for the opening faceoff Sunday afternoon, someone in the crowd yelled, "Go home! You don't belong here!"

Well, the Saints showed they did belong.

And when they went home, they took with them the Division II national championship trophy.

Limestone silenced its doubters and sent shock waves throughout the men's lacrosse world with a 10-9 win over top-ranked C.W. Post at Ludwig Field on the University of Maryland campus.

'Everybody looked down at Limestone. We have such a small enrollment. No one respected us.'

NICK CARLSON
MVP of championship game

With a full-time enrollment of only 463 students, Limestone became the smallest co-ed college to win an NCAA championship in any sport at any level.

Many questioned the Division II postseason format, which required that a team from the South b to the title game, and wheth stone's No. 3 ranking and 13 could be considered l because the Saints don't p talent indan Northeast.

"We know they are l because they beat a gre C.W. Post head coach To said.

Sophomore midfielder N son, who shattered Lin school scoring record th with 83 points, had three was named the Most Valuab He said the team was mo earn some respect.

LIMESTONE continued on B

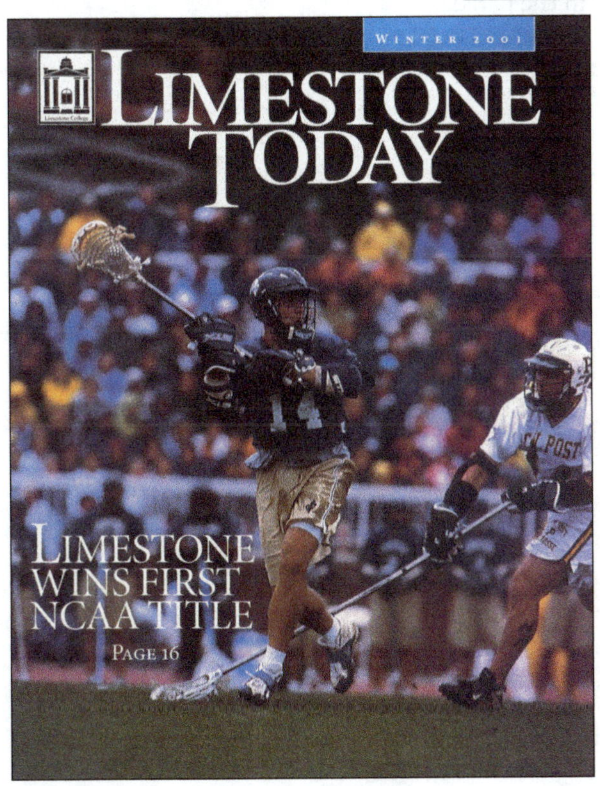

Limestone's campus magazine helped commemorate and honor the school's first ever NCAA national championship with this winter 2001 edition. Jake Lawson graced the cover, as the smallest coed school to ever win an NCAA team title celebrated its monumental achievement.

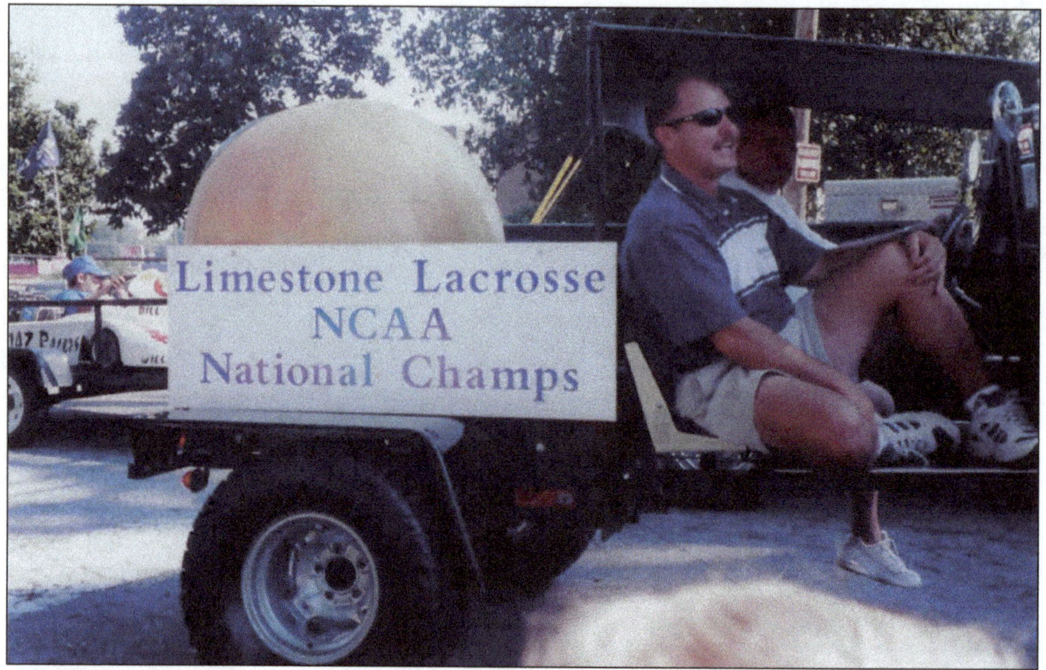

As part of Limestone's national championship celebration, the Saints were honored with a float in the Peach Festival Parade, held annually in downtown Gaffney. The festival attracts thousands of attendees from across the Upstate and Southeast region each year, and floats recognizing Limestone lacrosse have become a fixture in the parade.

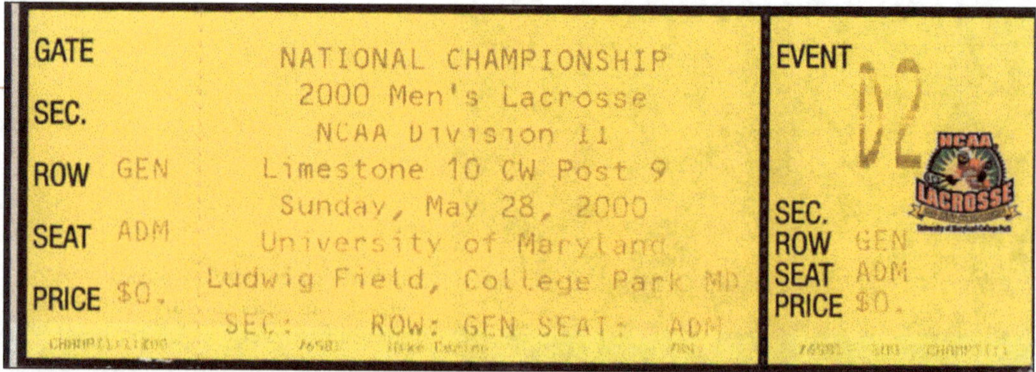

As a congratulatory token to the 2000 NCAA Division II national champions, the University of Maryland presented a select number of these tickets to the Saints after the team's 10-9 upset win over C.W. Post. The final score and game information printed on the tickets commemorate Limestone College's first ever team NCAA national title.

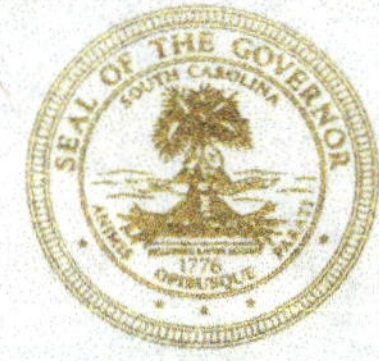

State of South Carolina

Office of the Governor

Jim Hodges
Governor

Post Office Box 11829
Columbia 29211

July 3, 2000

Mr. Mike Cerino
Head Coach
Limestone College
1115 College Drive
Gaffney, South Carolina 29340

Dear Coach Cerino:

On behalf of the State of South Carolina, I am pleased to extend my heartiest congratulations to you and the members of the Limestone College men's lacrosse team on winning the 2000 NCAA Division II Championships.

This achievement is the direct result of your outstanding leadership and commitment to excellence in athletics. You have proven that goals can be accomplished through teamwork and perseverance and I am certain you are very proud of the talent and skill your team exhibited. All South Carolinians join me in thanking you for your leadership and guidance in teaching our young people to become productive citizens and future leaders.

Rachel joins me in extending our personal congratulations to you on this well-deserved accomplishment. Please let me know if I can ever be of help to you in any way.

Sincerely,

Jim Hodges

Jim Hodges

Gov. Jim Hodges expressed his congratulations on the 2000 NCAA Division II national championship to Limestone head coach Mike Cerino with this letter. Hodges was later visited by the Saints at the South Carolina State House in Columbia.

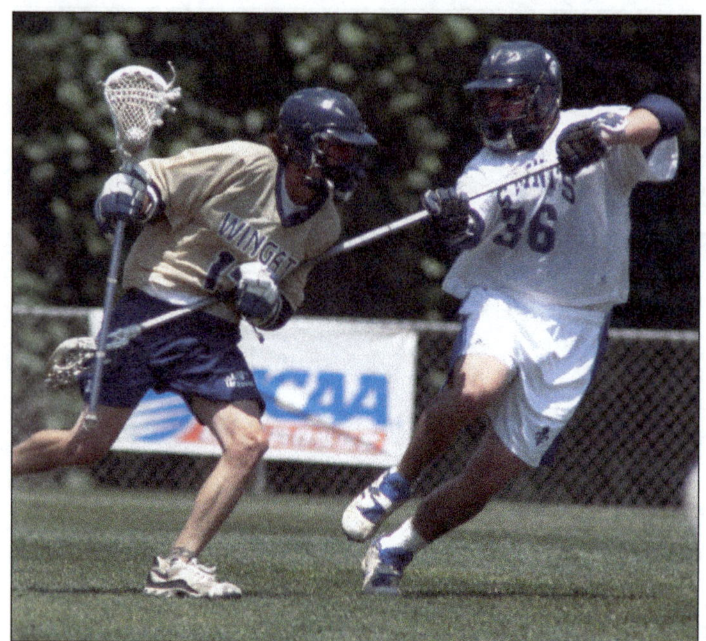

Things got ugly in the lone NCAA tournament meeting between Limestone and the Wingate University Bulldogs in 2001. Josh Rudder (No. 36) and the Saints ran over and through the Bulldogs en route to a 20-2 slaughter, which propelled the Blue & Gold to a second consecutive appearance in the NCAA Division II national championship game. Going for two in a row after their 2000 title win over C.W. Post, the Saints would have to go through another traditional power in 2001, with the Adelphi University Panthers also vying for the trophy.

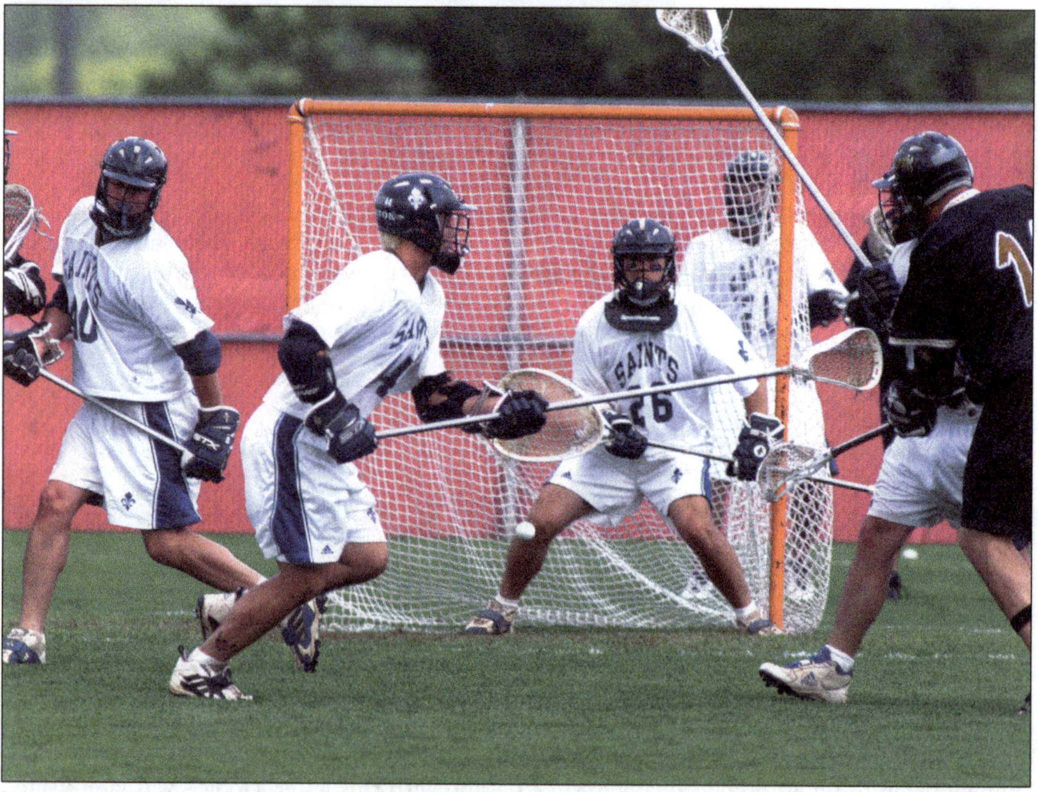

Limestone College squares off with Adelphi University in the 2001 national championship game, hoping to bring home a second straight national championship. An Adelphi shot bounces toward two-time All-American Matt Malloy's goal as Travis Gillespie (No. 44) and Tim Cober (No. 40) defend.

Three-time All-American Nick Carlson tries to work his way around an Adelphi defender as a high check is delivered.

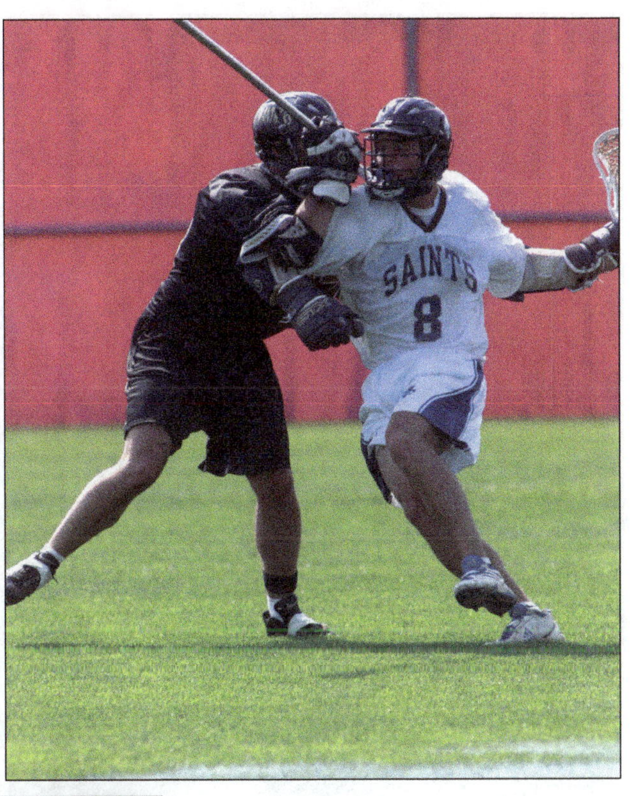

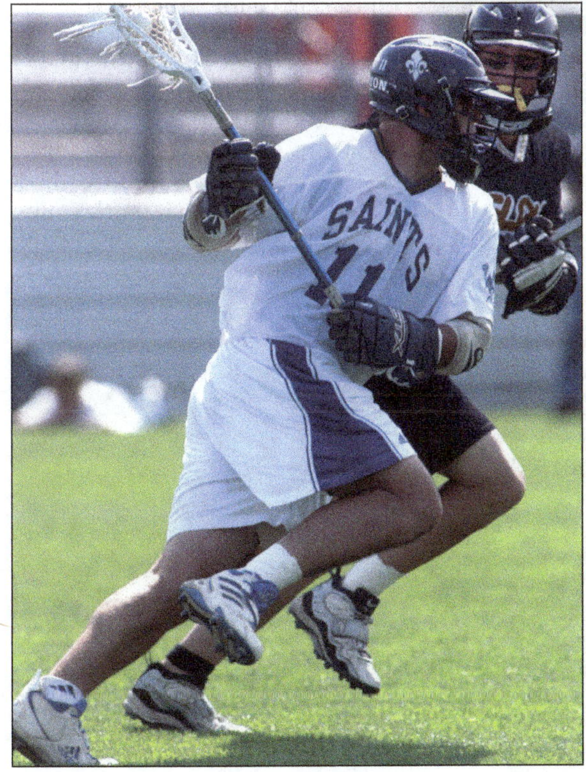

Jon Riley moves to his right and looks for a teammate as the Panther defense closes in. The Limestone offense was forced to work hard for everything it got on this afternoon.

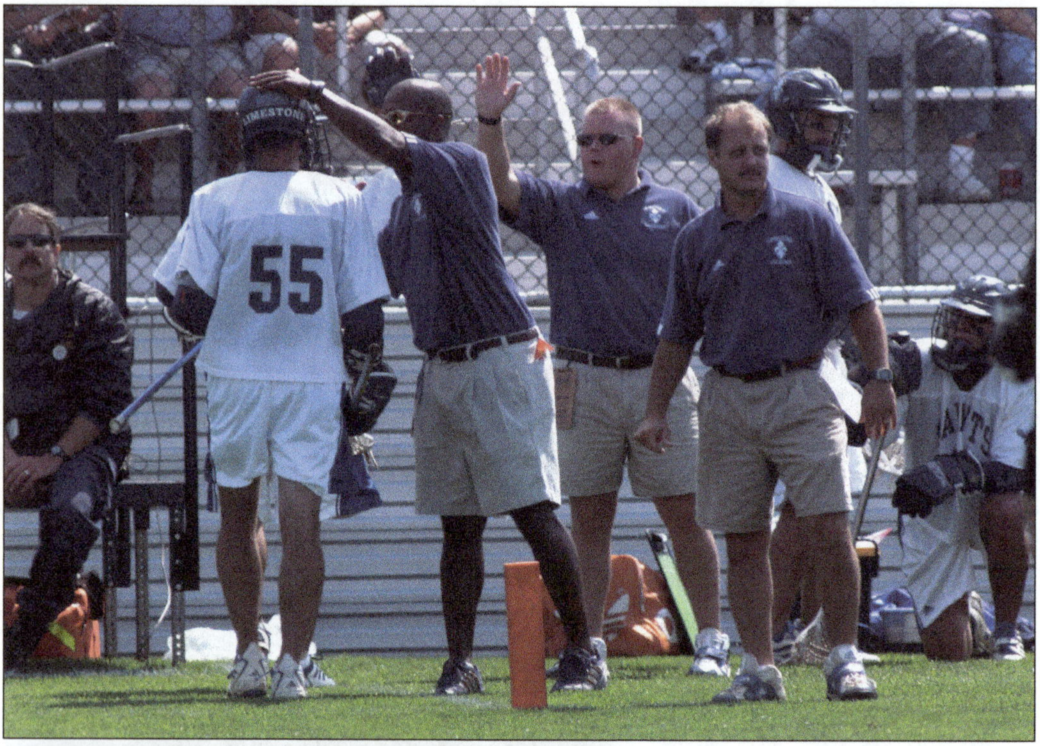

All-American Greg Hiltz comes off the field during the 2001 national championship game and is welcomed by Limestone College assistant coaches, from left to right, Ricky Matthews, John Donahue, and Chris Phenicie. Head coach Bill Milone led the Saints to a 13-3 record and this national title game appearance during his only season at the helm.

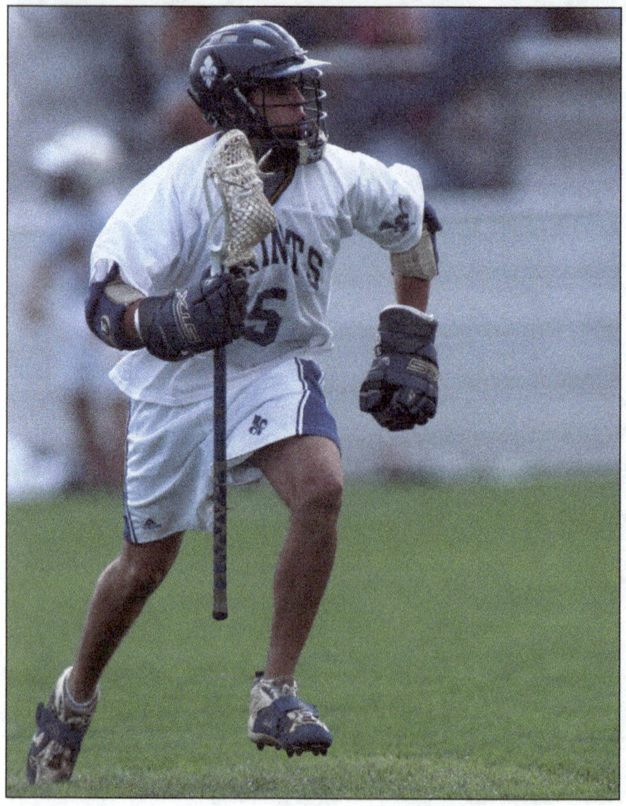

Johnny Navarro, known by teammates as "Johnny Five," examines the defense in front of him before he makes a move.

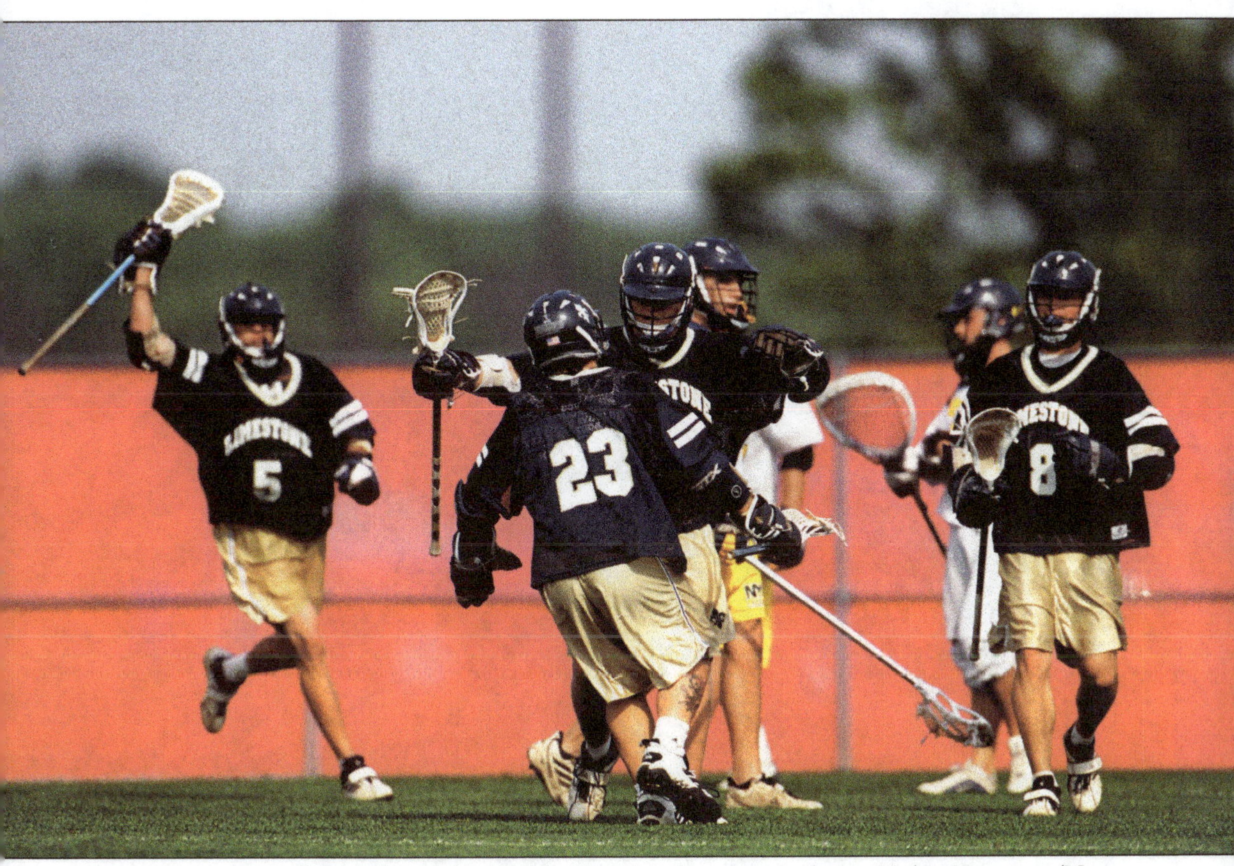

One of Limestone College's all-time leading point and goal scorers, freshman Nolan Heavener (No. 23) runs to celebrate with a teammate during the 2002 NCAA Division II national championship. The Saints knocked off the New York Tech Bears in a thrilling 11-9 finish to capture the program's second title in three years. (Courtesy of NCAA.)

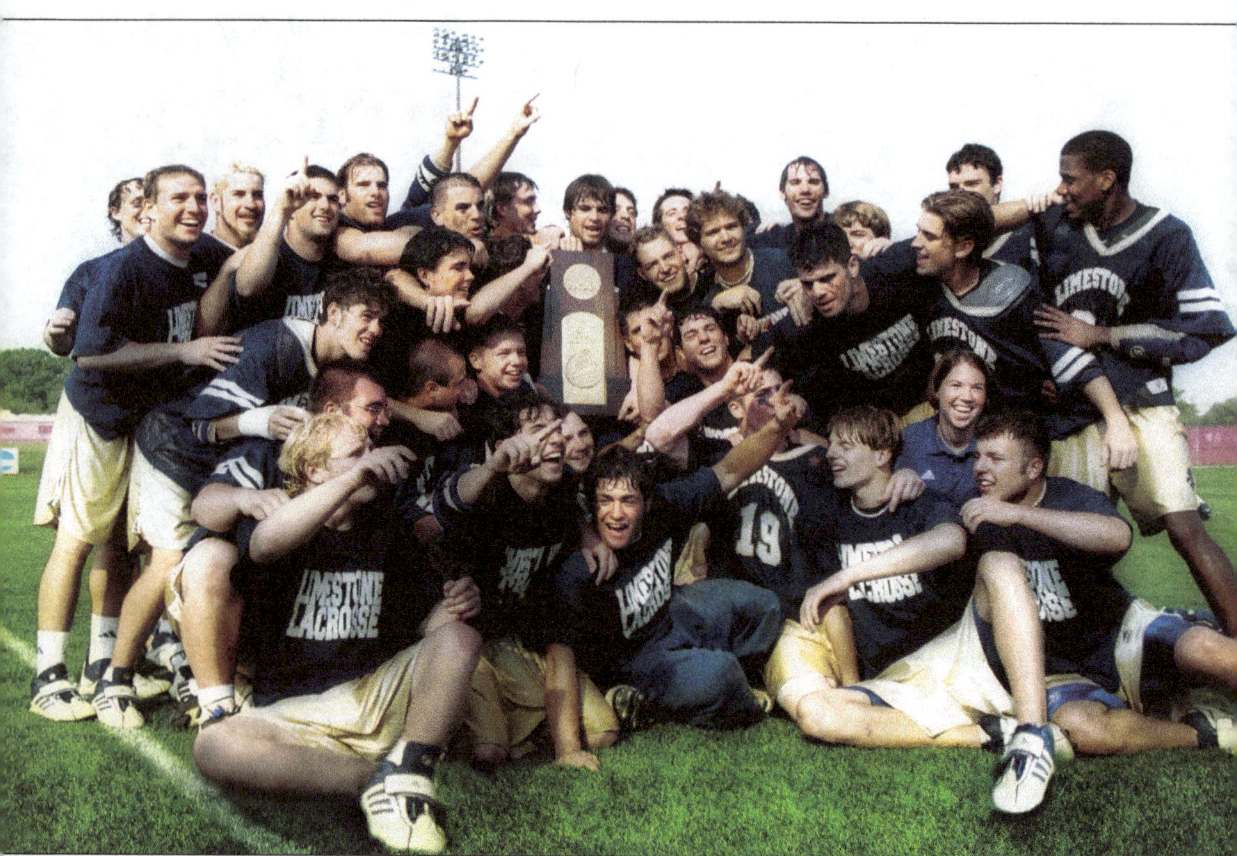

The entire team joined in the celebration as the victorious Limestone Saints were handed their NCAA Division II national championship trophy for the second time in three seasons. (Courtesy of NCAA.)

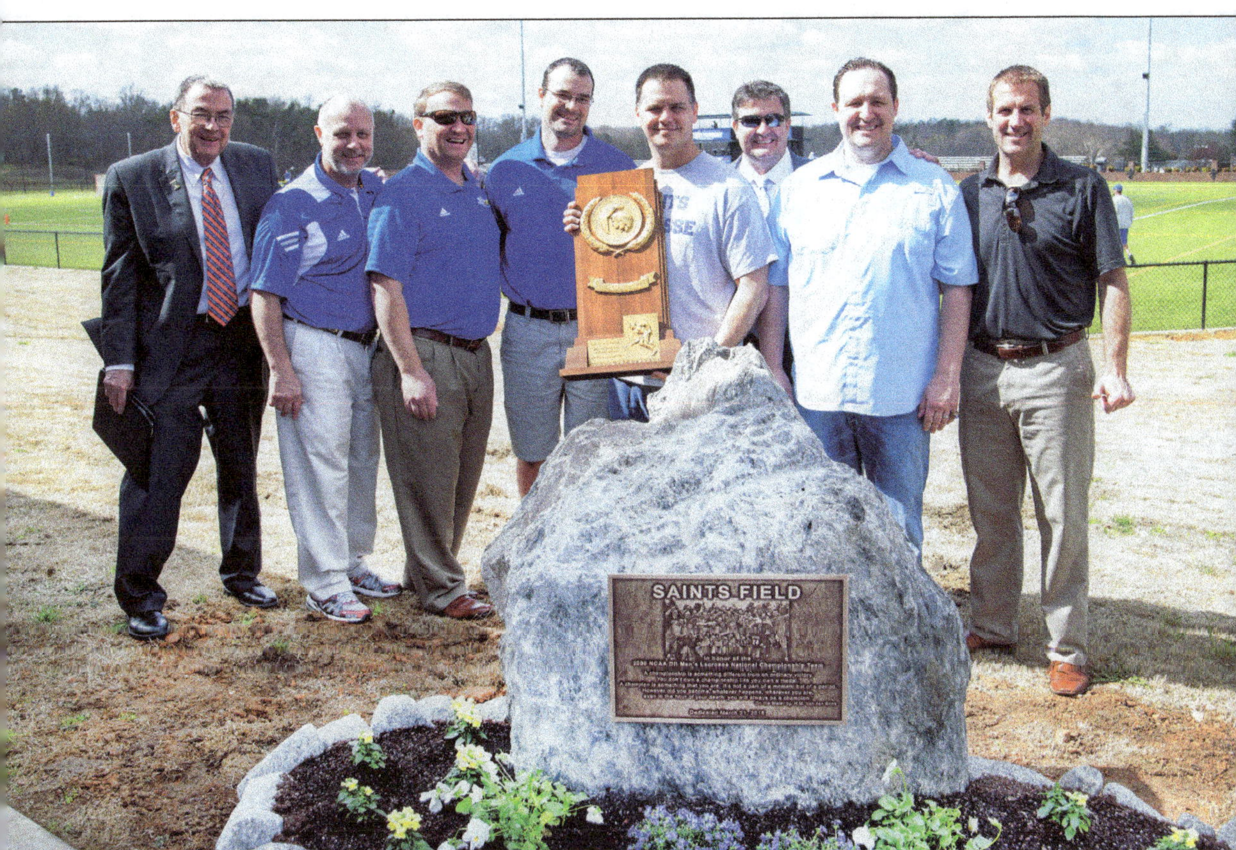

Limestone College president Dr. Walt Griffin (far left) and members of the 2002 national championship team and coaching staff get together with the national title trophy for the dedication of Saints Field in 2015. Saints Field is home to Limestone lacrosse as well as soccer and field hockey.

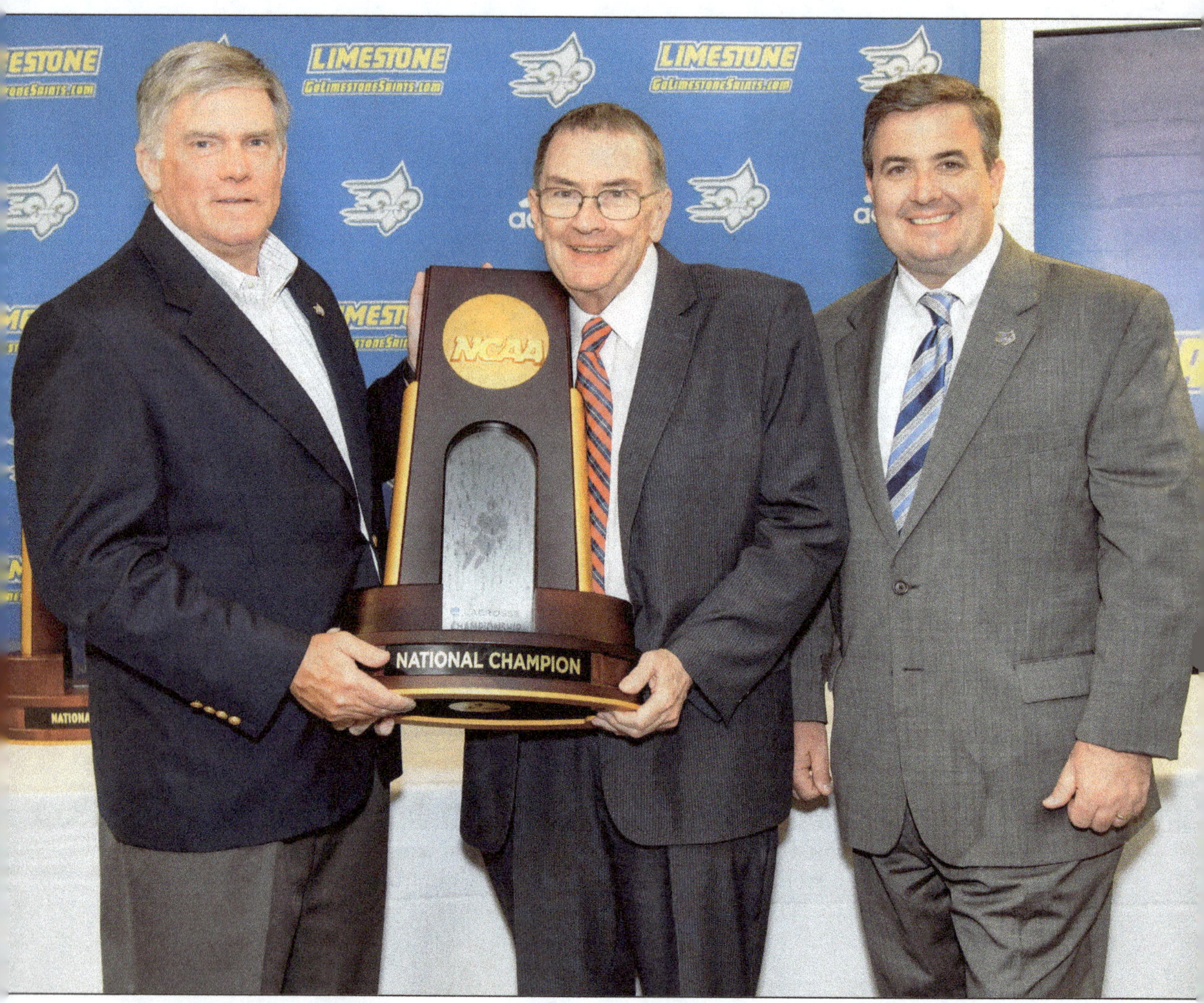

Another trophy was brought home later that spring when Limestone celebrated its first season on Saints Field with the program's fourth national championship. From left to right, head coach J.B. Clarke, president Dr. Walt Griffin, and vice president for intercollegiate athletics Mike Cerino pose during the celebration.

Three

Breaking Through to National Prominence

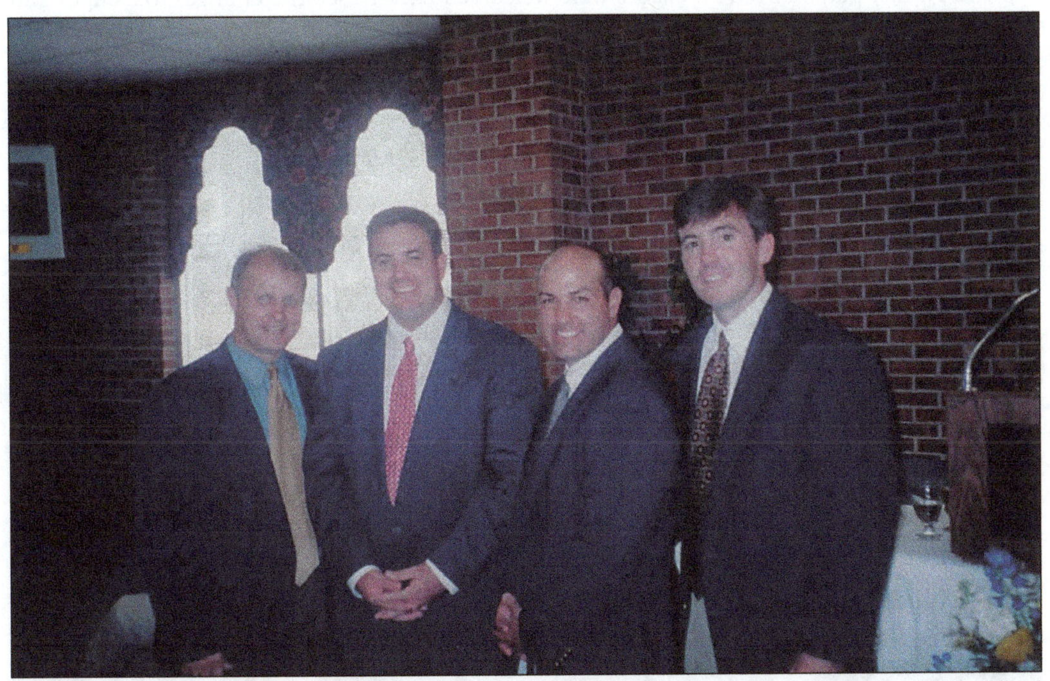

As the founding coach of the Limestone College lacrosse program and one of the most accomplished coaches in the sport's history, Mike Cerino (second from left) was inducted into the Limestone College Athletics Hall of Fame in 2004. He is pictured here with assistant coach Chris Phenicie (far left), Mike Sessa (second from right) and brother Tom Cerino (far right).

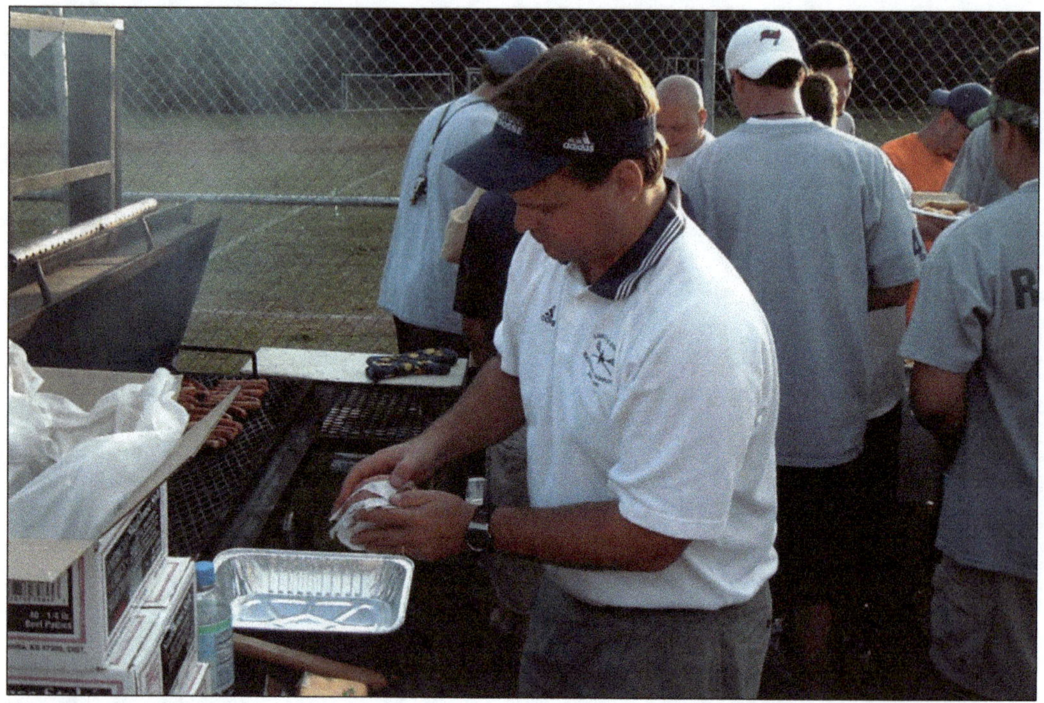

Head coach T.W. Johnson and the Saints treat themselves to lunch after an alumni game on campus. Former players from all classes were welcomed back to see the changes to campus and celebrate the program's achievements.

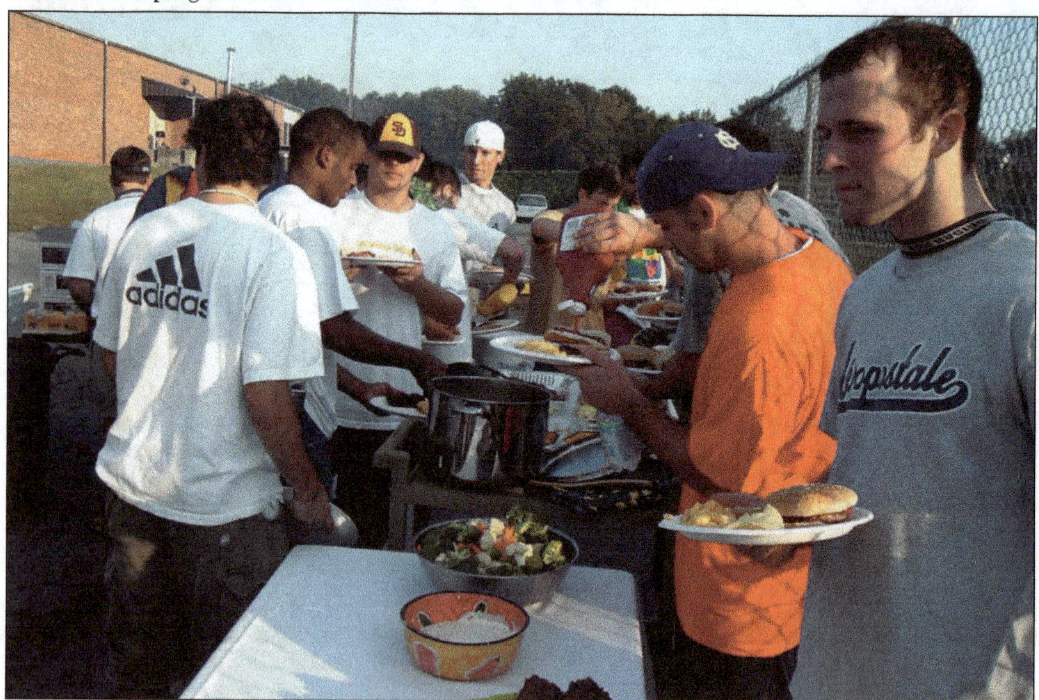

Current and former players gather for an alumni game in the early 2000s while head coach T.W. Johnson mans the grill in the background.

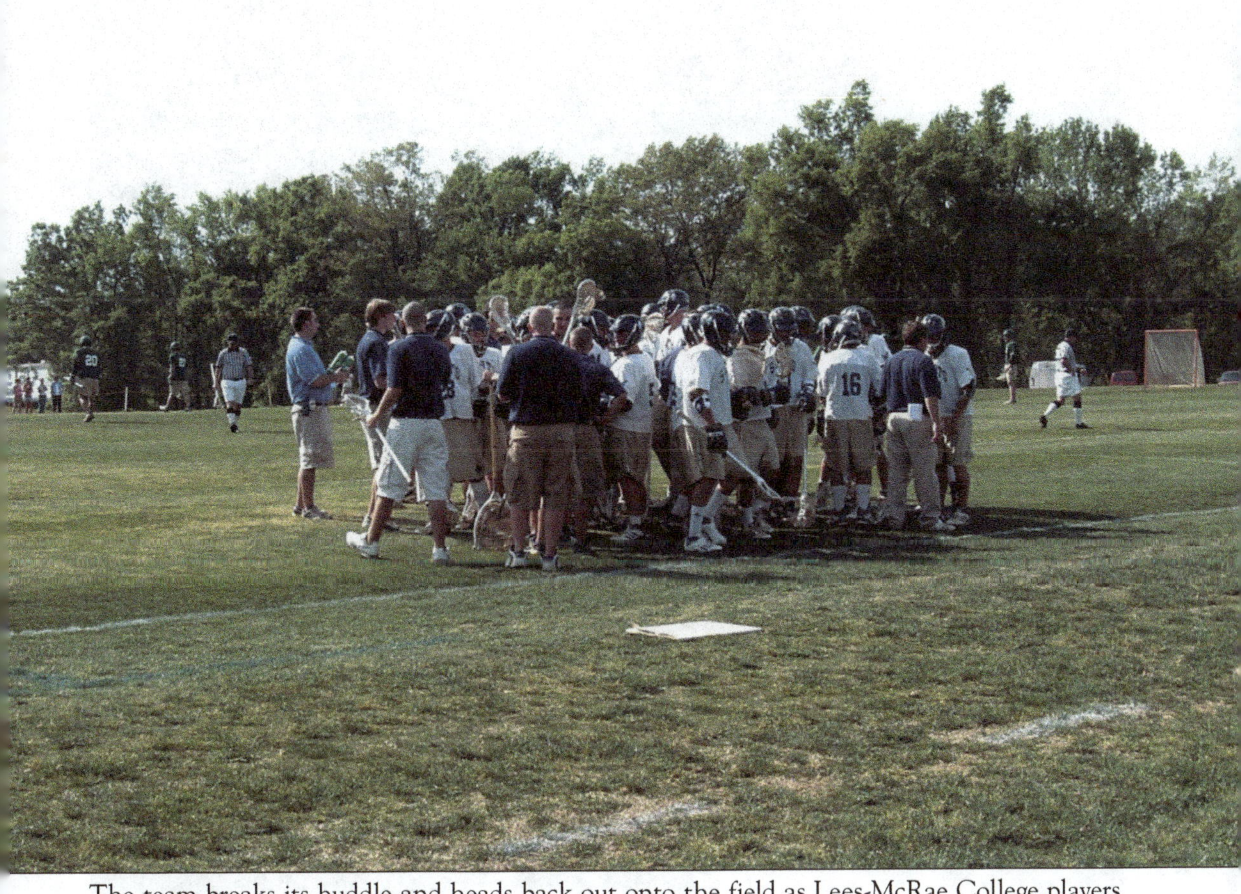

The team breaks its huddle and heads back out onto the field as Lees-McRae College players wait for play to resume.

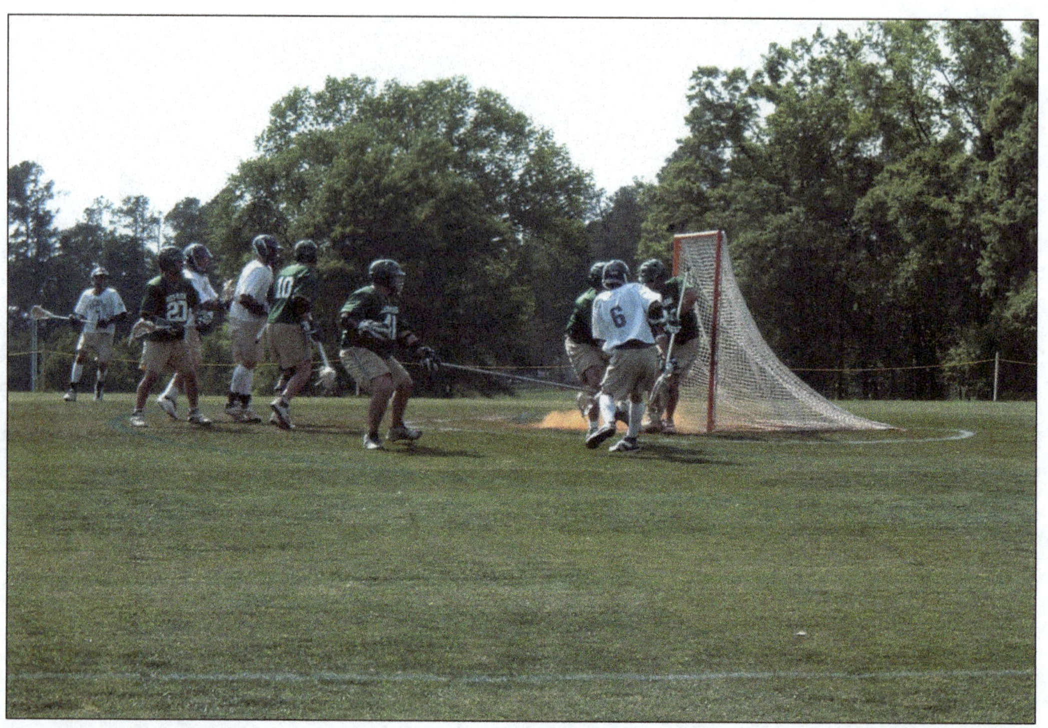

Limestone College's David Wooster punches in a goal during a 2004 matchup against conference foe Lees-McRae. The Saints went on to a comfortable 31-6 win and registered what is still the second highest goal total in a single game in team history.

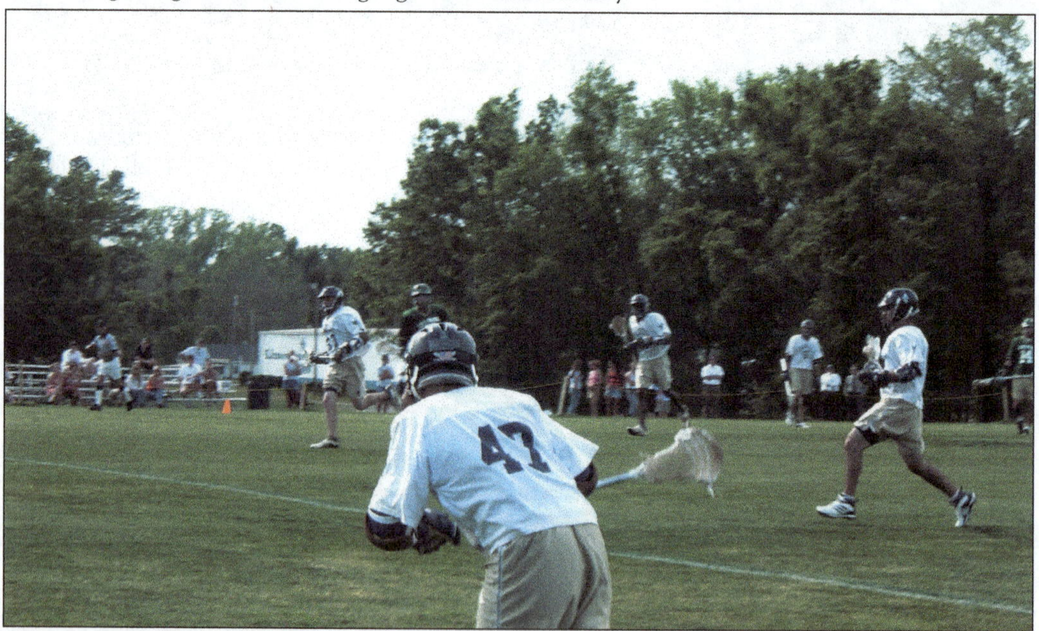

Plenty of Saints saw action in this 25-goal win over the Lees-McRae College Bobcats, as freshman Ryan Collins can be seen racing down the field with a host of unguarded teammates. Limestone College has enjoyed one of the most lopsided rivalries in college sports against Lees-McRae, with 23 wins and no losses all-time.

Johnny Navarro scans the St. Andrews defense during this 25-8 Limestone win in Laurinburg, North Carolina, later during the 2004 season.

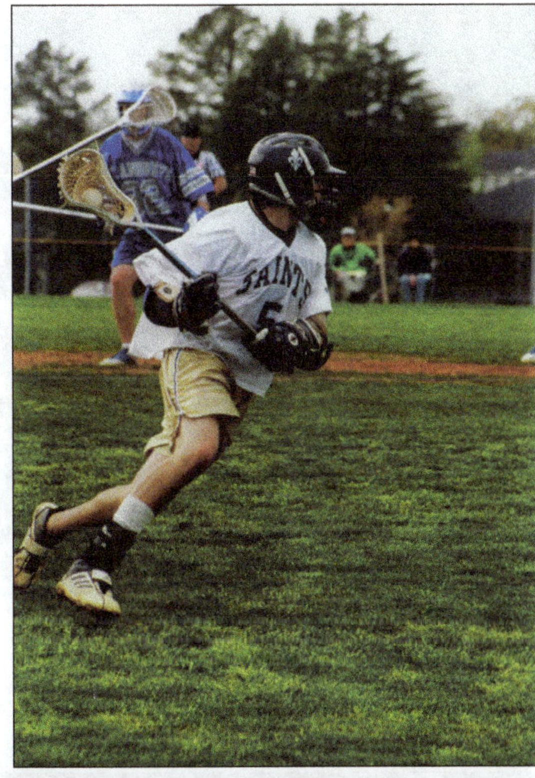

The 2004 team gathers together for a watch party as the brackets are announced for the NCAA tournament. Longtime program supporters C.R. Horton and Brenda Watkins, who rarely miss a game, helped put together the watch party and can be seen with the team as the Saints await their postseason fate.

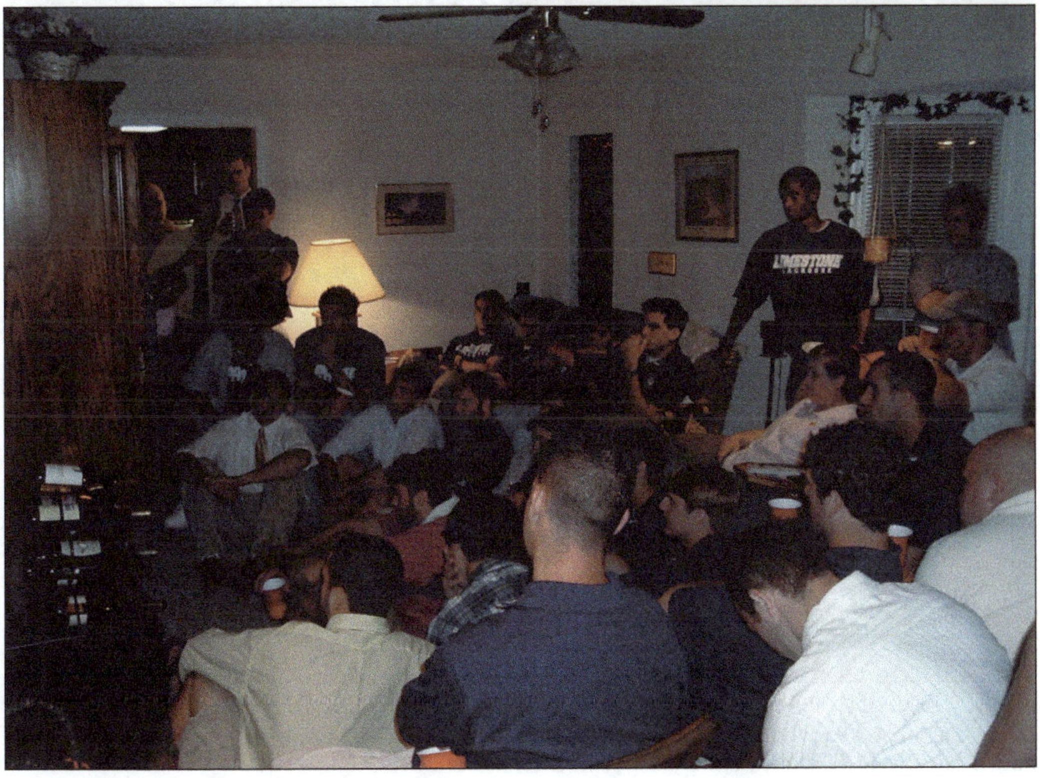

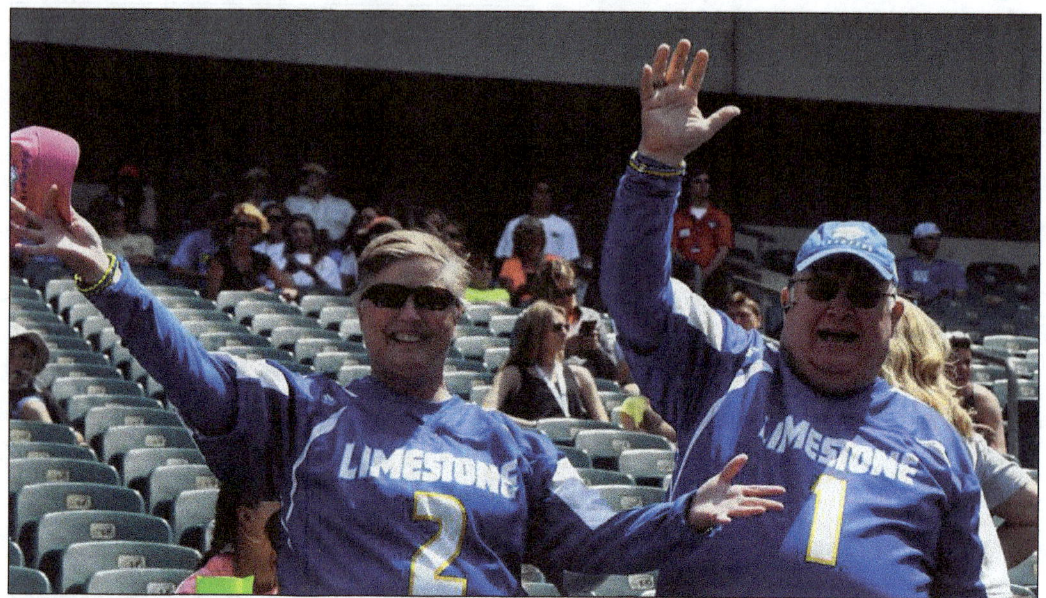

Watkins and Horton continue to be the program's biggest fans and can be seen here at the 2015 national championship game in Philadelphia.

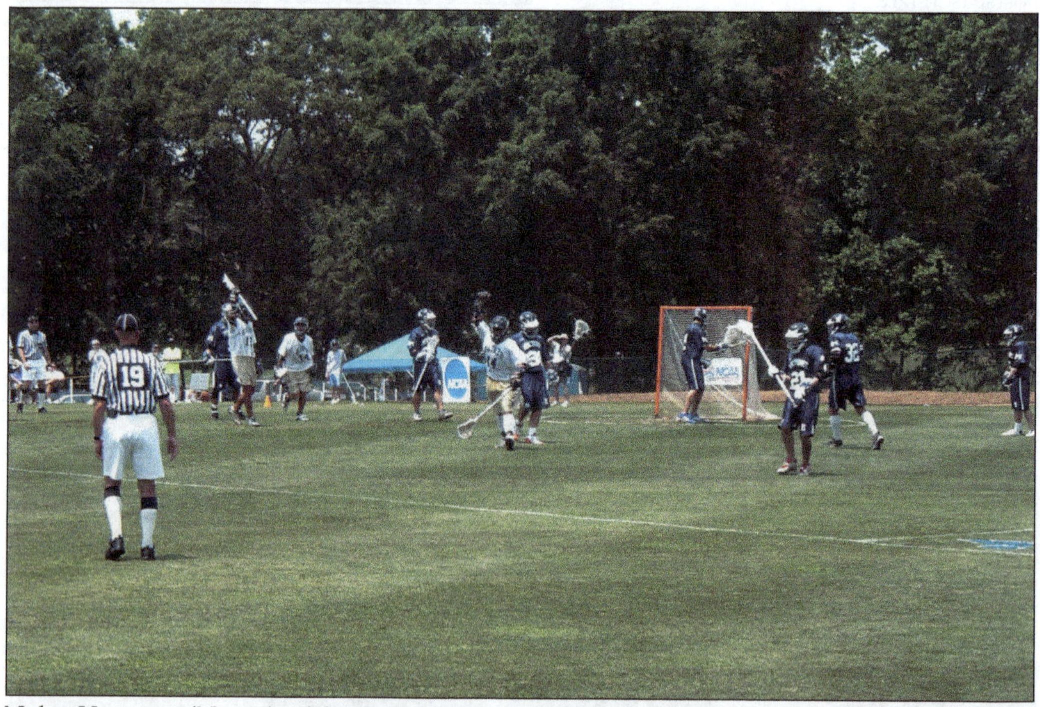

Nolan Heavenor (No. 44) celebrates a Limestone College goal during a 2004 NCAA tournament contest against Mercyhurst College. The Saints used the home crowd to their advantage and pulled out the 14-12 win to clinch a spot in the national title game.

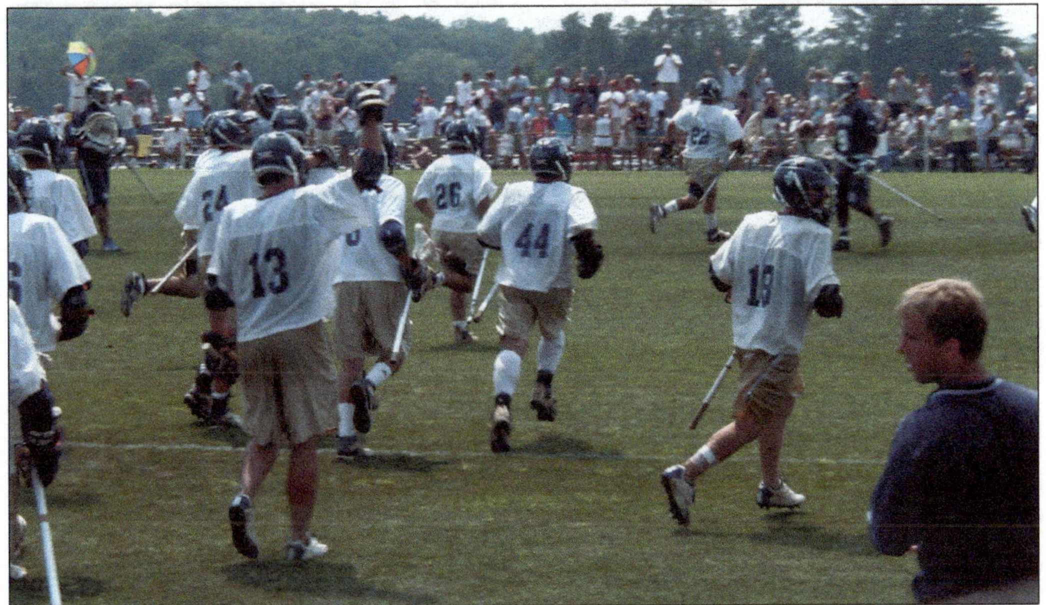

Teammates storm the field to celebrate the win over the Lakers as fans look on in excitement. The win set up another showdown between classic powerhouse programs as Limestone College clinched its spot against Le Moyne College in the title fight.

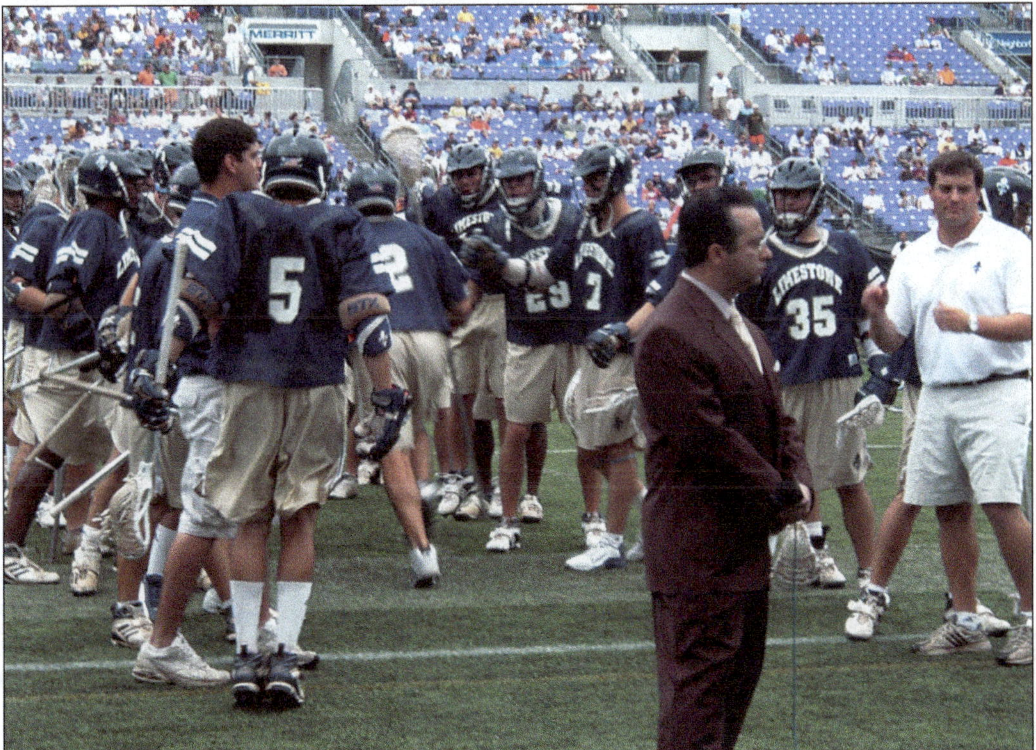

The Saints showed up in Baltimore ready to roll and looking to secure the program's third national title in five seasons. As shown here, starting lineups against the Le Moyne Dolphins were announced with the team forming a tunnel onto the field.

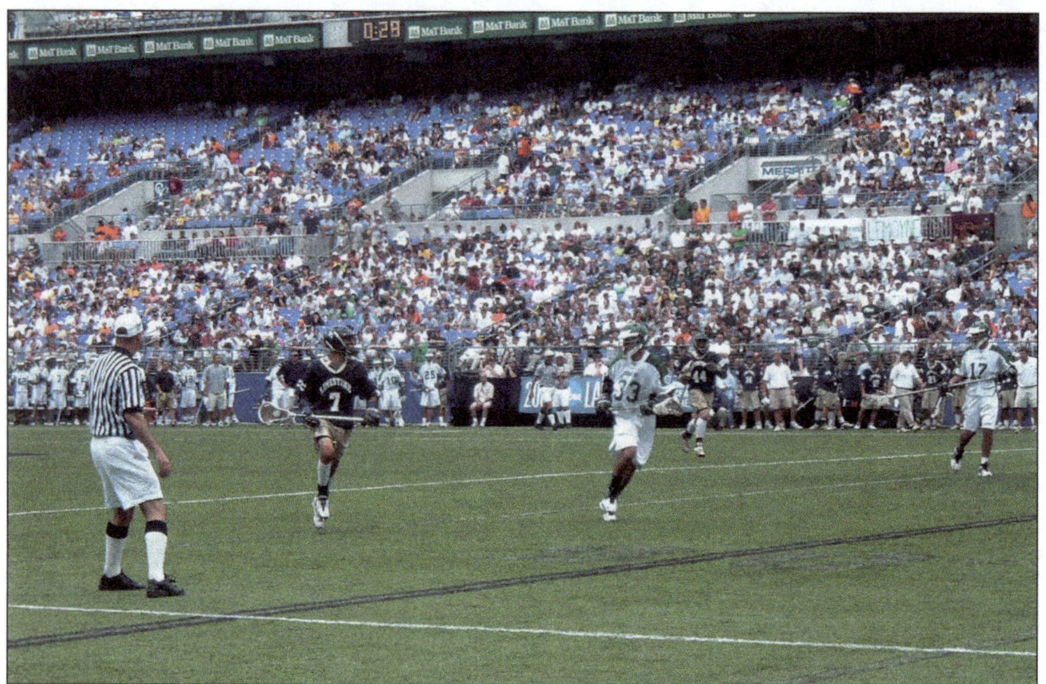

Senior Chris Barrett runs the Limestone College offense against defensive powerhouse Le Moyne College inside M&T Bank Stadium in Baltimore during the 2004 NCAA Division II national championship game.

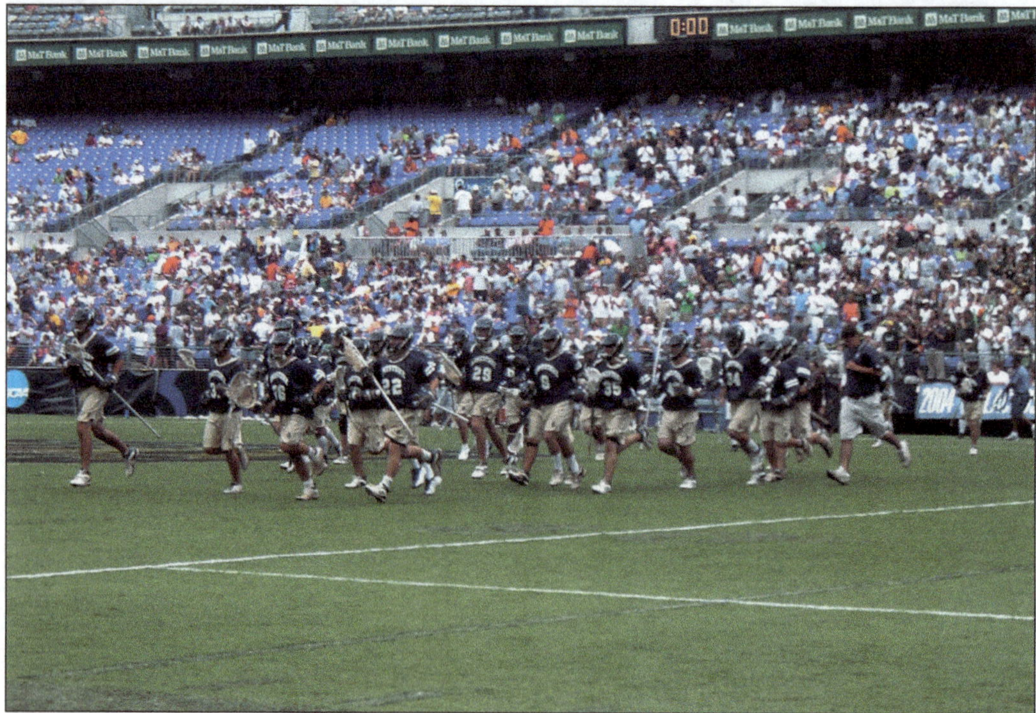

The Saints come off the field at halftime in a tight game where either side could come away with a victory.

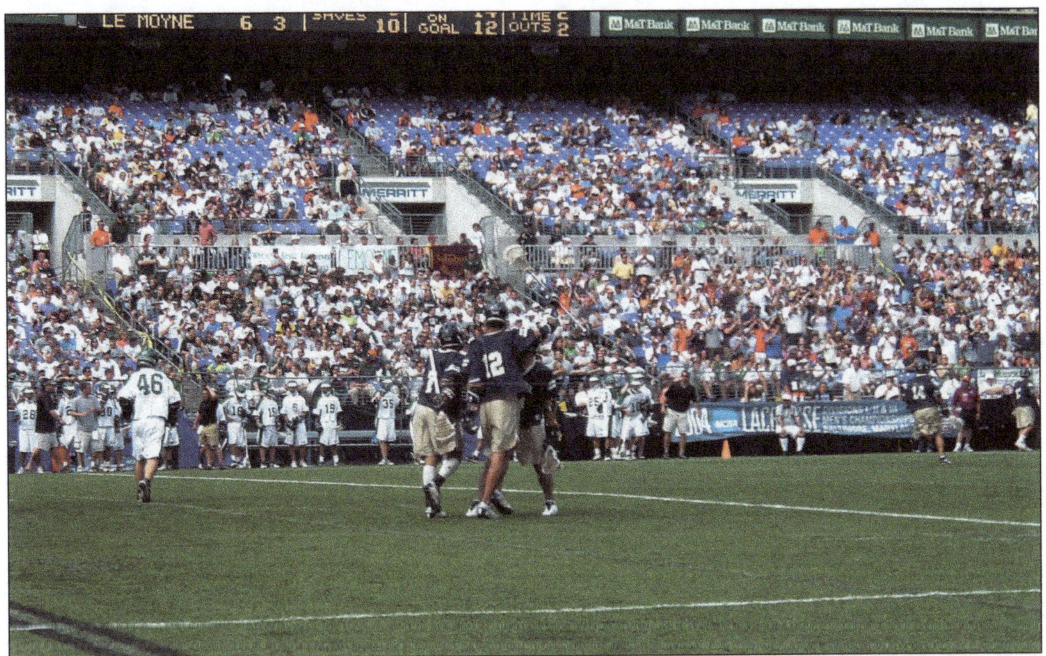

Chris Barrett and fellow senior Jason Randolph celebrate a second half goal with a teammate as time winds into the final stretch.

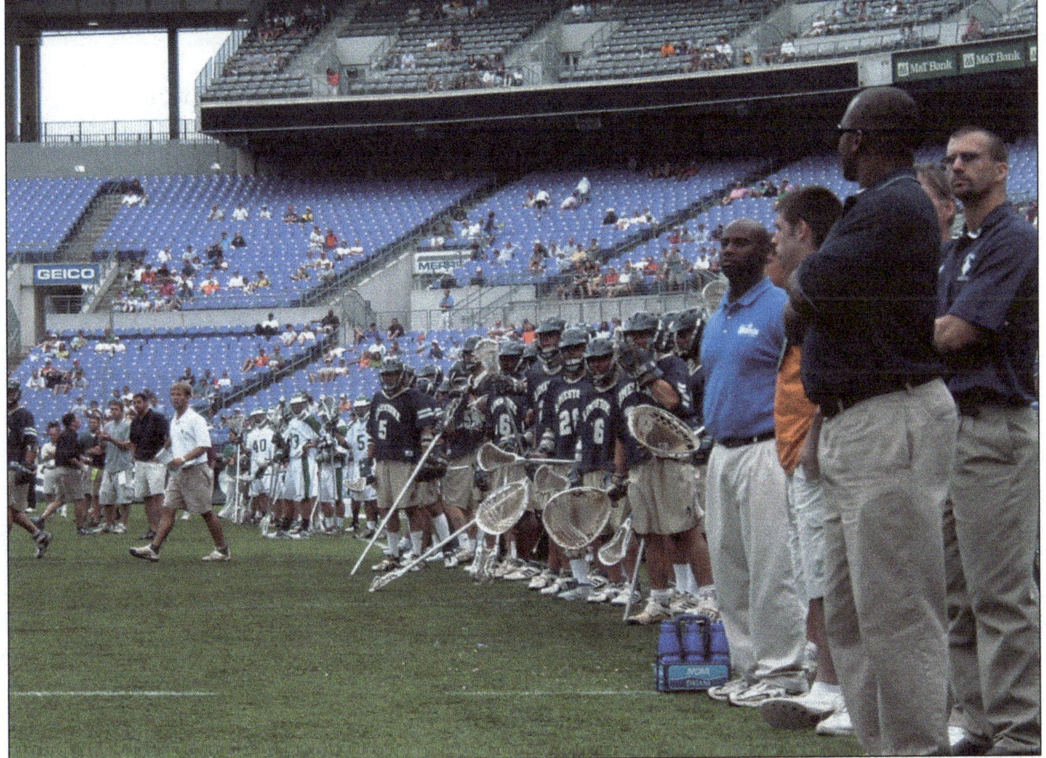

Both sidelines were on edge throughout the full 60 minutes of this heavyweight fight, as overtime was needed to declare a winner.

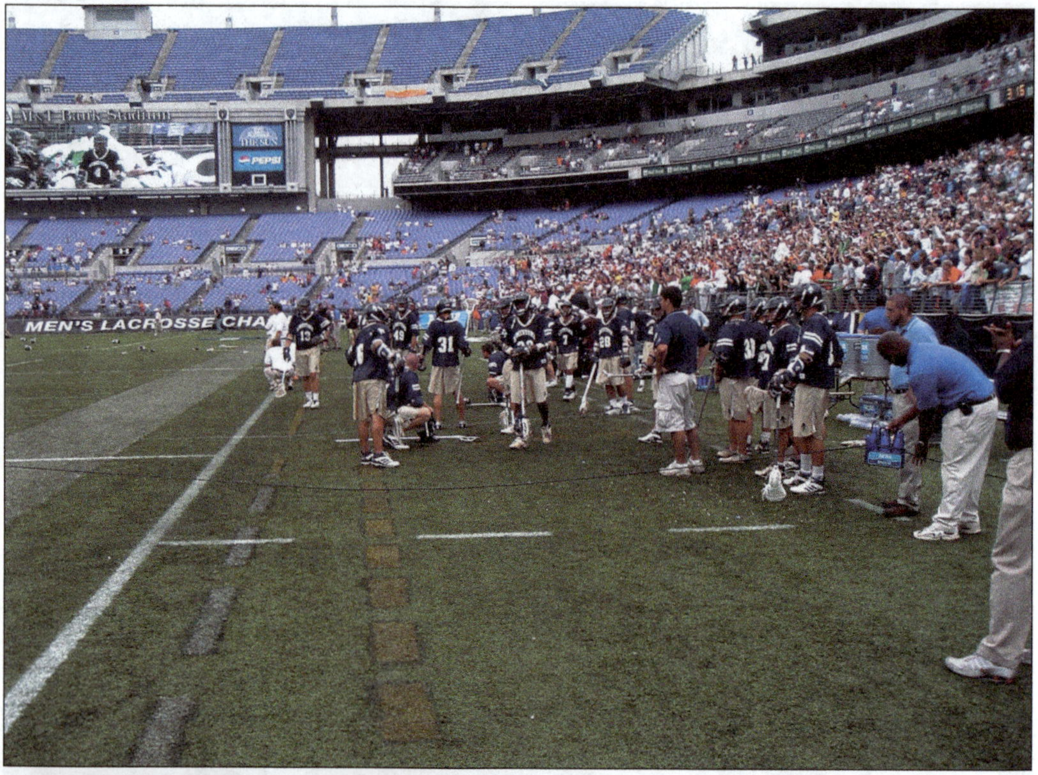

Le Moyne College's overtime goal sent the Dolphins rushing onto the field while Limestone was forced to watch from the sideline.

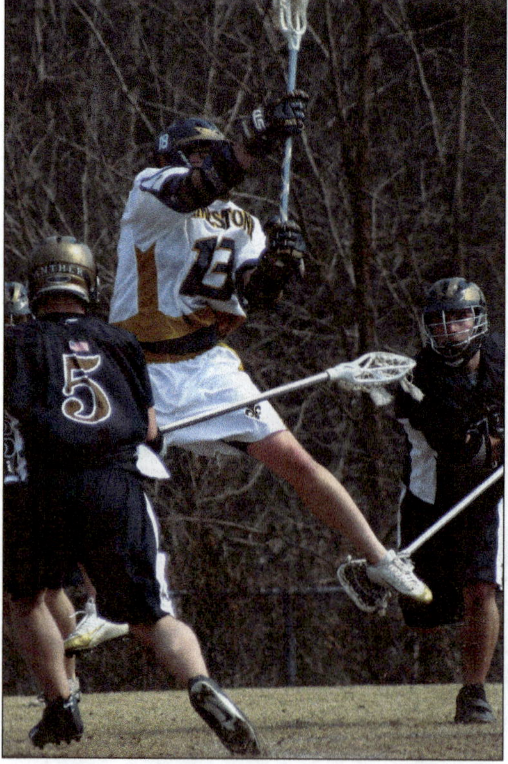

A senior at the time, All-American Bobby Woody is seen here propelling the Saints to victory over Adelphi University in Annapolis, Maryland, during a 2005 contest. Woody finished his Limestone College career with 101 goals and played in four straight national title games.

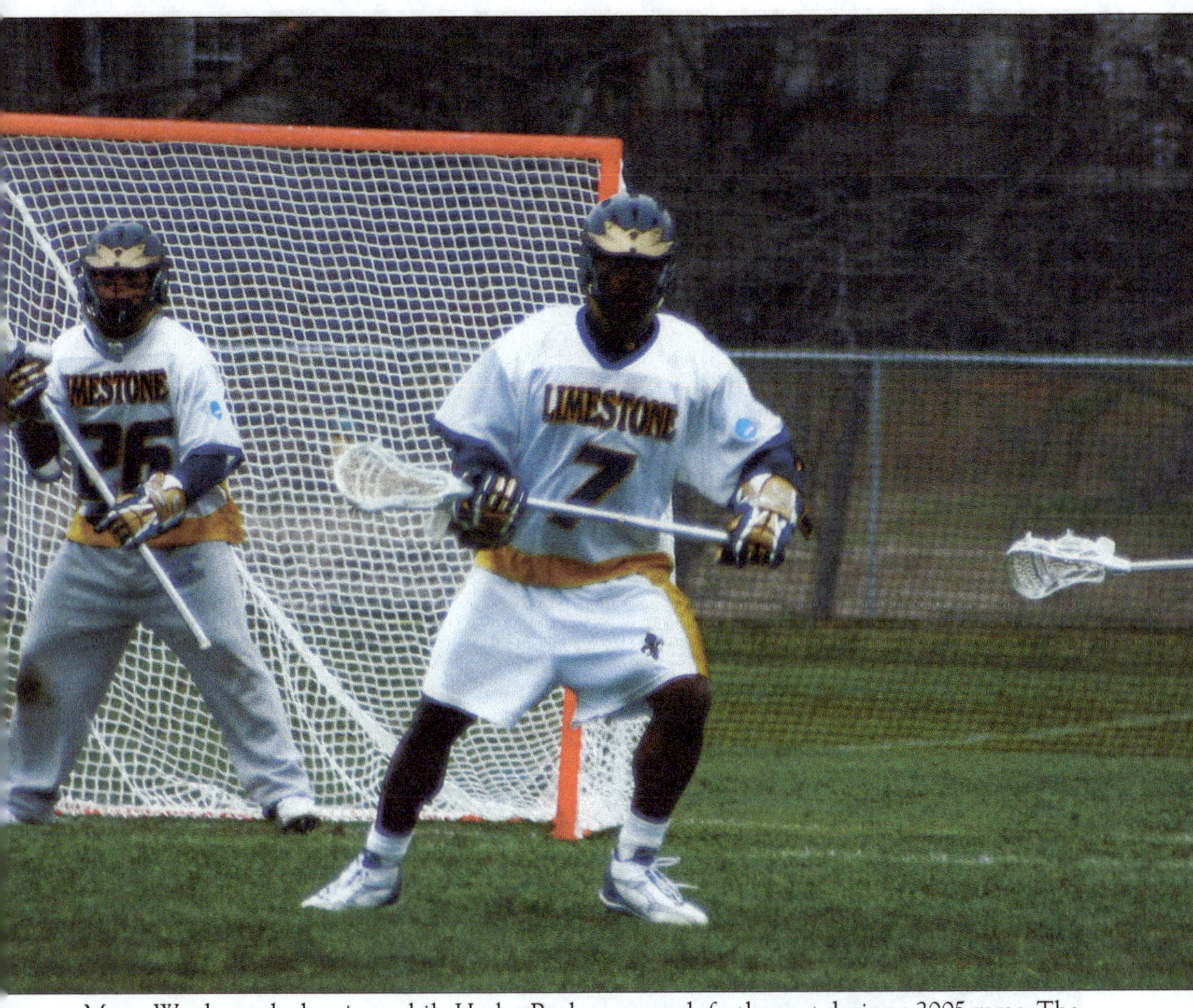

Marty Ward patrols the pipes while Harley Beekman guards farther out during a 2005 game. The Saints began the season 14-0 before dropping two of the last three, including a one-goal loss to New York Tech in the national championship.

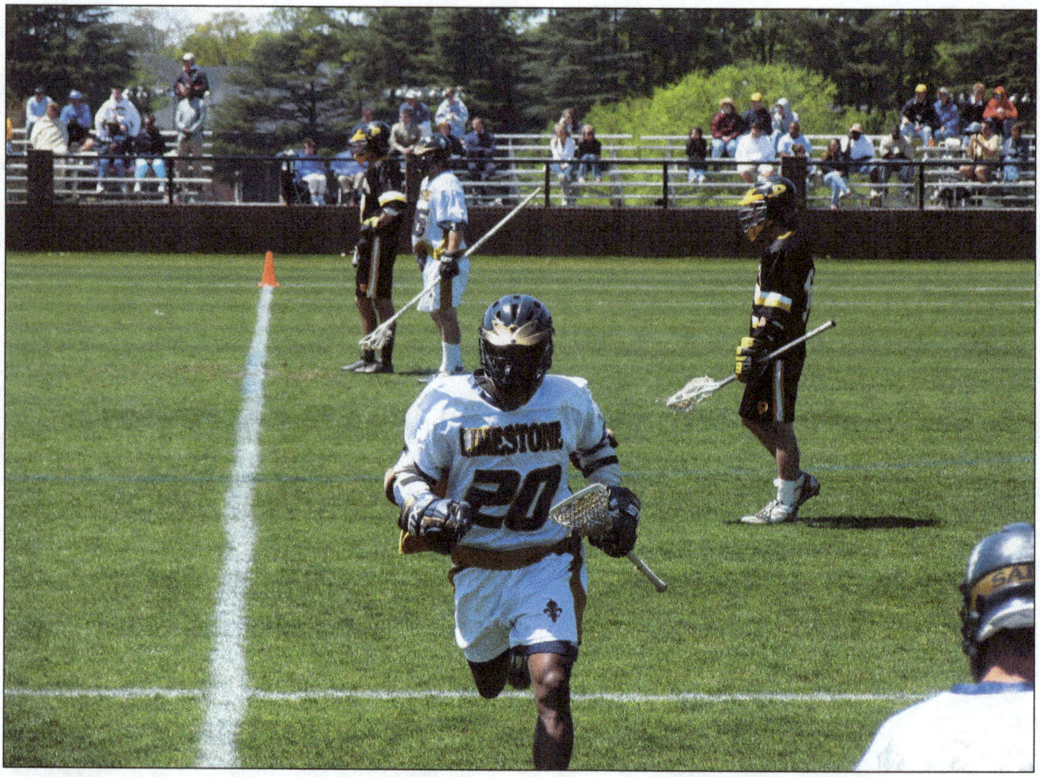

Phil Thompson rushes off the field in a 2005 win against Pfeiffer University. Limestone College has met the Falcons more than any other team in the program's history, with a 29-5 all-time record.

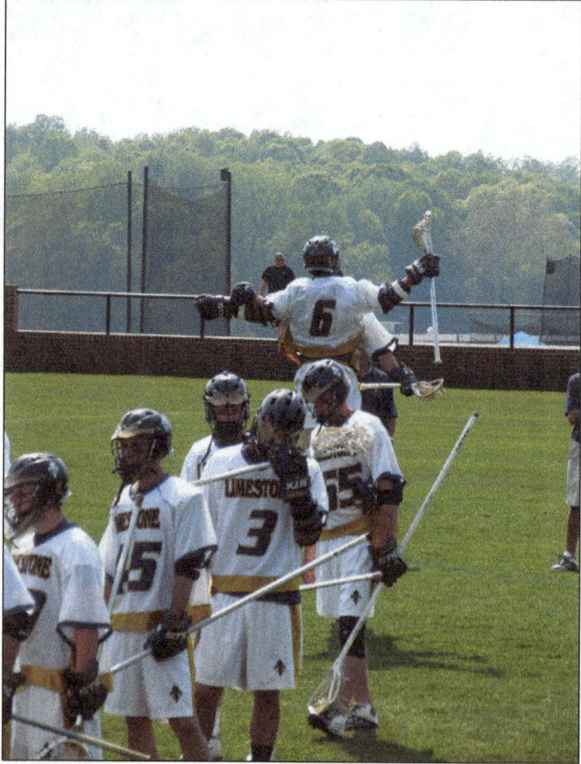

David Wooster and a teammate celebrate after Limestone College's win at home over rival Pfeiffer University to wrap up an undefeated Deep South Conference slate in 2005.

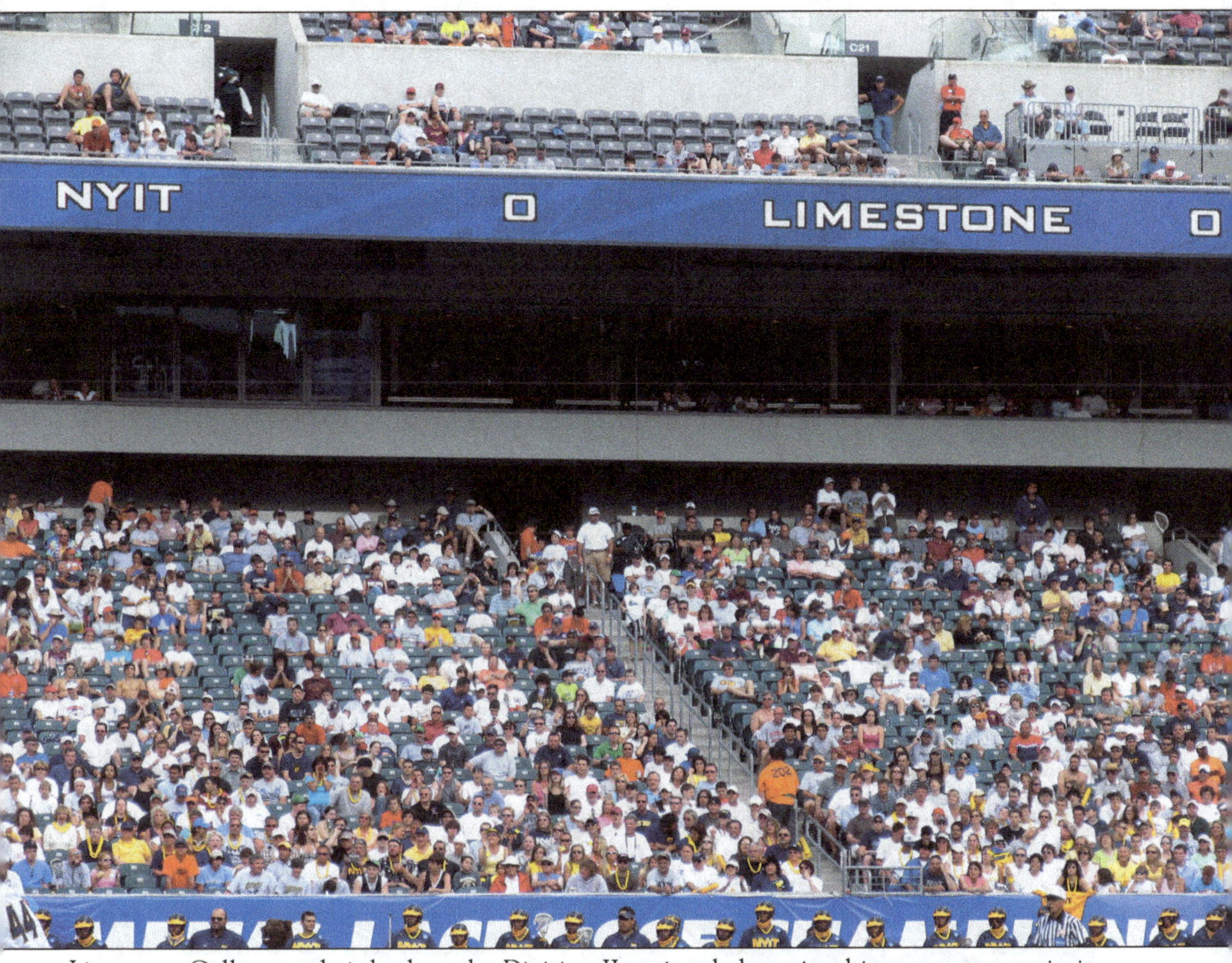

Limestone College made it back to the Division II national championship game once again in 2005 after a thrilling 9-8 win over Le Moyne College in the semifinals. This marked Limestone's sixth title game appearance and third against New York Institute of Technology.

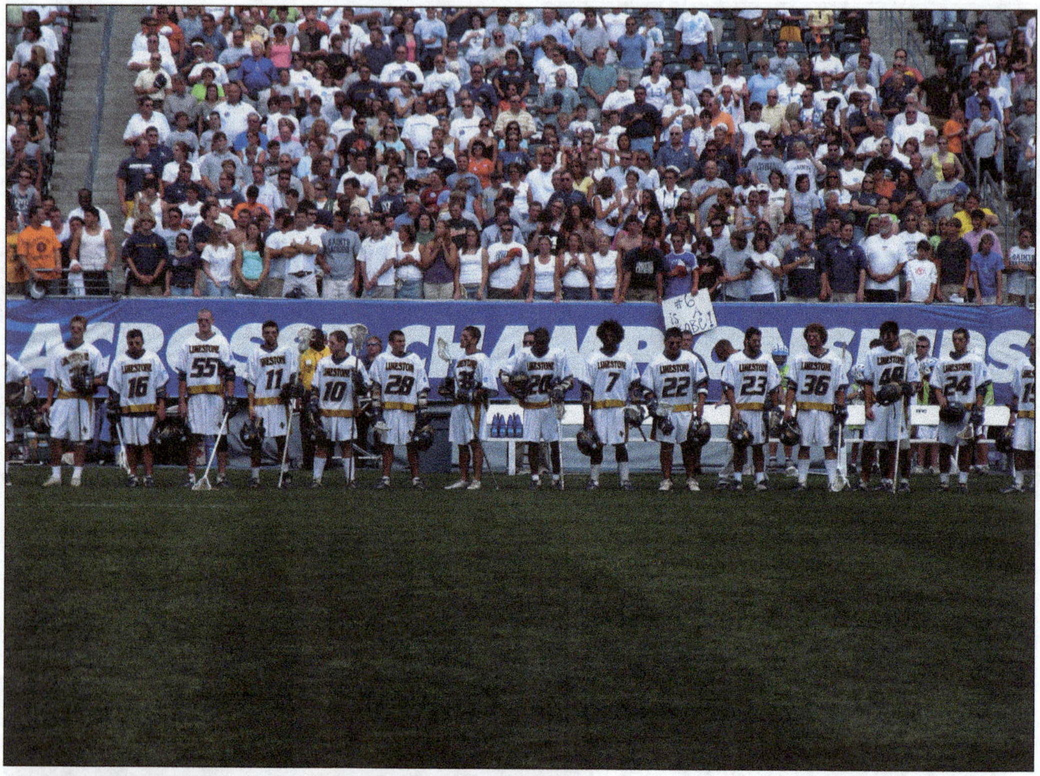

No stranger to the national spotlight and big stage, the Saints are lined up here just before the program's sixth consecutive NCAA Division II national championship appearance, a record that no other program has been able to match.

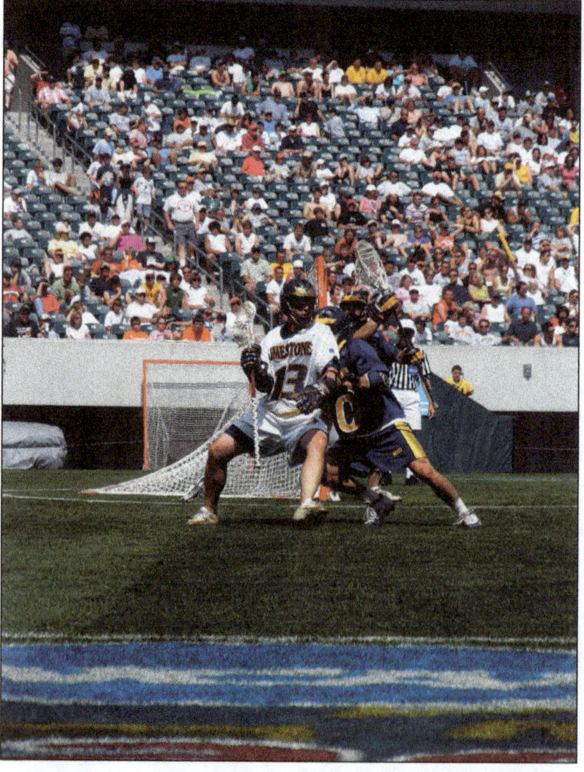

Bobby Woody backs down a New York Tech defender and looks for a path toward goal.

A New York Tech defender is unable to stay with Limestone's Patrick Cardiff as the Saints put the pressure on the Bears early.

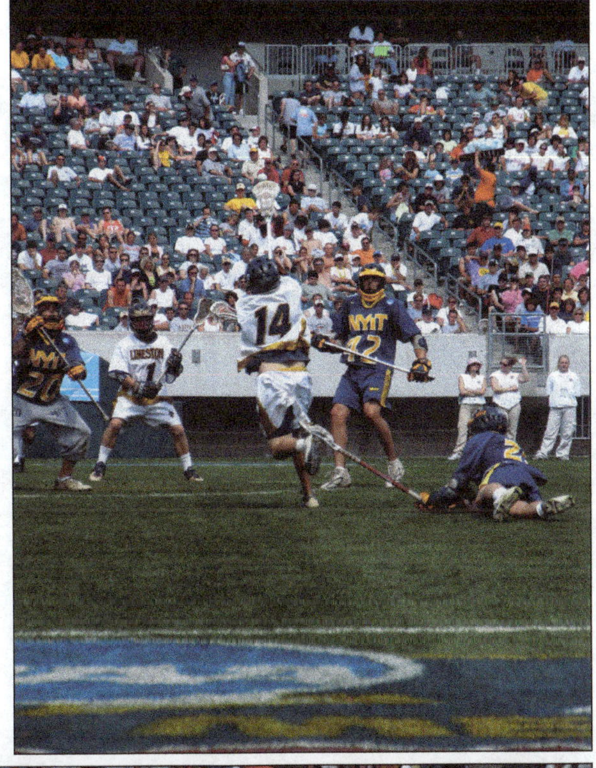

Unfortunately for the Blue & Gold, the Saints fell short of adding a third national title for the second consecutive year by just one goal. The 14-13 loss to New York Tech in 2005 followed Limestone College's heartbreaking 11-10 overtime loss to Le Moyne College the previous year.

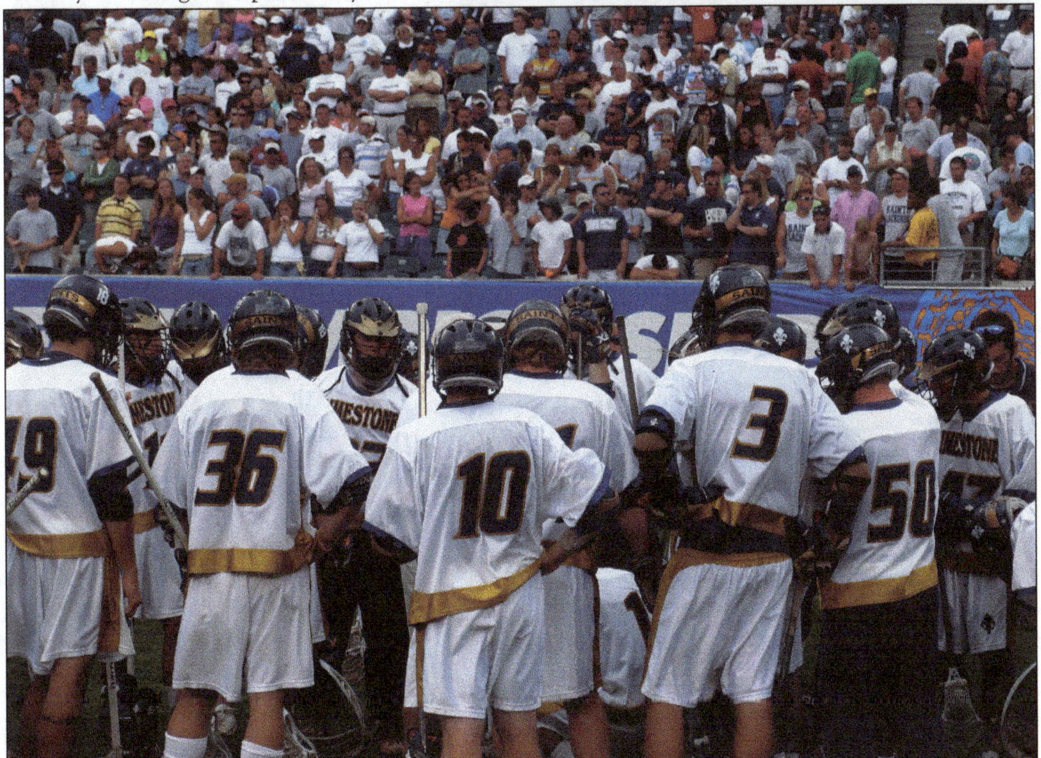

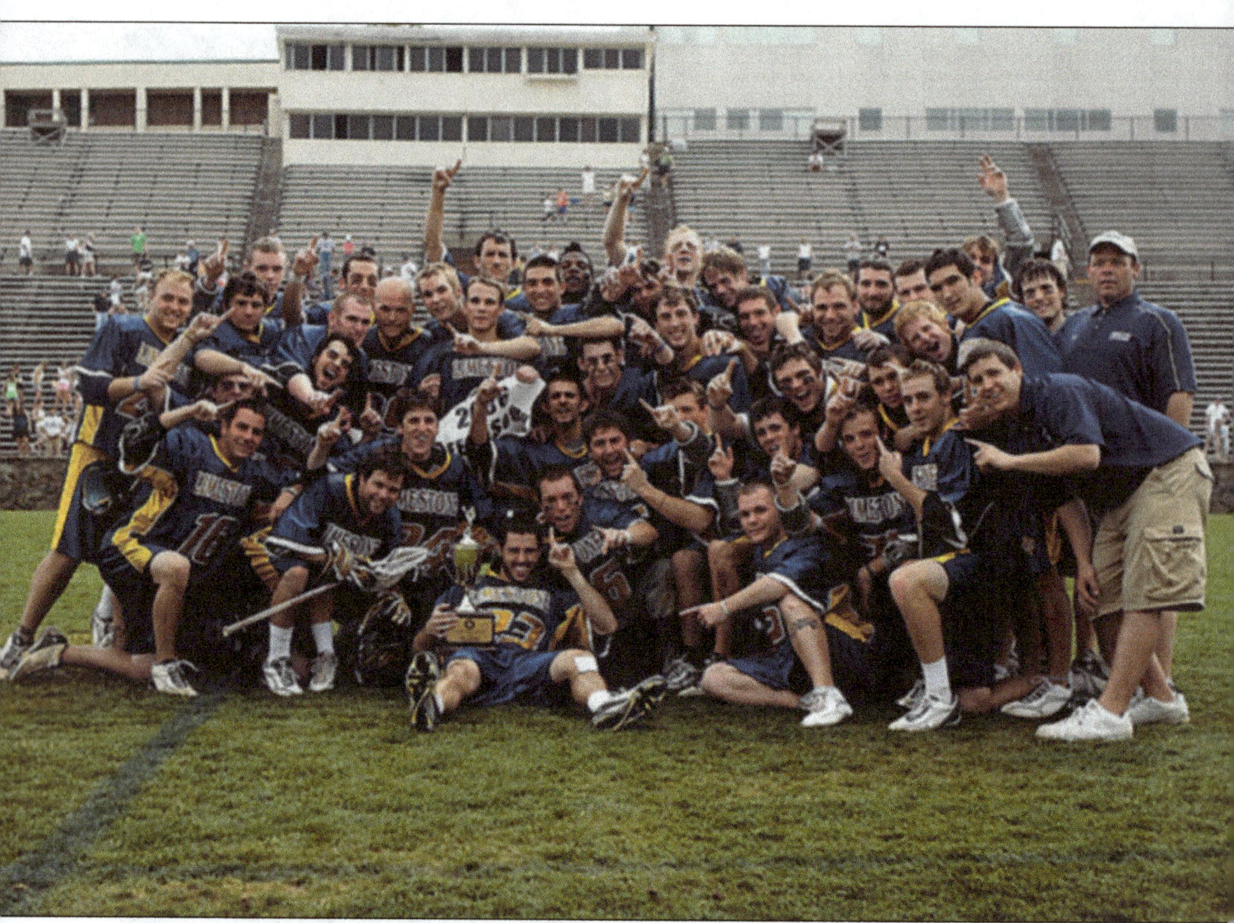

The final year of the Deep South Conference in 2006 saw Limestone College raise yet another banner after a 14-9 victory over Queens University of Charlotte in the conference tournament title game. Head coach Chris Hasbrouk and the Saints, led by Brad Patridge and Drew Comeau, got revenge on the Royals from their regular season loss and combined for seven goals on the day. Coach Hasbrouck racked up a 26-7 record including a pair of conference championships and an appearance in the 2005 national championship game.

Four

Restoring the Order

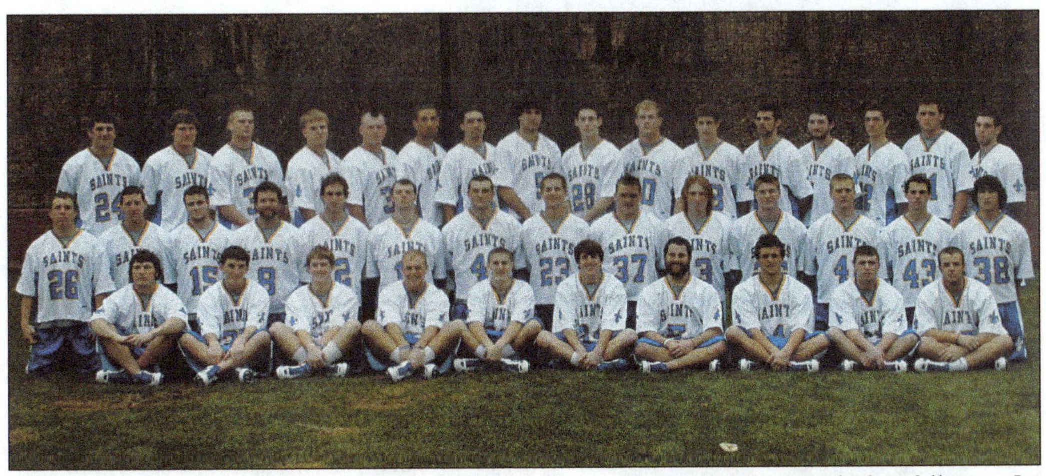

This 2007 team finished the season 14-2 with a win over Bryant University before falling to Le Moyne College in the national championship game.

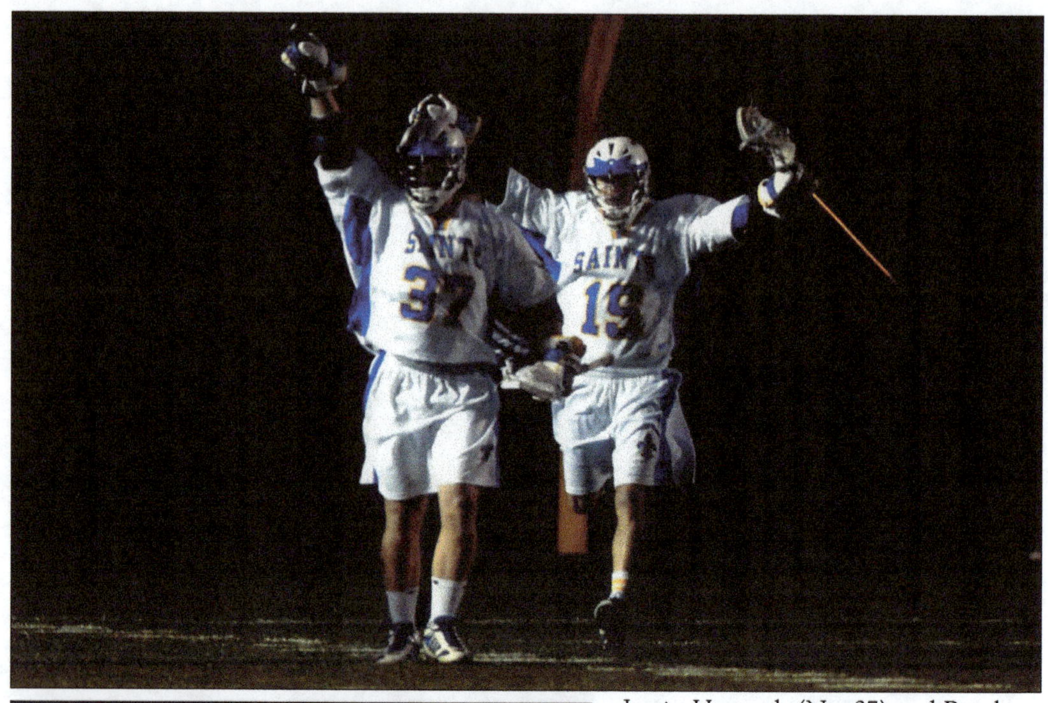

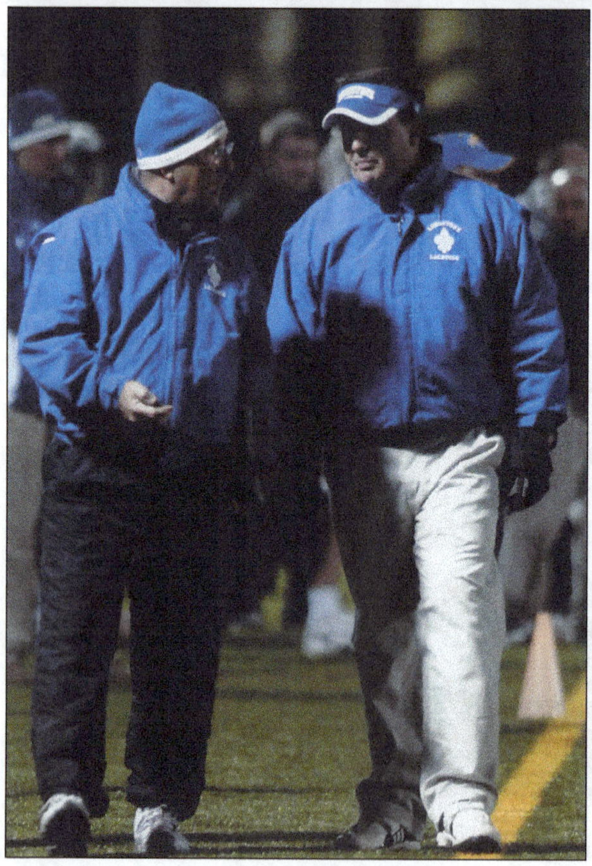

Justin Haworth (No. 37) and Brock Spilker (No. 15) celebrate a goal against Adelphi University in 2007. Playing a neutral site game at Broadneck High School in Arnold, Maryland, just outside of Annapolis, the Saints suffered their only regular season defeat in a low-scoring 7-4 affair. Haworth went on to be named an All-American that season and again in 2008.

Head coach Mike Cerino paces the sidelines with assistant coach Jim Dietsch during the game against Adelphi.

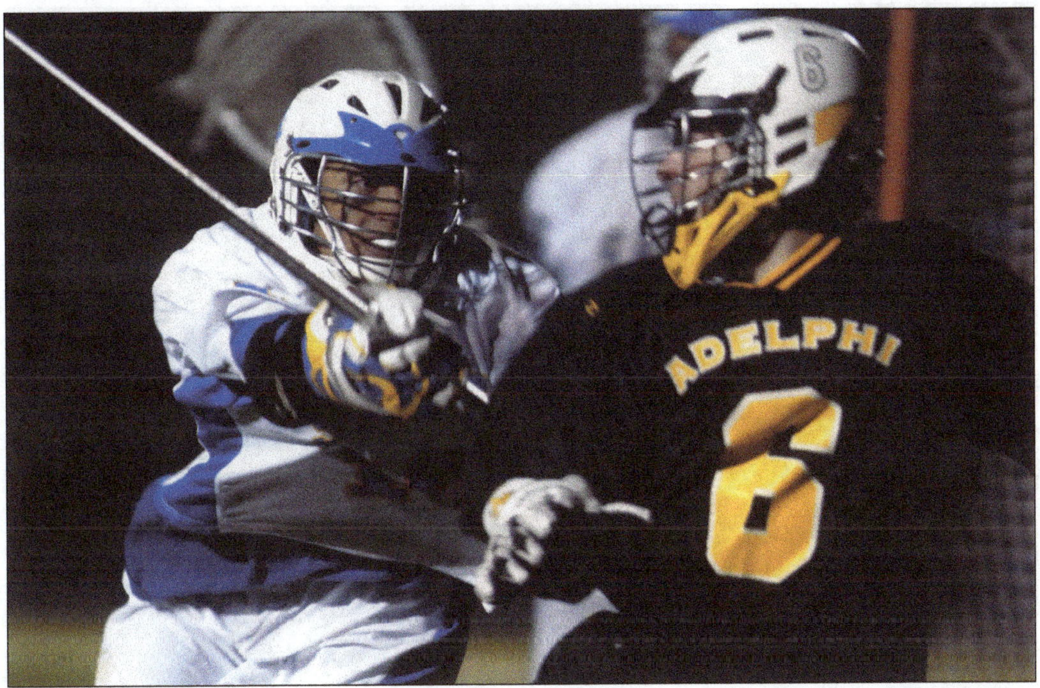

A first-team All-American in 2009, Spencer Wims is shown here making life tough on the Adelphi University Panthers. Wims still ranks sixth all-time at Limestone College with 37 career caused turnovers and was an enforcer for the Blue & Gold defense.

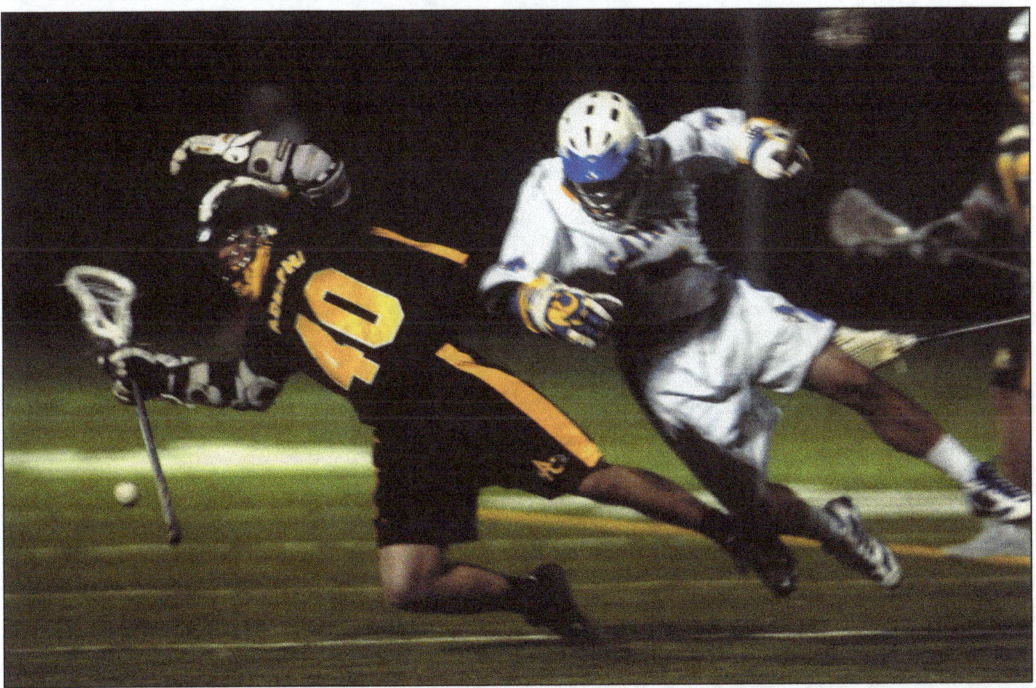

Goals were difficult to find in this 2007 low-scoring slugfest with Adelphi University. Limestone came into the game looking for revenge against the Panthers after their loss in the previous season, but the Saints were once again turned away in a 7-4 defeat.

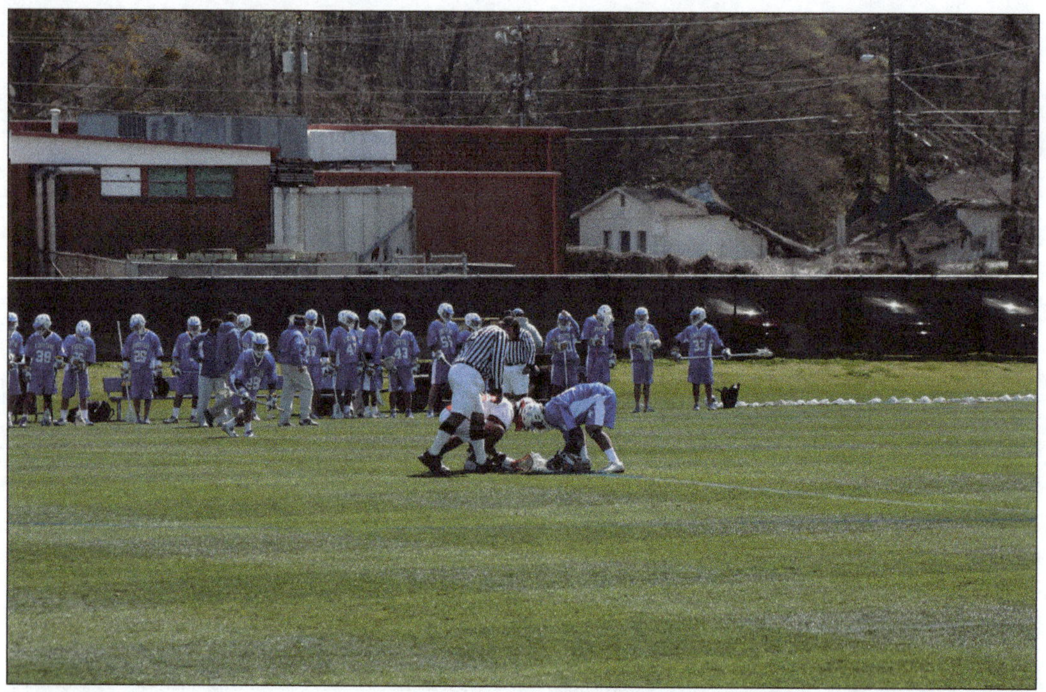

Another longstanding conference rival, Belmont Abbey College has enjoyed little success in its series history against the Saints. Here, the teams are set for the opening face-off in a 2007 mid-season tilt.

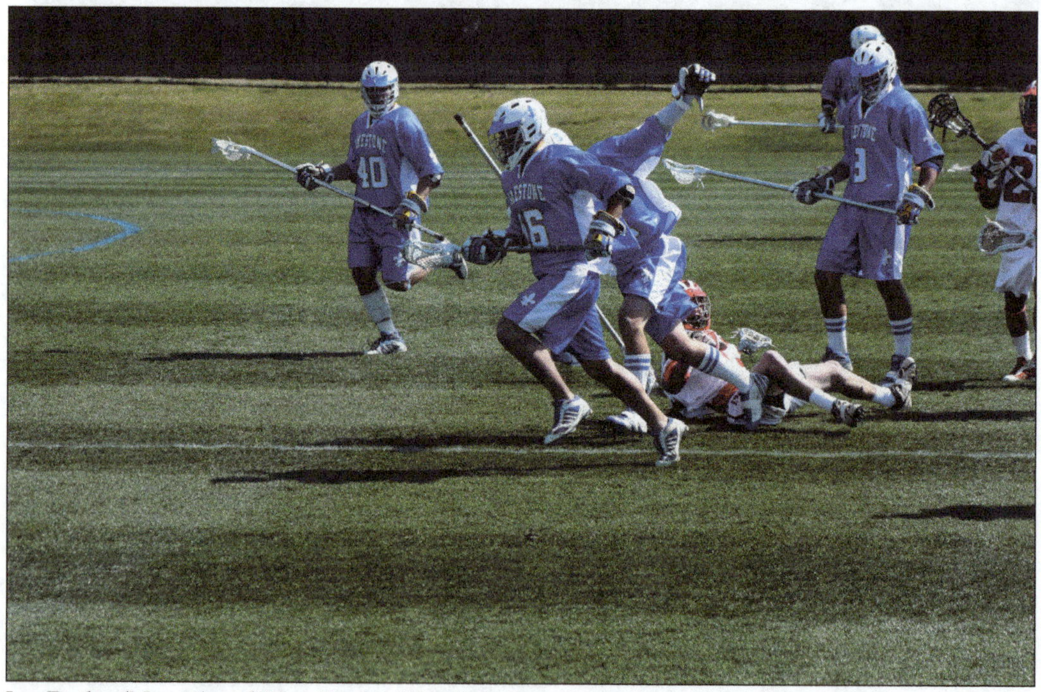

Jan Dailey (No. 40) and Matt Pinder (No. 9) look on as Nick Chandler (No. 46) comes away with a loose ball and looks to get on the attack against Belmont Abbey's Crusaders.

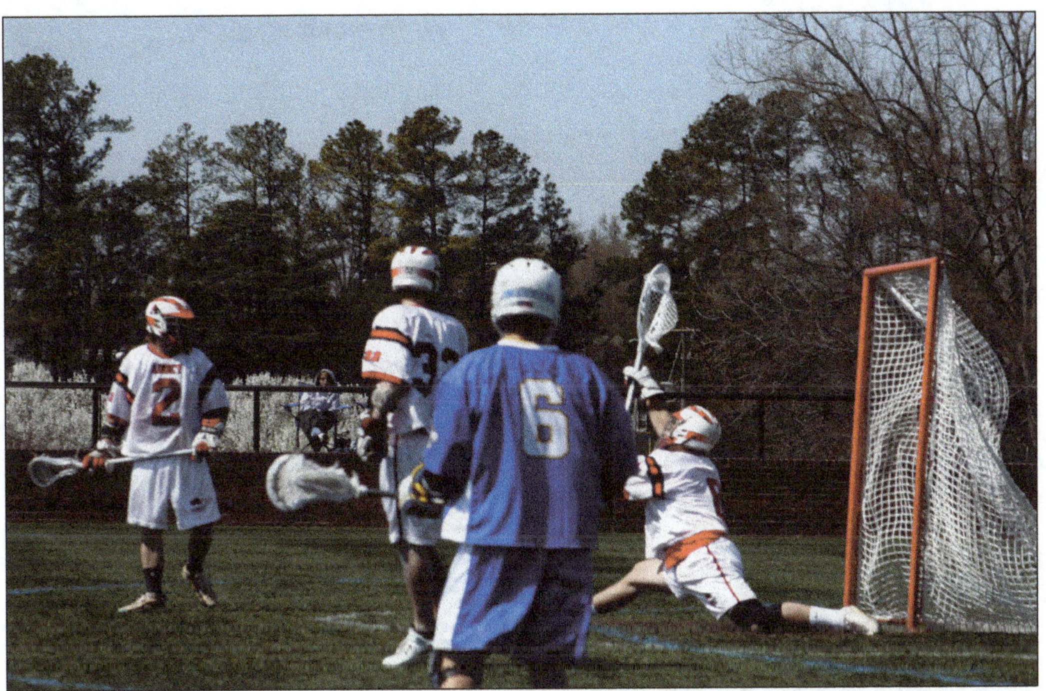

A Limestone shot flies by the Belmont Abbey goalie and into the net for one of 13 Blue & Gold scores in the six-goal victory.

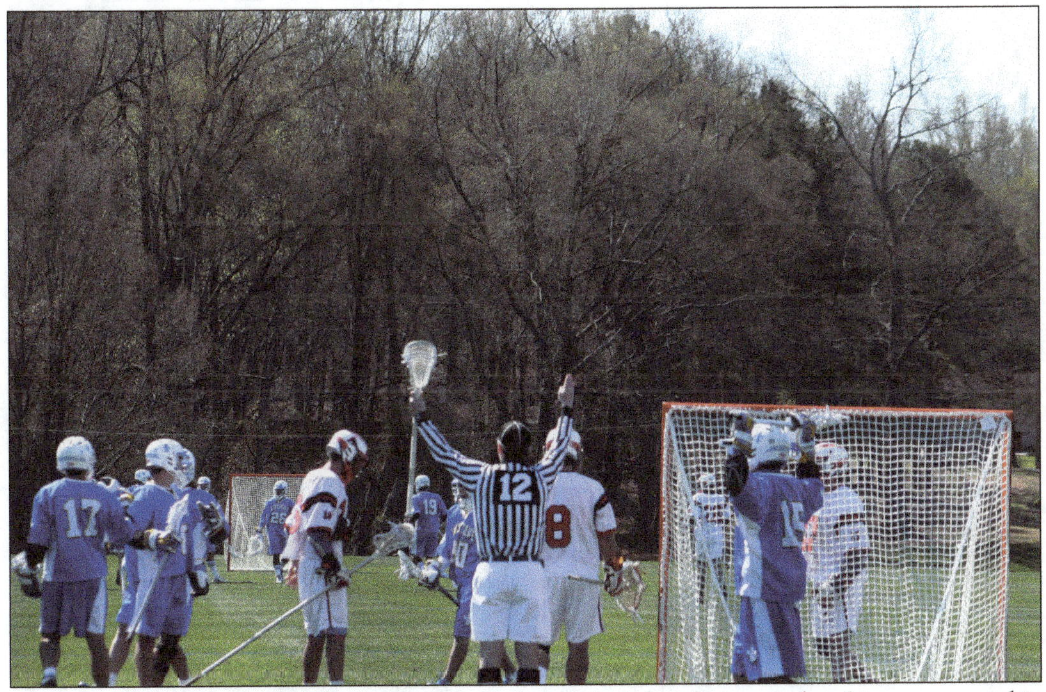

Belmont Abbey College defenders can only hang their heads as another Limestone goal is confirmed by the official and the Saints continue to pound away.

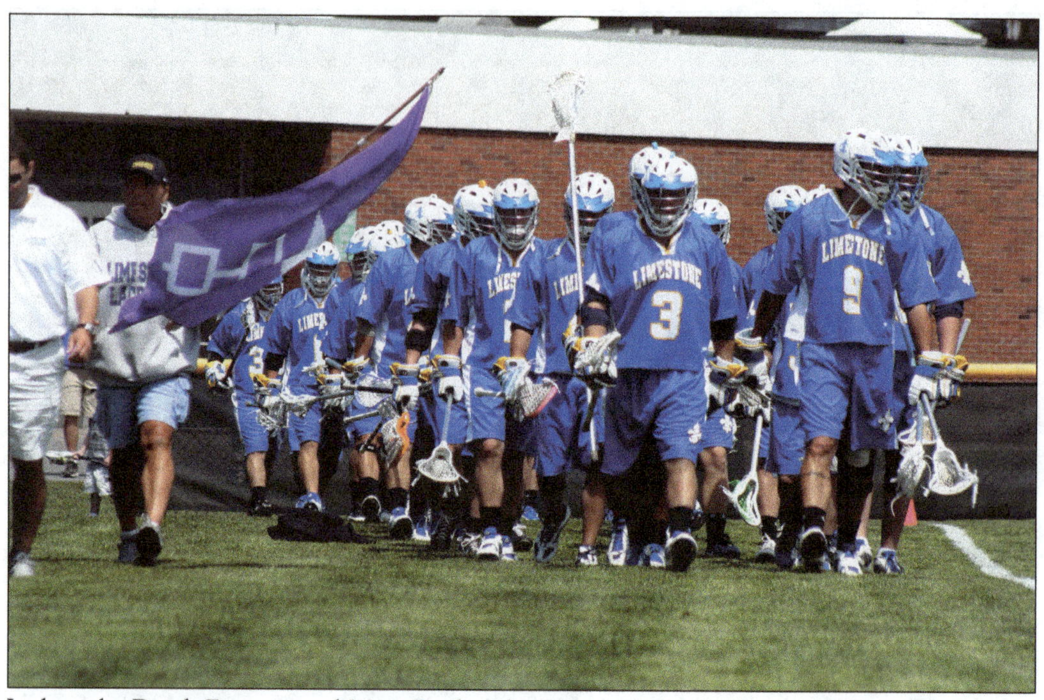

Led out by Derek Franzen and Matt Pinder, the Saints went marching into the 2007 NCAA tournament fresh off an impressive 13-8 win over Bryant University and hoped to earn another bid to the title contest. (Courtesy of Greg Wall.)

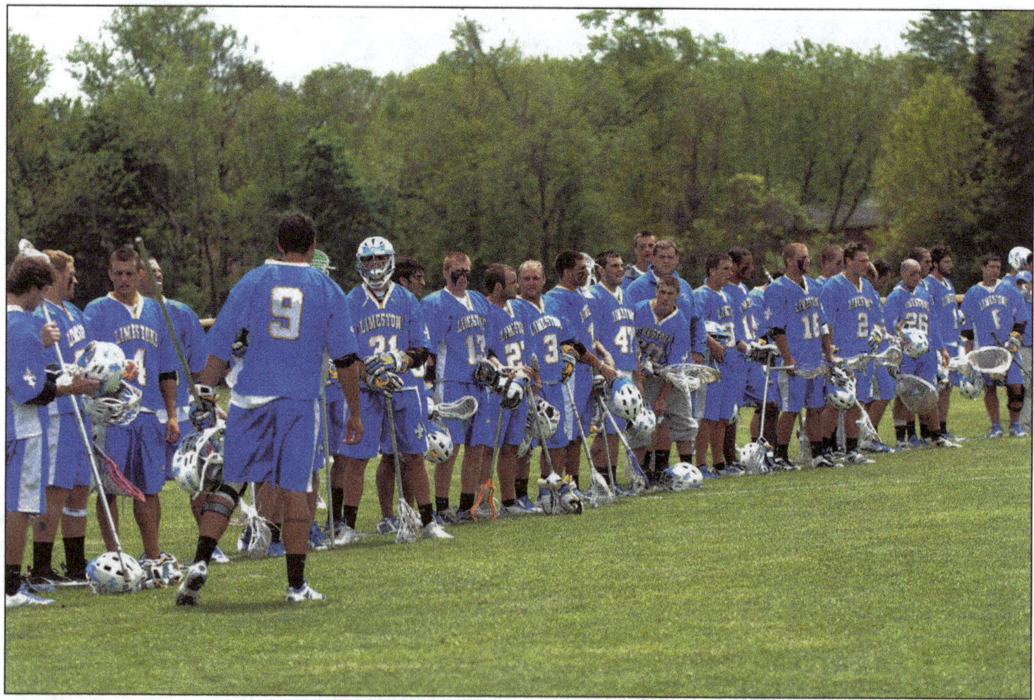

With a 14-1 record, Limestone made the trip to Syracuse, New York, where it once again faced Le Moyne College with title implications on the line. (Courtesy of Greg Wall.)

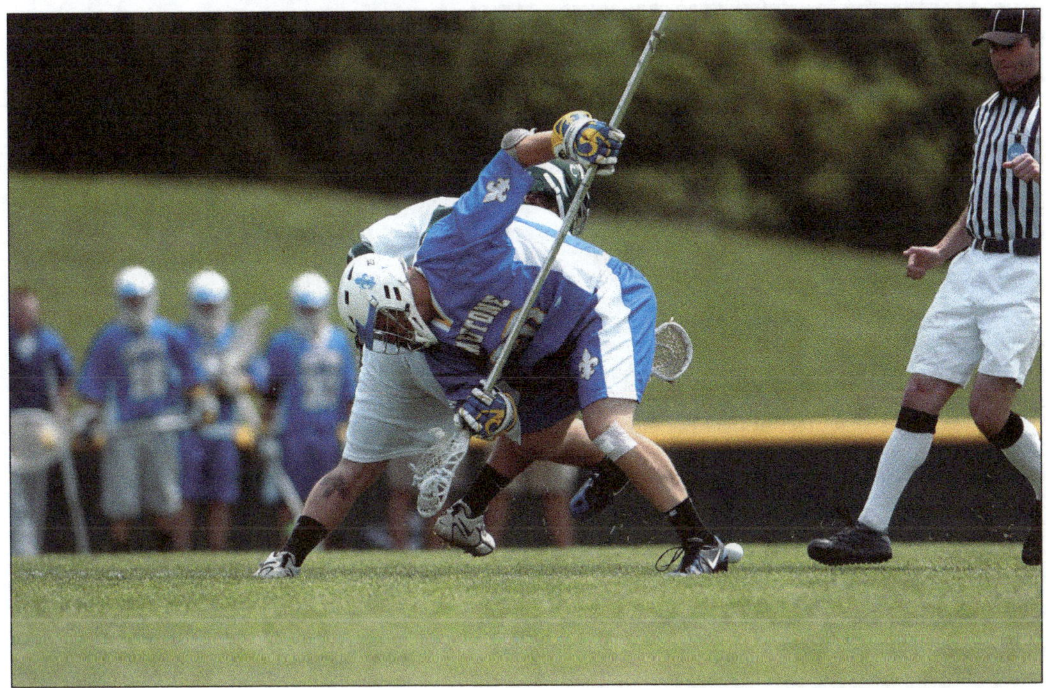

Jan Dailey looks to take the face-off to start off against the Le Moyne College Dolphins. (Courtesy of Greg Wall)

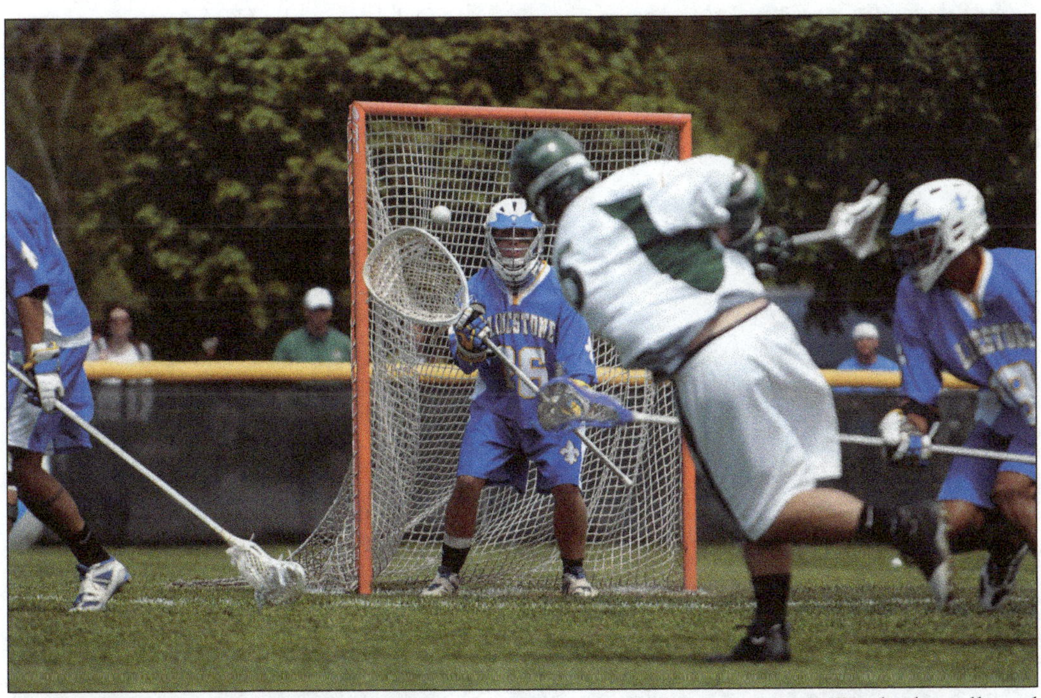

A Le Moyne College shot gets fired in directly at two-time All-American Marty Ward, who collected 11 saves that afternoon and kept the Dolphins offense in check. (Courtesy of Greg Wall.)

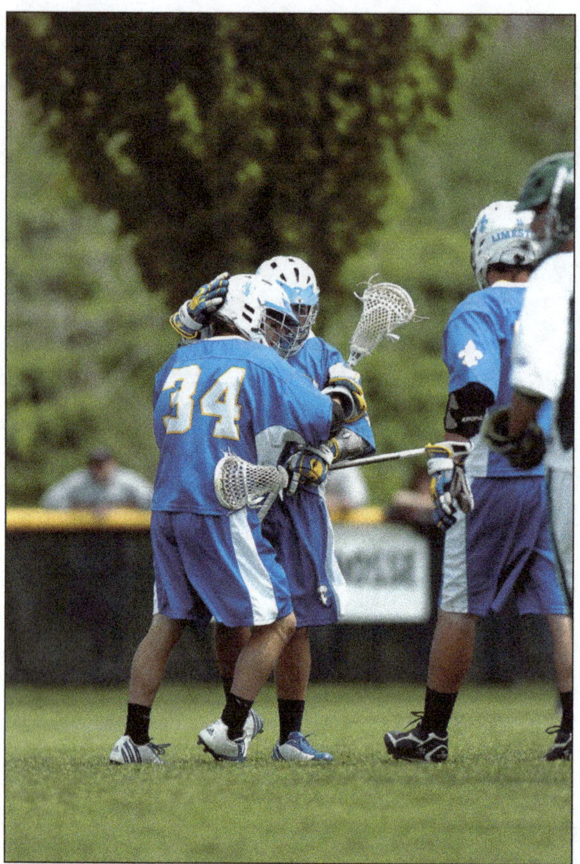

Greg Kacinko celebrates a Limestone College goal with a teammate as Allen Vaughn runs over to join. The Saints trailed 4-1 at halftime but came charging back with three goals in the third quarter. (Courtesy of Greg Wall.)

In a display of toughness, Matt Pinder (No. 9) finished out the season with a torn ACL in his left knee and can be seen here with a supportive brace as he defends against the Dolphins in the NCAA tournament semifinals. (Courtesy of Greg Wall.)

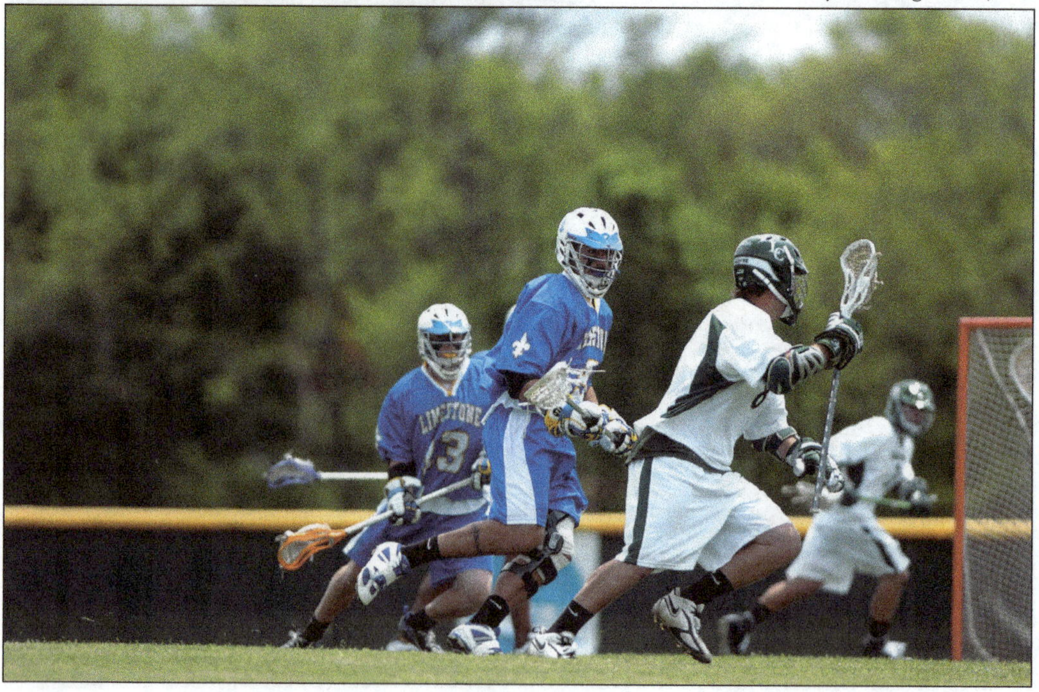

Allen Vaughn fights on in a grueling game that wore out both teams. Goals were difficult to come by for either side, as they usually are in a Limestone College matchup with Le Moyne, and players spent all their energy working for each goal. (Courtesy of Greg Wall.)

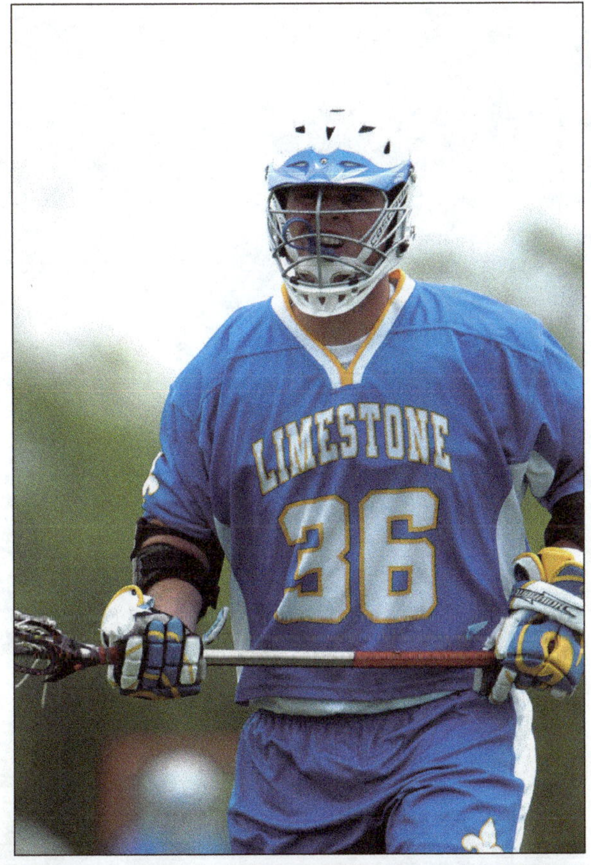

Head coach Mike Cerino and assistant Chris Phenicie look on from the sidelines as they try to construct a plan to get by Le Moyne's historically tough defensive unit. (Courtesy of Greg Wall.)

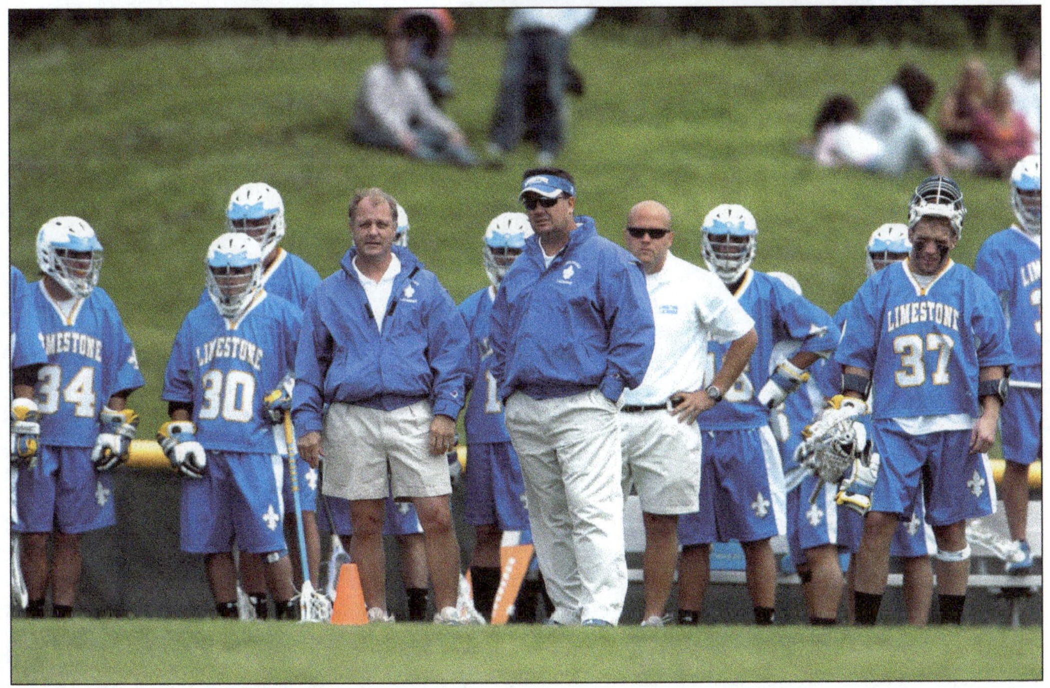

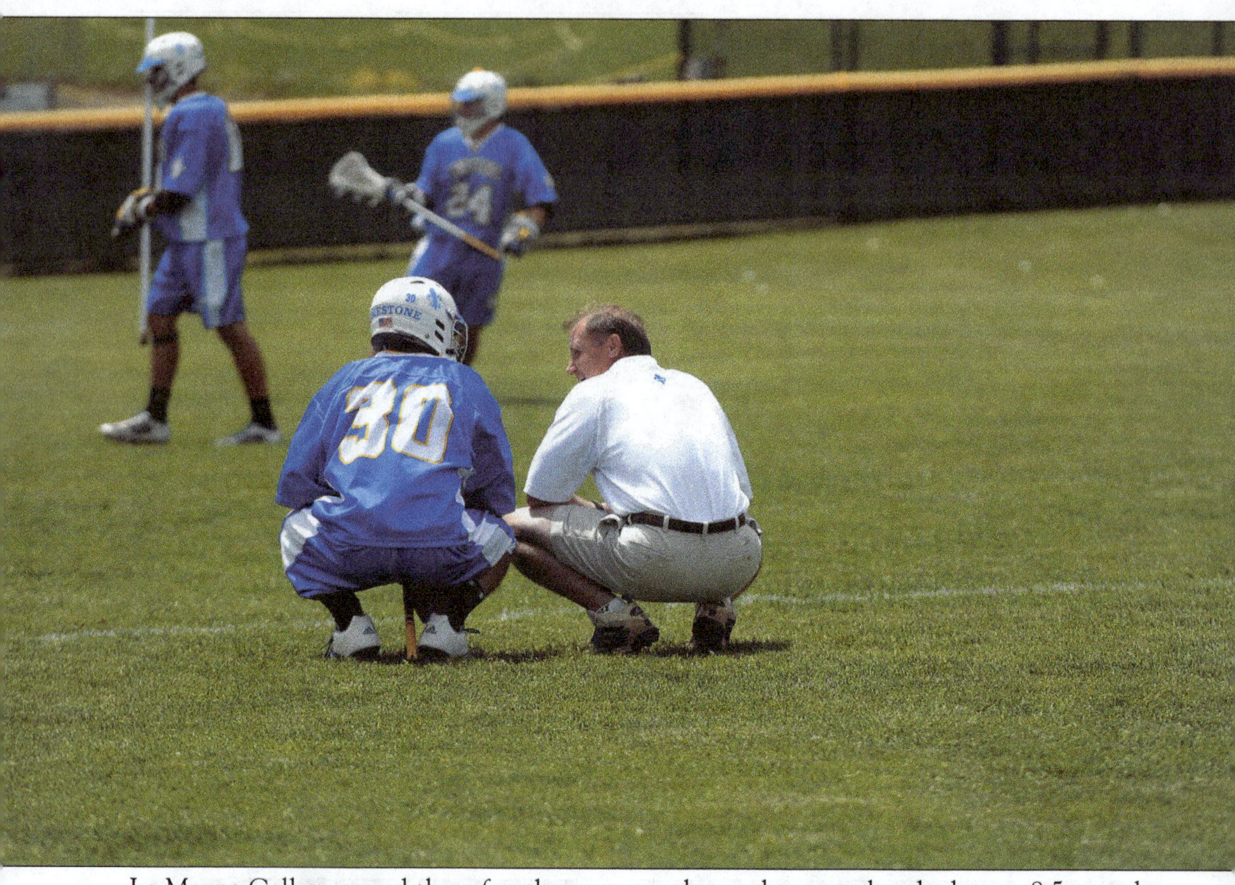

Le Moyne College scored three fourth-quarter goals to take control and advance 8-5 past the Saints. Assistant coach Chris Phenicie (right) has a talk with Jay Tranello as time winds down and the Blue & Gold begins to look toward next season. (Courtesy of Greg Wall.)

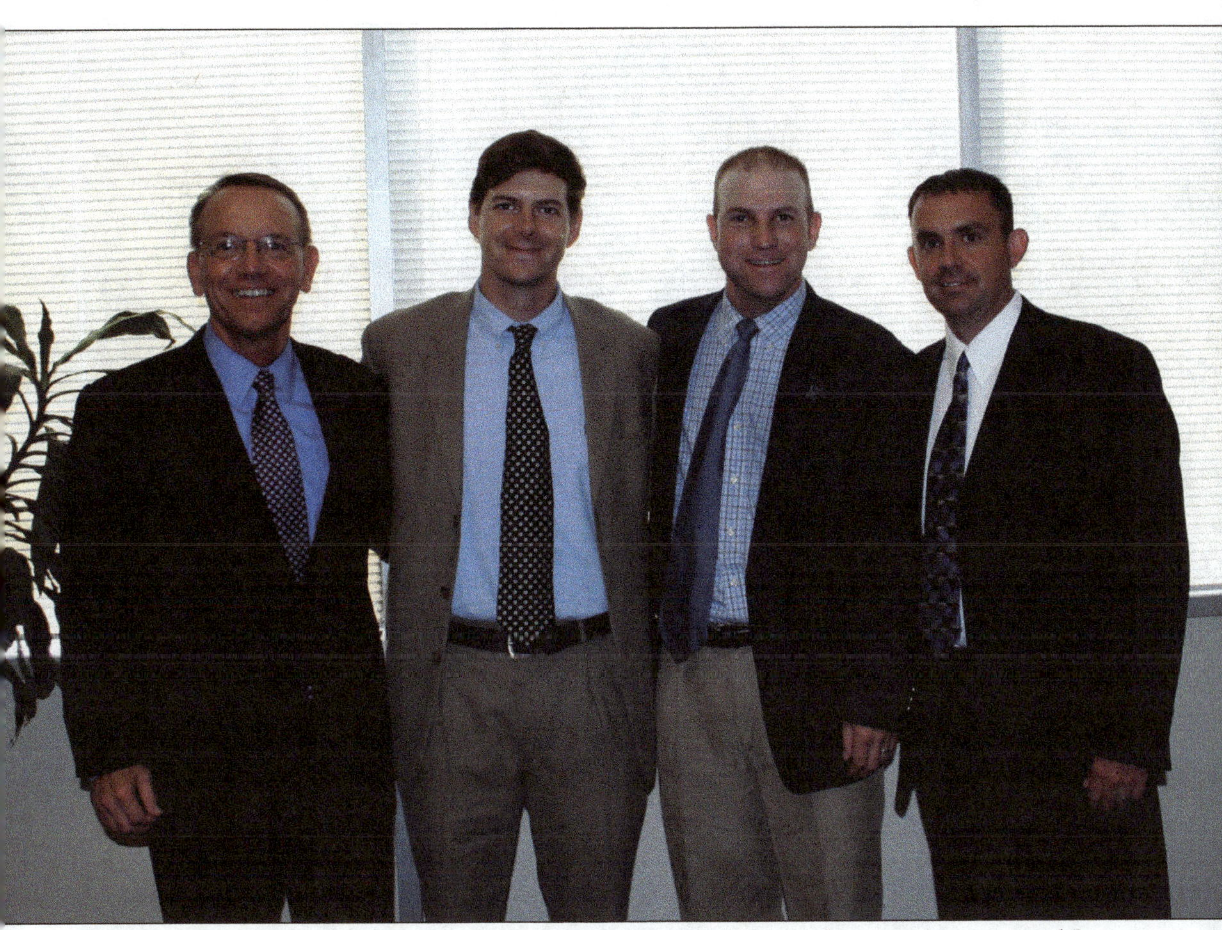

The Limestone Hall of Fame class of 2007 was a memorable one for many reasons, and Joe Monmonier (second from left) of the men's lacrosse team certainly played a part in making the class stand out. A stone wall between the pipes during his Limestone College career, Monmonier joined Ralph Pim (far left; men's basketball), Kris Ruckelshaus (second to right; men's soccer), and Michael Scerbo (far right; women's lacrosse) in the 2007 Hall of Fame class.

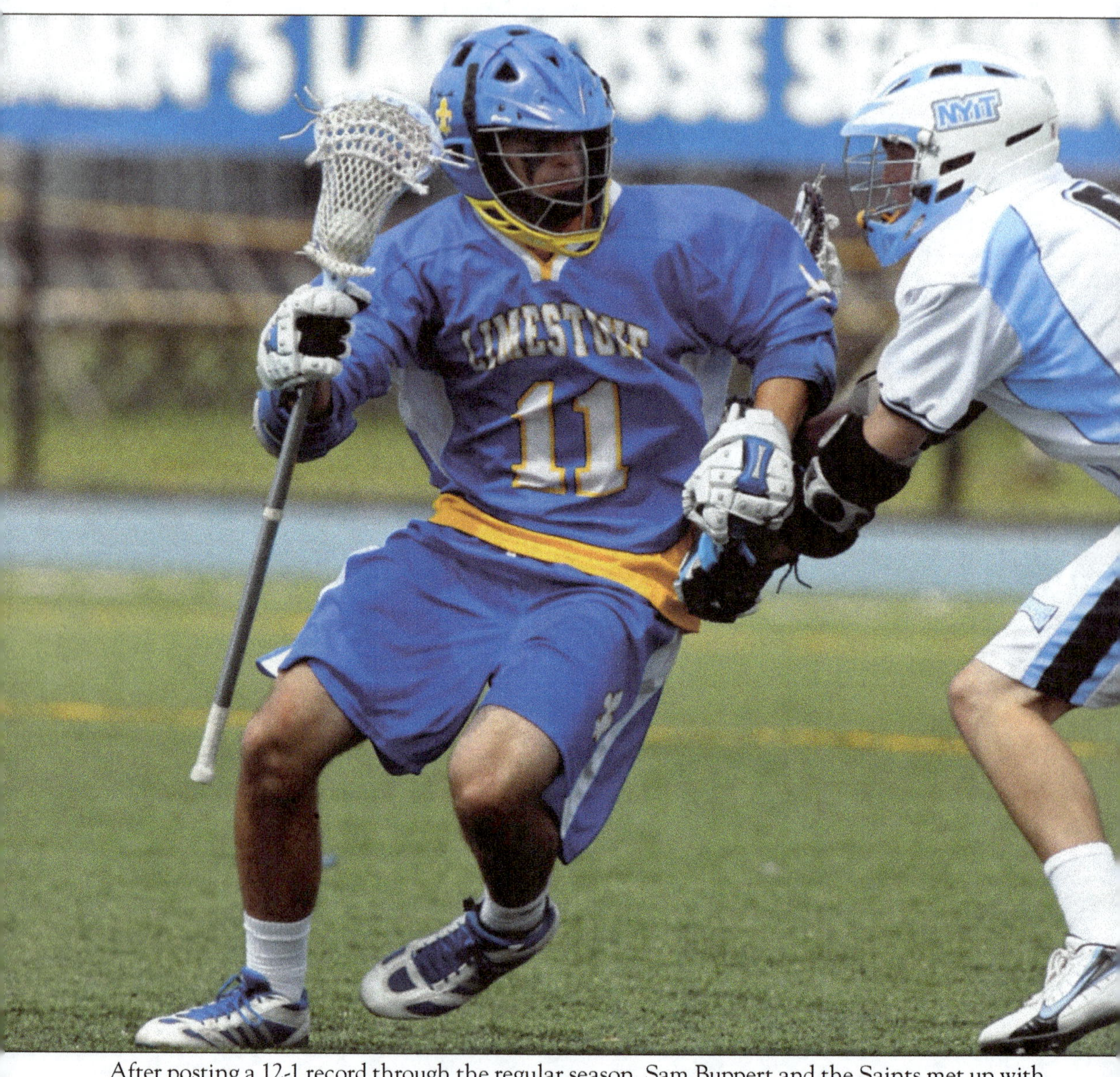

After posting a 12-1 record through the regular season, Sam Buppert and the Saints met up with New York Tech in the opening round of the 2008 NCAA tournament.

Jake Rogalia (No. 6), Thomas Langan (No. 41), and Mike Medrano (No. 5) celebrate with a teammate after one of Limestone's eight goals on the day. The Blue & Gold eventually dropped their third straight national semifinal game, this time by a final score of 11-8.

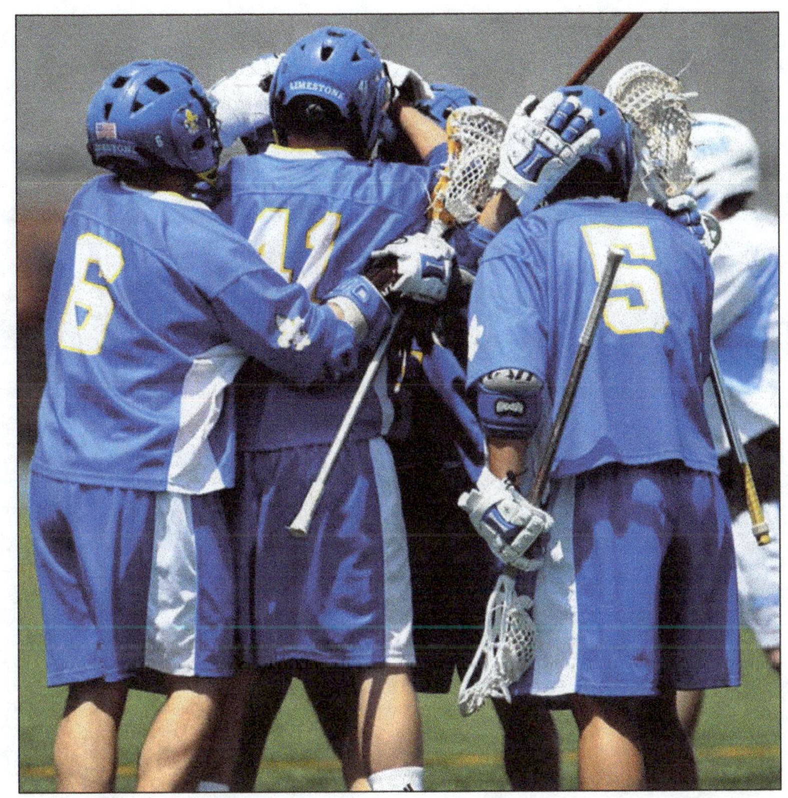

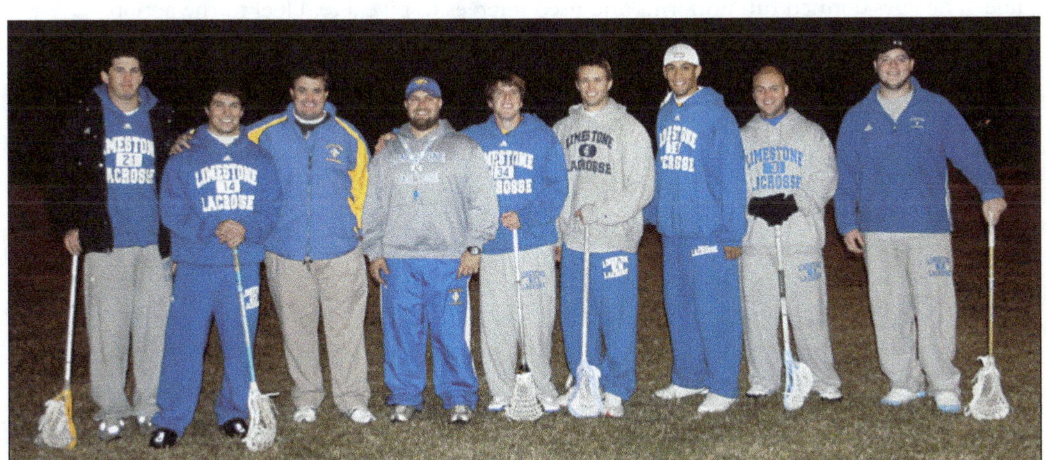

A fall camp in 2008 brought coaches, alumni, and players together. From left to right are James Touhy, C.J. Ciaravino, Mike Cerino, Drew Delaney, Greg Kacinko, Jason Brammall, Spencer Wims, Derek Franzen, and Brendan Storrier.

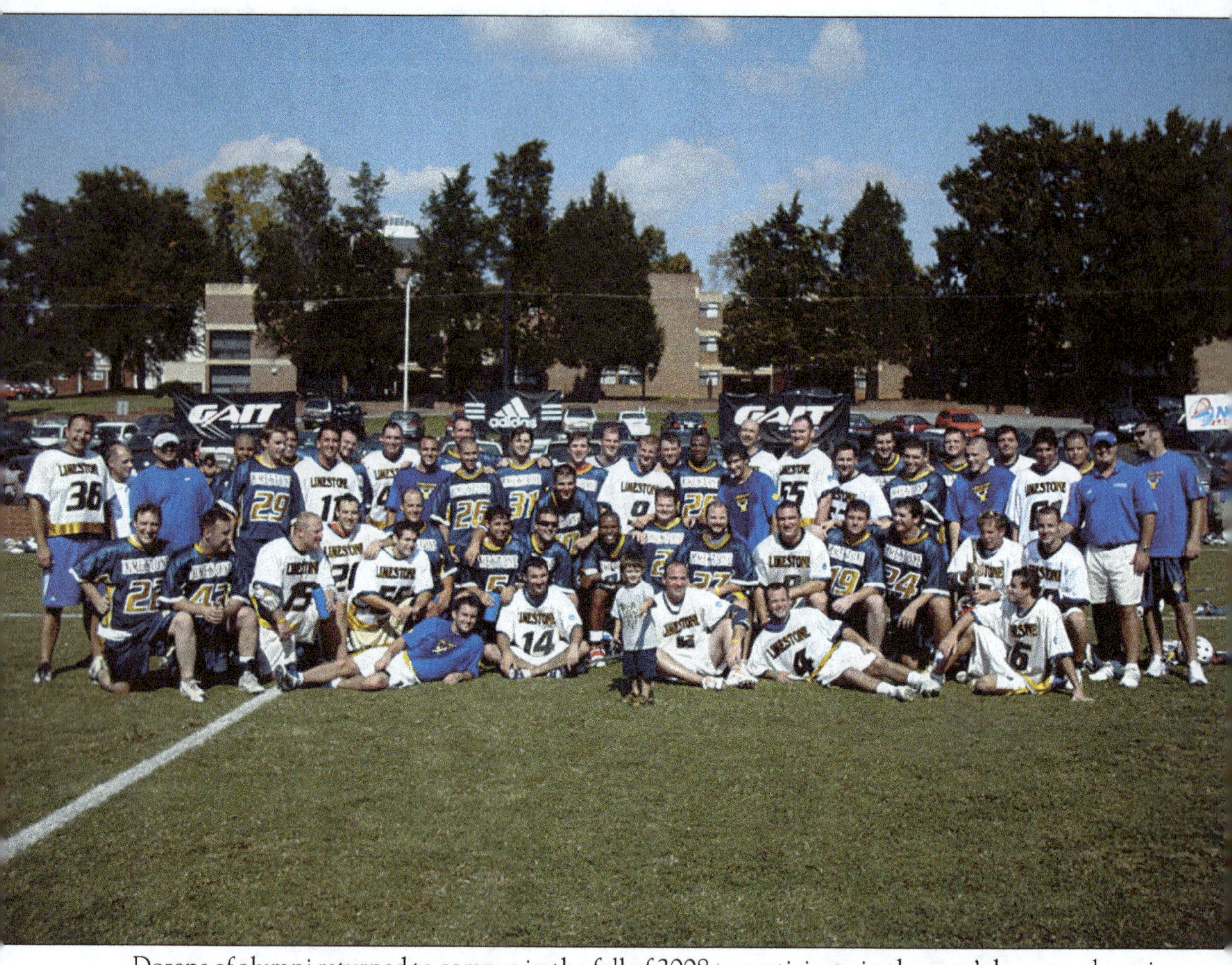

Dozens of alumni returned to campus in the fall of 2008 to participate in the men's lacrosse alumni game. The guys donned full uniforms and used referees to give a real feel to the action.

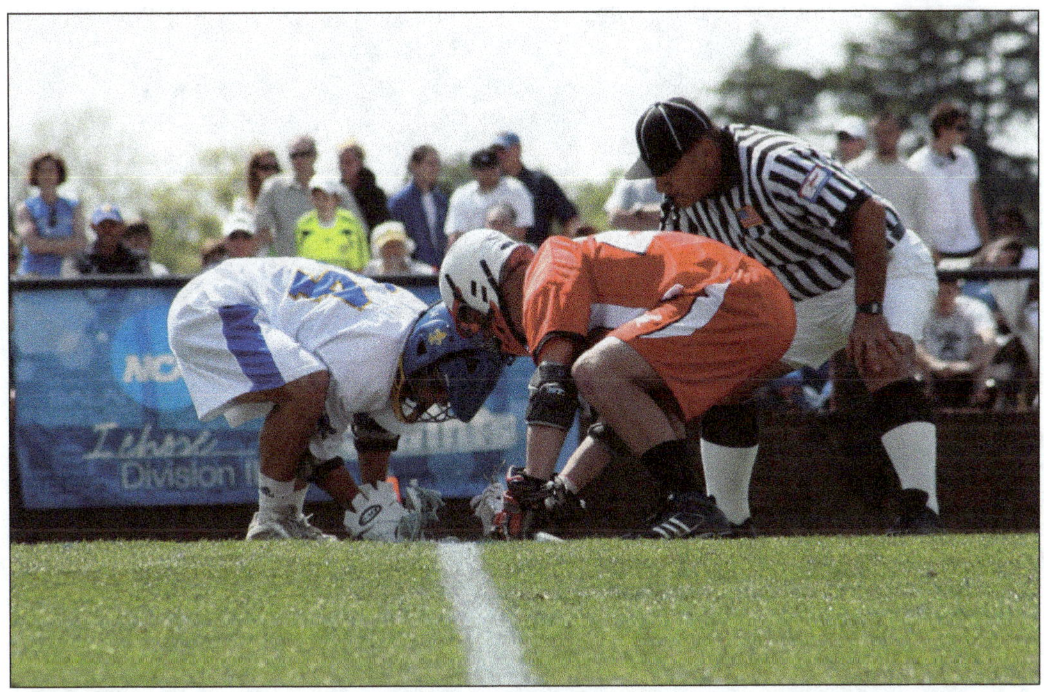

Limestone opened the 2009 season with Belmont Abbey and fell victim to the upset, losing against the Crusaders for the second straight time. However, the Saints have reeled off 14 straight wins against Abbey since this loss, including one victory later in this 2009 campaign.

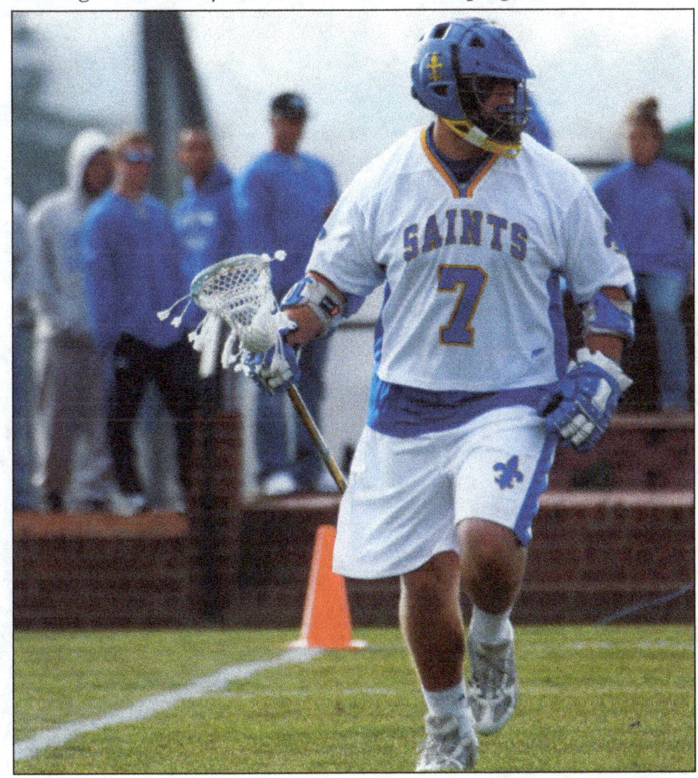

Brendan Storrier was an All-American in 2008 and made his way onto the coaching staff in 2011. Storrier has remained on the Limestone coaching staff for the last six seasons and has helped lead the Saints to two national championships.

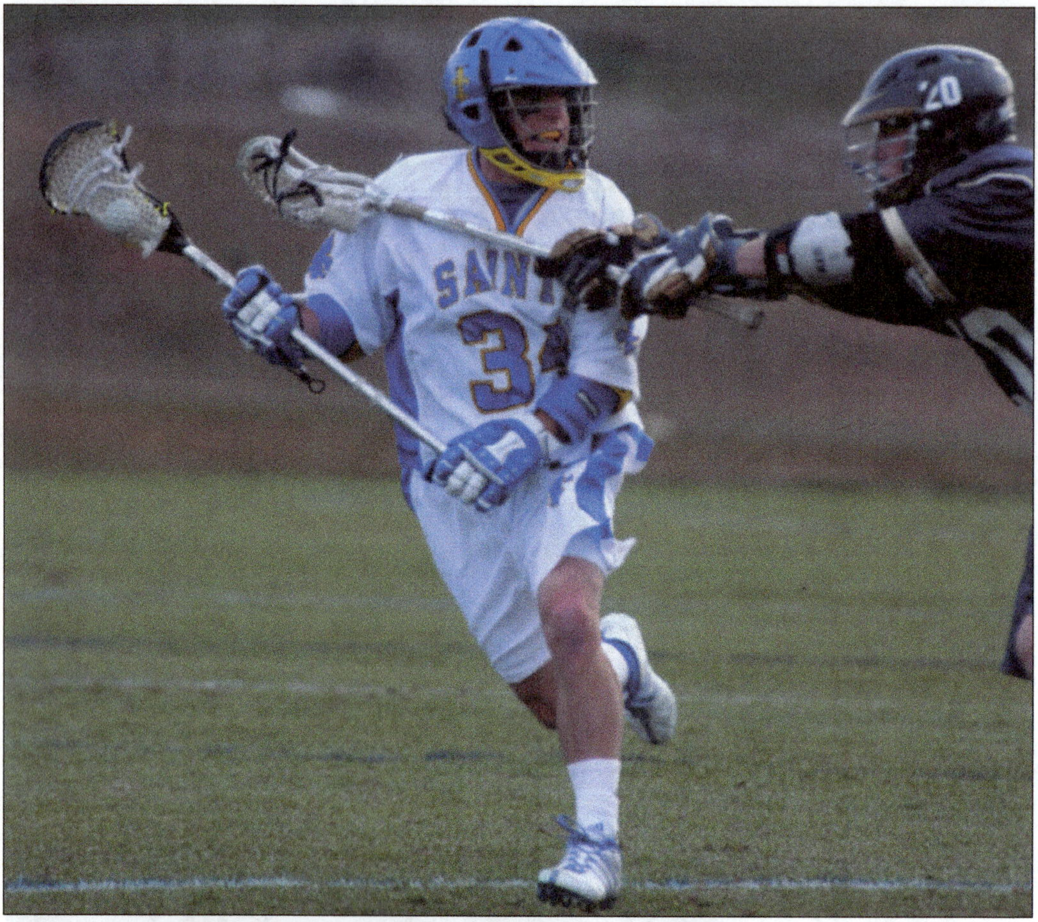

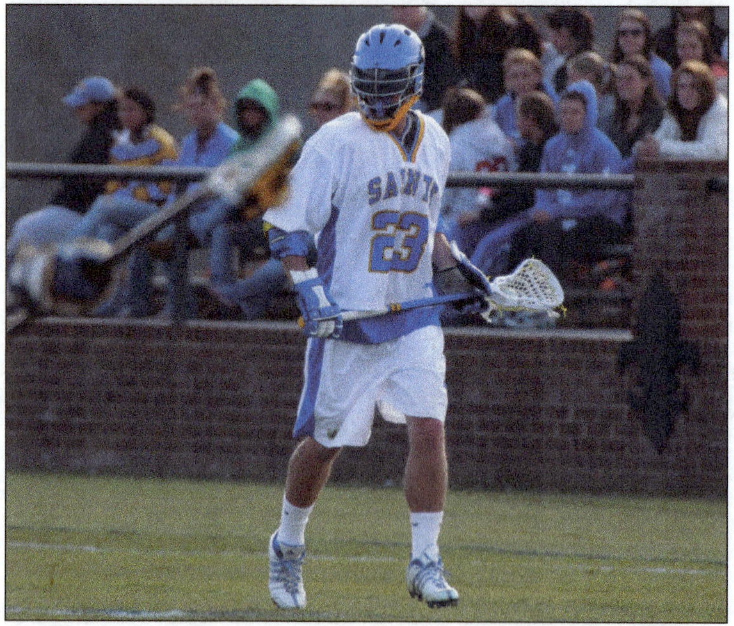

Team captain Greg Kacinko is seen here dodging a Queens University defender in a 2009 home game. The Saints won 14-8 thanks to a game-high five goals from Brendan Storrier and four each from Mike Poerstel and Thomas Langan.

First-team All-American Mike Poerstel, in his signature black visor, looks to take on a defender during the 2009 home game against Queens University.

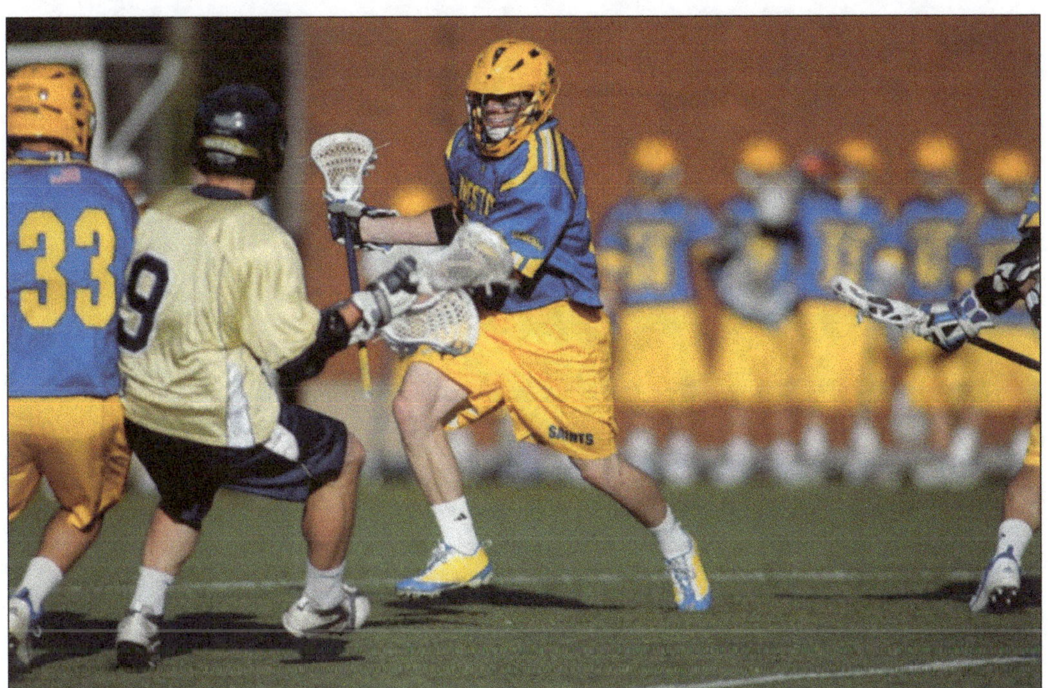

Another matchup against Queens University, this time in the 2010 season, saw Teddy Prager and Limestone College come away with a 15-10 victory. The Saints are 15-1 all-time against the Royals and have not dropped a game in the series in over 10 years.

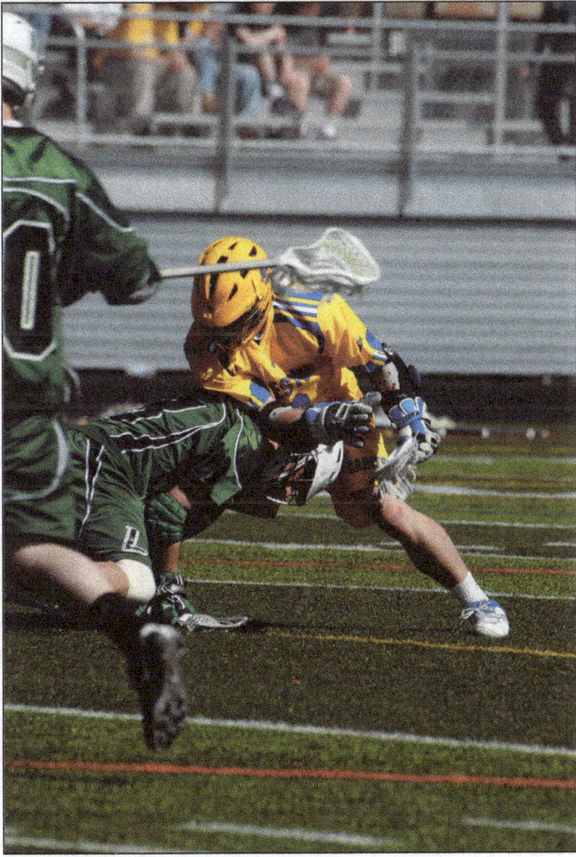

Limestone and Le Moyne Colleges met in Severna Park, Maryland, for a mid-season clash between two programs looking to make a statement in their march to a title.

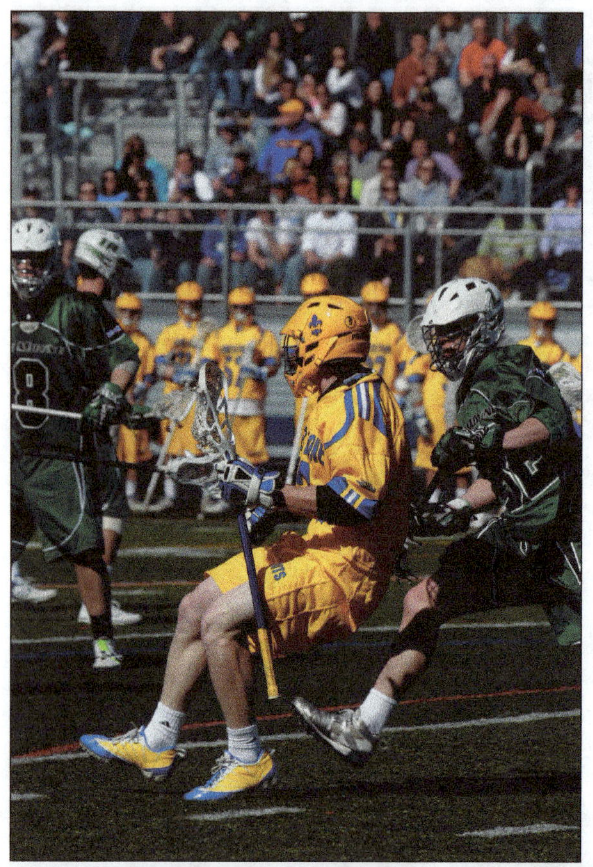

The Saints scored three goals in the fourth quarter but were unable to complete the comeback. As seen here, room to roam was tough to find on the offensive side.

Limestone College's quick 2-0 start to the season was derailed by the Dolphins, who came away with the early season victory in a tight 8-6 battle. However, the Saints would go on to win 10 straight to head into the postseason with a 12-1 mark.

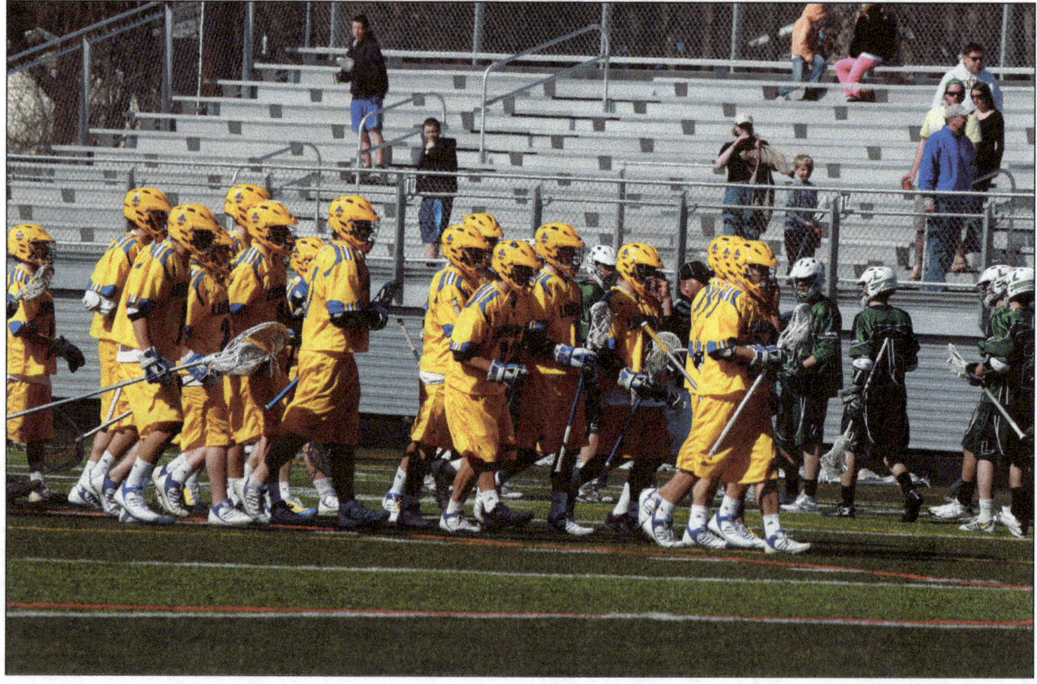

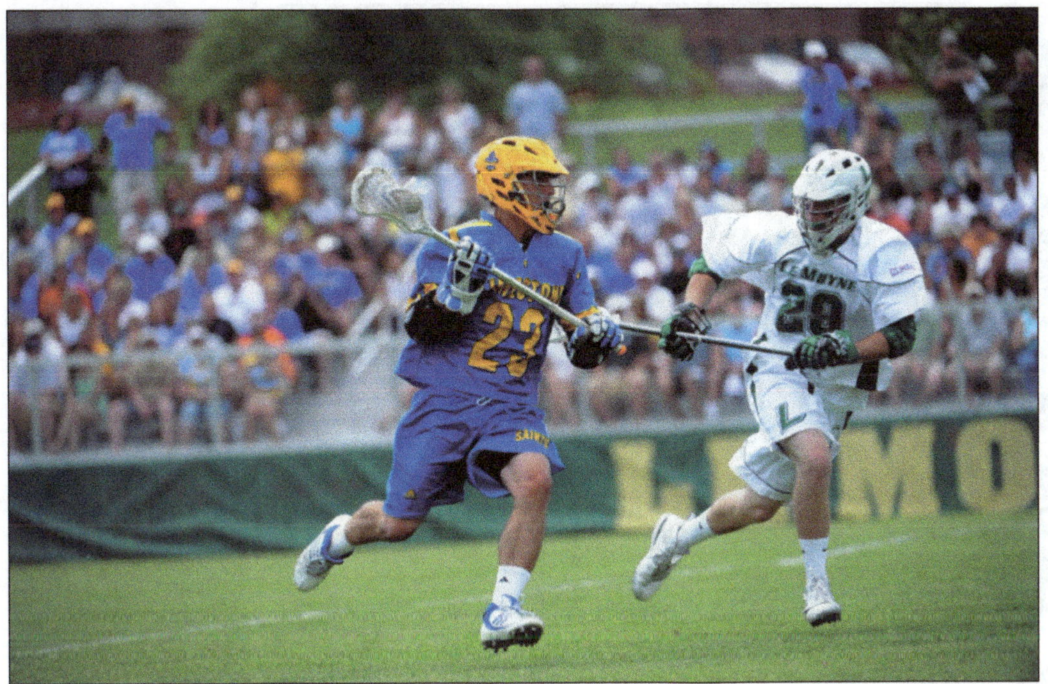

Mike Poerstel and the Saints made the trip to Syracuse in May for another battle with the Dolphins in the NCAA national semifinals that season, but Le Moyne College was able to defend home turf and put an end to Limestone's title dreams one game short.

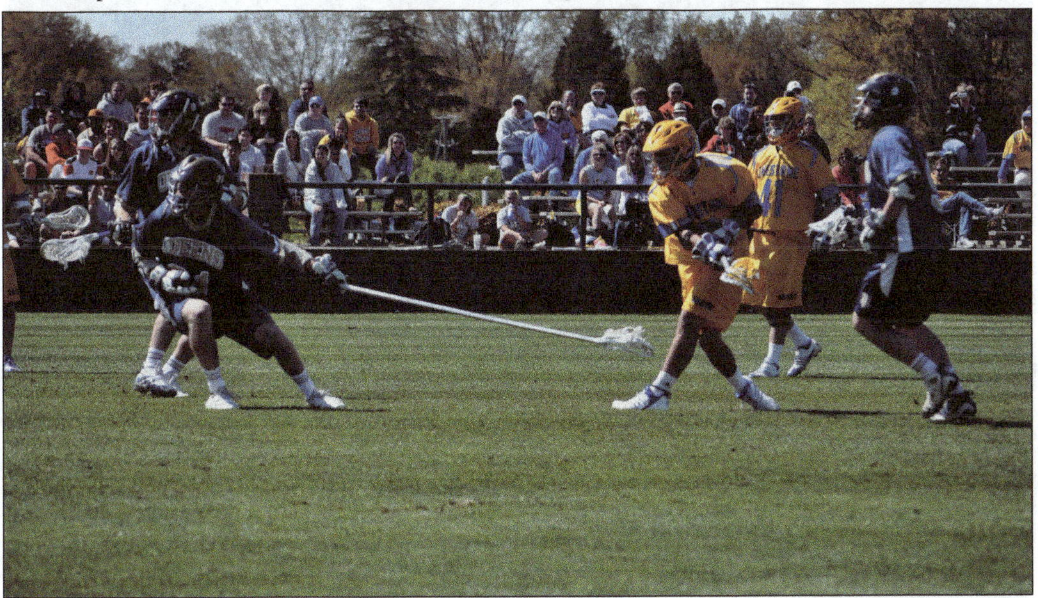

Seen here against long time conference foe Queens University of Charlotte, the Saints thrashed the Royals 24-3 in their 2011 meeting, thanks to four goals each from Shayne Jackson, Riley Loewen, and Desi Gonzalez. Sam Buppert finished with three assists but takes a shot here against a worn-out defense. The win was Limestone's 10th straight to open up the season, and the Saints went on to reach 14-0 after a win over Pfeiffer University in the Conference Carolinas Tournament. (Courtesy of Joshua Darling.)

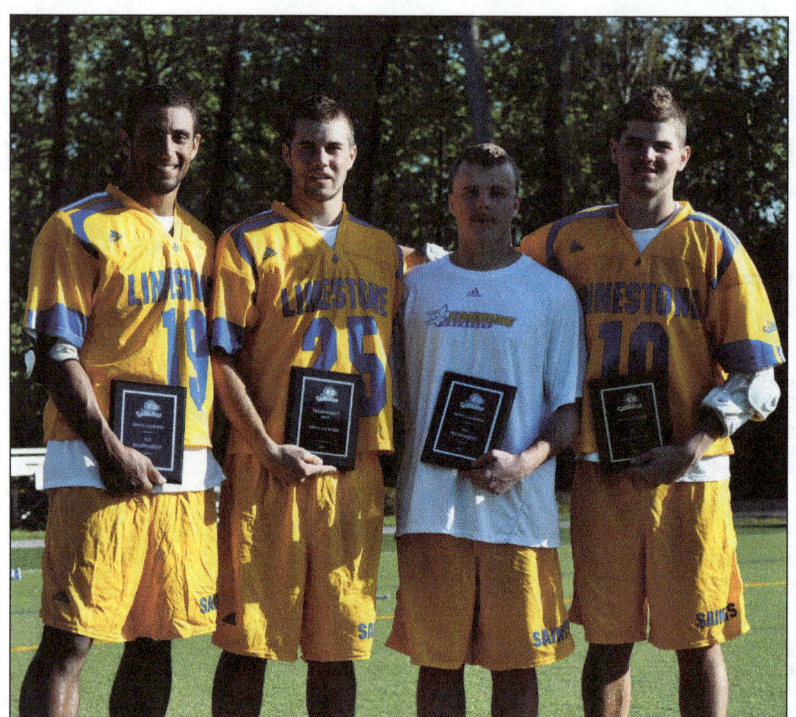

Spencer Wims (No. 19), Jackson Decker (No. 25), Steve Gartleman, and Riley Loewen (No. 10) pose with their hardware from the Conference Carolinas after winning another league title at the Queens University sports park. The Saints breezed to an undefeated season against the conference slate and took down nationally 11th-ranked Pfeiffer University in the tournament championship game. (Courtesy of Joshua Darling.)

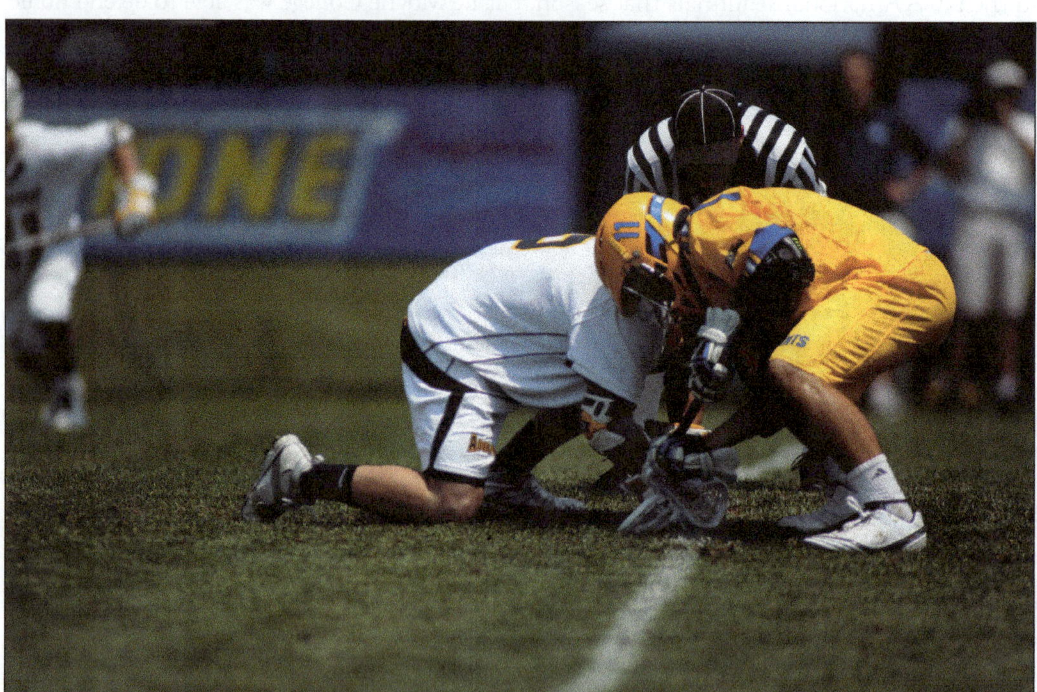

Senior team co-captain Sam Buppert faces off against an Adelphi University player in the 2011 NCAA Division II national semifinal, a game in which the No. 2 nationally ranked Saints went on to lose by a final score of 14-11. Despite the loss, the 2011 squad tied Limestone College's program record with 15 wins on the season. (Courtesy of Mike Slade.)

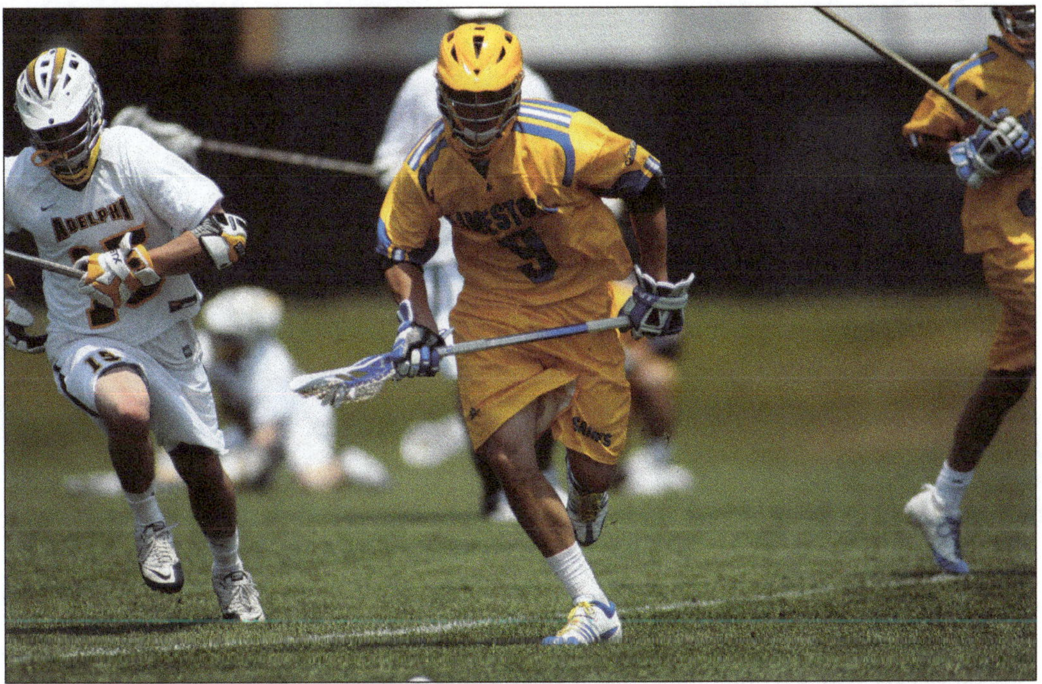

Mason Mundell and the No. 2 Saints entered the 2011 postseason as one of the favorites to bring home a national title. Unfortunately for the Blue & Gold, that dream fell short in the quarterfinal round as Limestone College was eliminated by No. 5-ranked Adelphi University despite five goals from Thomas Langan.

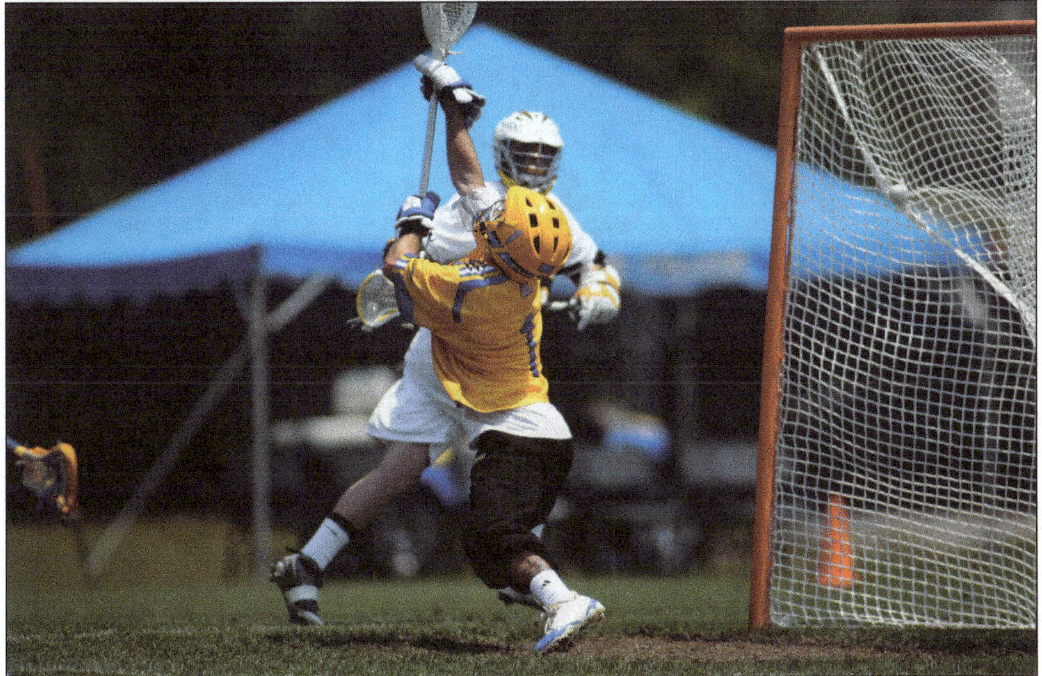

One of the most experienced and decorated goalies in Blue & Gold history, Steve Gartleman misses out on a save here in an NCAA tournament game against Le Moyne College.

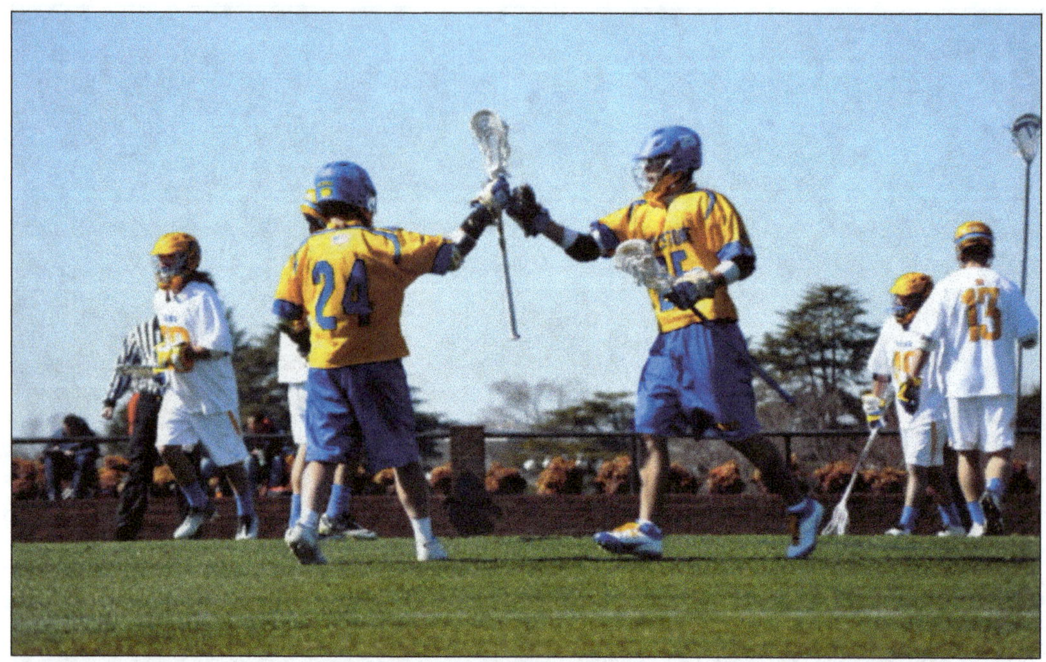

Jackson Decker (No. 25) and Shayne Jackson (No. 24) enjoy a quiet celebration against Rollins College as the Tars try to figure out a way to slow down the Blue & Gold attack during the 2012 season opener.

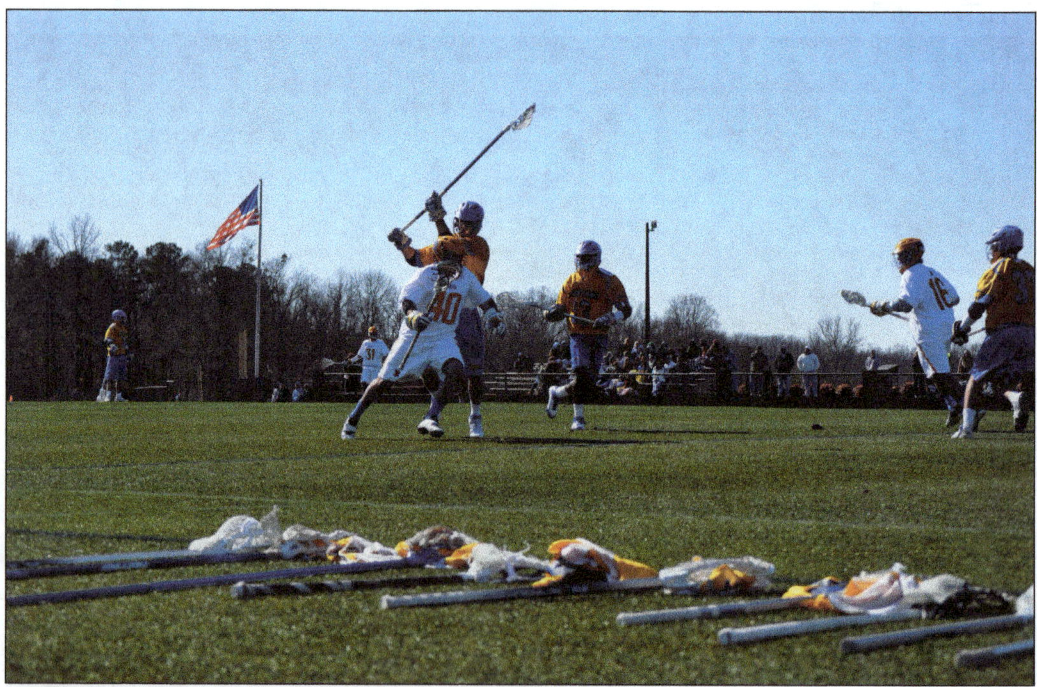

Sticks line the sideline in the 2012 opener against Rollins College. Saints Field has since taken on a subtle change with benches swapping sides due to the additions to the Bob Campbell Field House leading out to the playing surface.

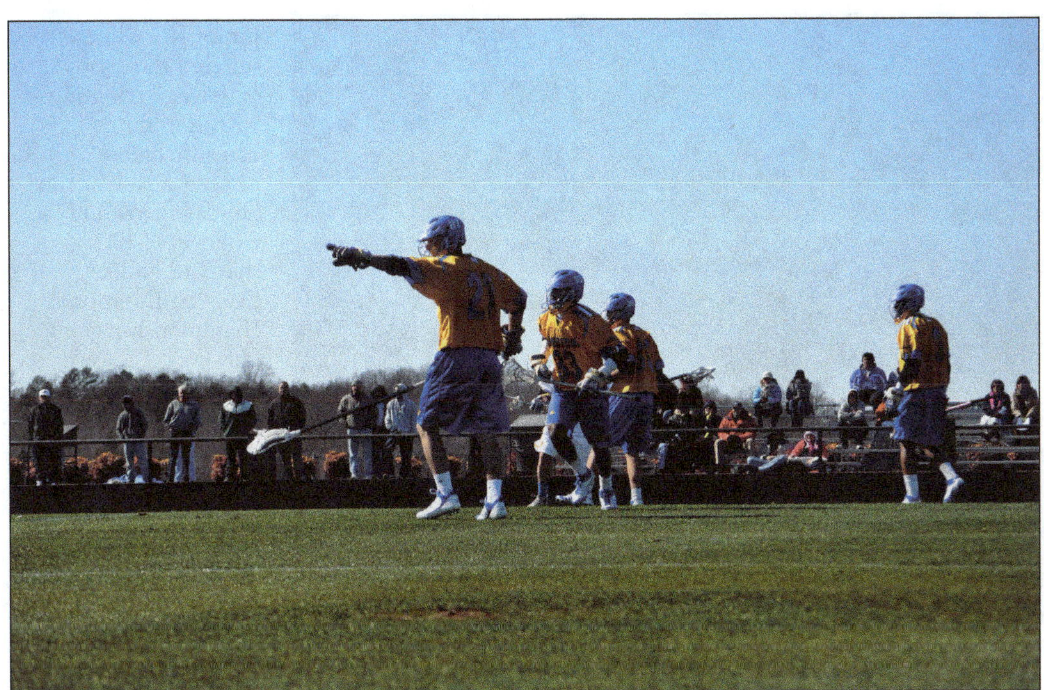

Anthony Starnino (No. 27) directs traffic along the defensive unit as Ahmaad Simmons (No. 33), Glenn Trovato (No. 35), and Jamar Peete (No. 3) prepare to keep the Rollins attack in check.

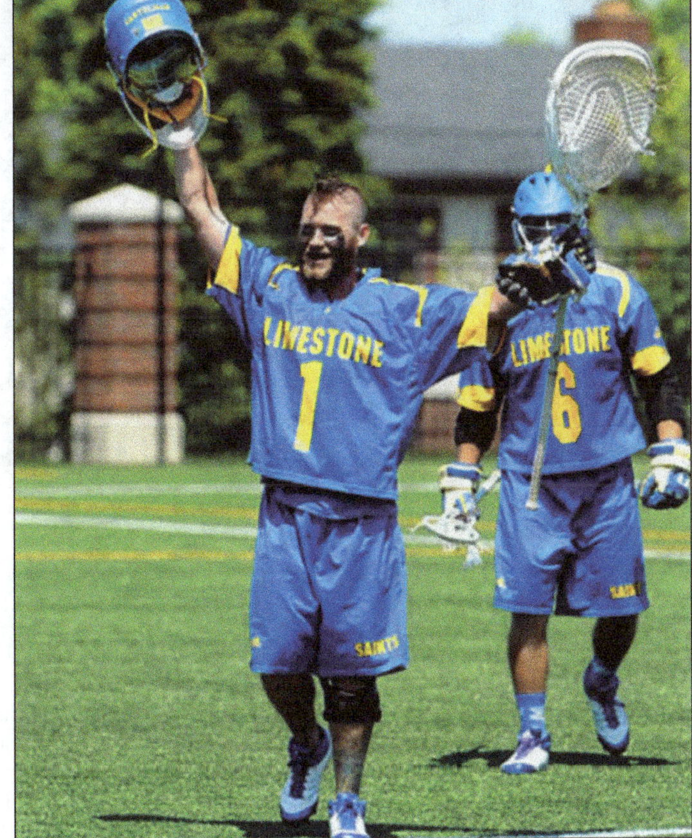

Goalkeeper Steve Gartelman celebrates Limestone's 10-8 win over Le Moyne College in the 2012 NCAA semifinals. The victory moved the Saints to 16-1 on the year and put the Blue & Gold in their first national championship game since the 2006 season.

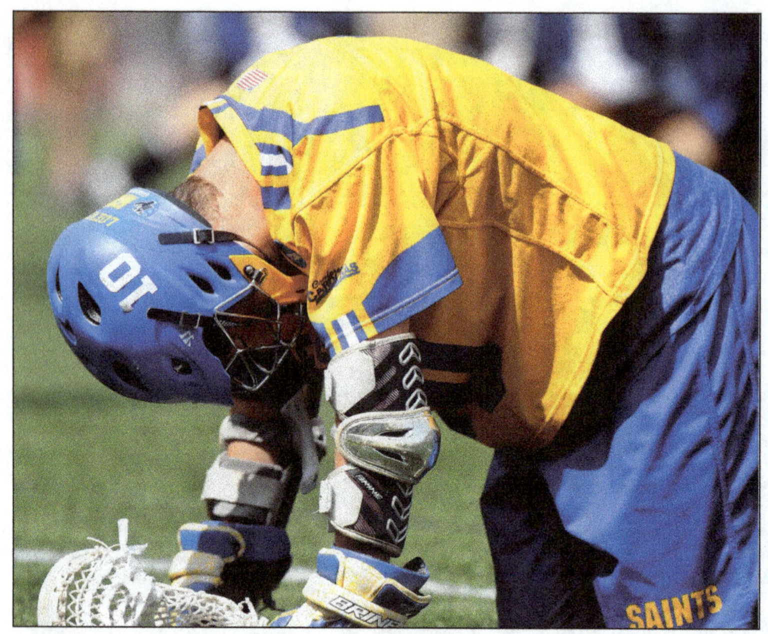

Junior Riley Loewen suffered the agony of defeat by coming within minutes of a title before Limestone fell at the hands of Dowling College, 11-10, in the 2012 NCAA Division II national championship game. However, Loewen went on to become a three-time United States Intercollegiate Lacrosse Association All-American and set a new school record with 184 career goals—a mark that still stands today.

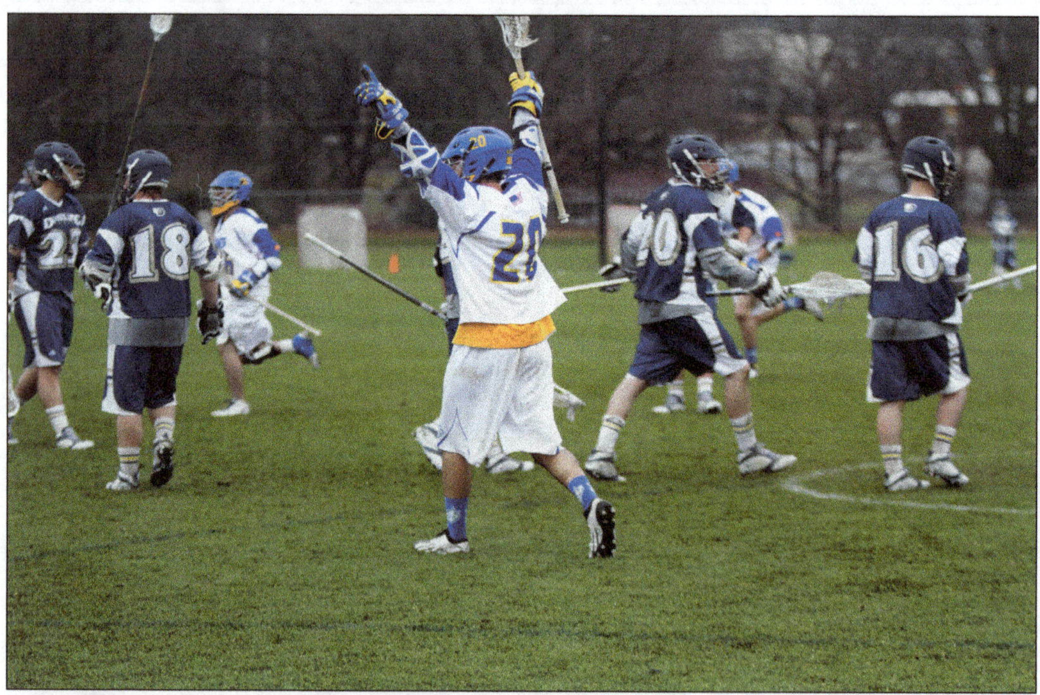

Looking for the program's third national championship in 2012, the Saints fell short in the title game as Dowling University walked away with the crown. Fortunately for Limestone, the 2013 squad would have its revenge. Dowling made its way down to The Rock for an early season clash and the Saints were ready. Corey Rich, celebrating the 10-7 win here with arms raised, poured in a game-high three goals and two assists to lead Limestone in knocking off the top-ranked defending national champions.

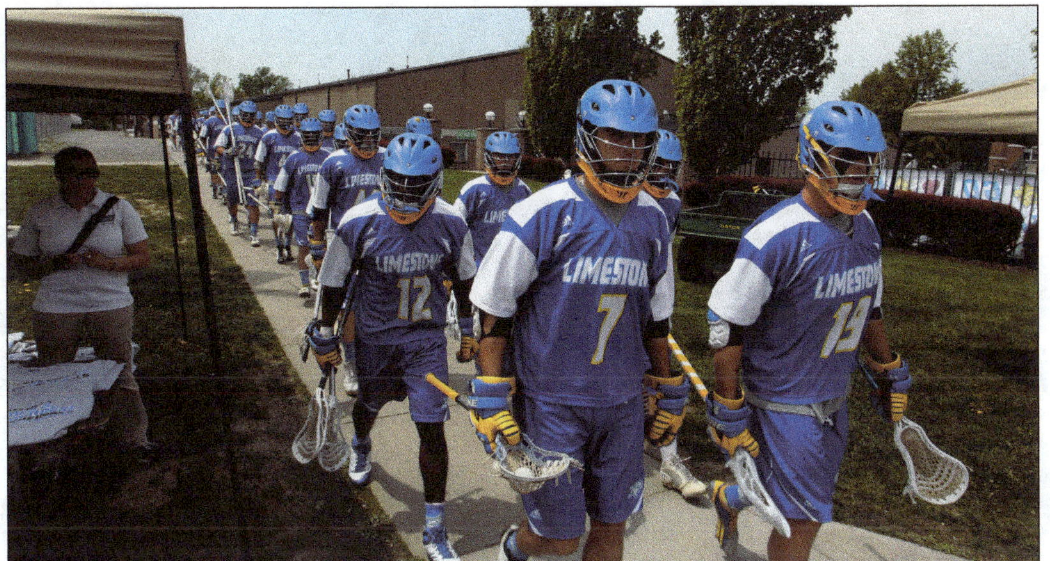

Limestone College suffered just one regular season setback that year and earned yet another trip to the NCAA postseason. After handling No. 8 Seton Hill University at home in the quarterfinals, the Saints traveled to the South's top seed, the Mercyhurst University Lakers. Tor Reinholdt (No. 7) and Zach Cummings (No. 19) are seen here leading the upset-minded Saints out of the locker room and onto the field at game time.

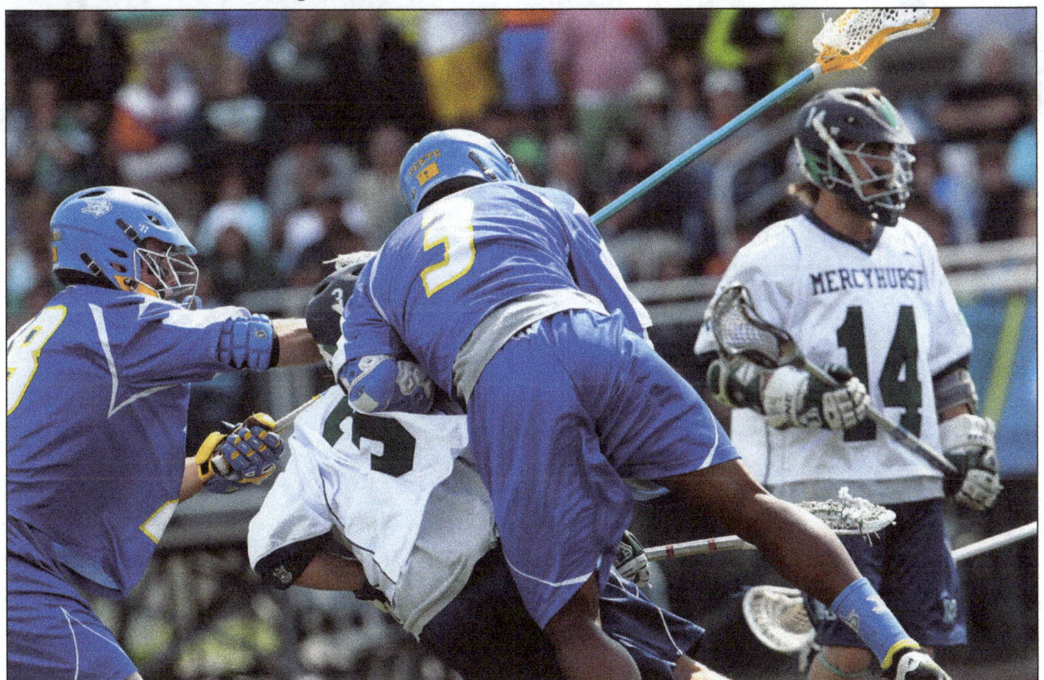

The physical play of Jamar Peete (No. 3) on the defensive end mixed with Todd Nakasuji, Corey Rich, and Riley Loewen on the offensive end gave Limestone a one-goal lead on the road heading into the fourth quarter. A win would guarantee the Saints a spot in their second straight national title game and give the team a chance to finish off what could not be accomplished the previous season.

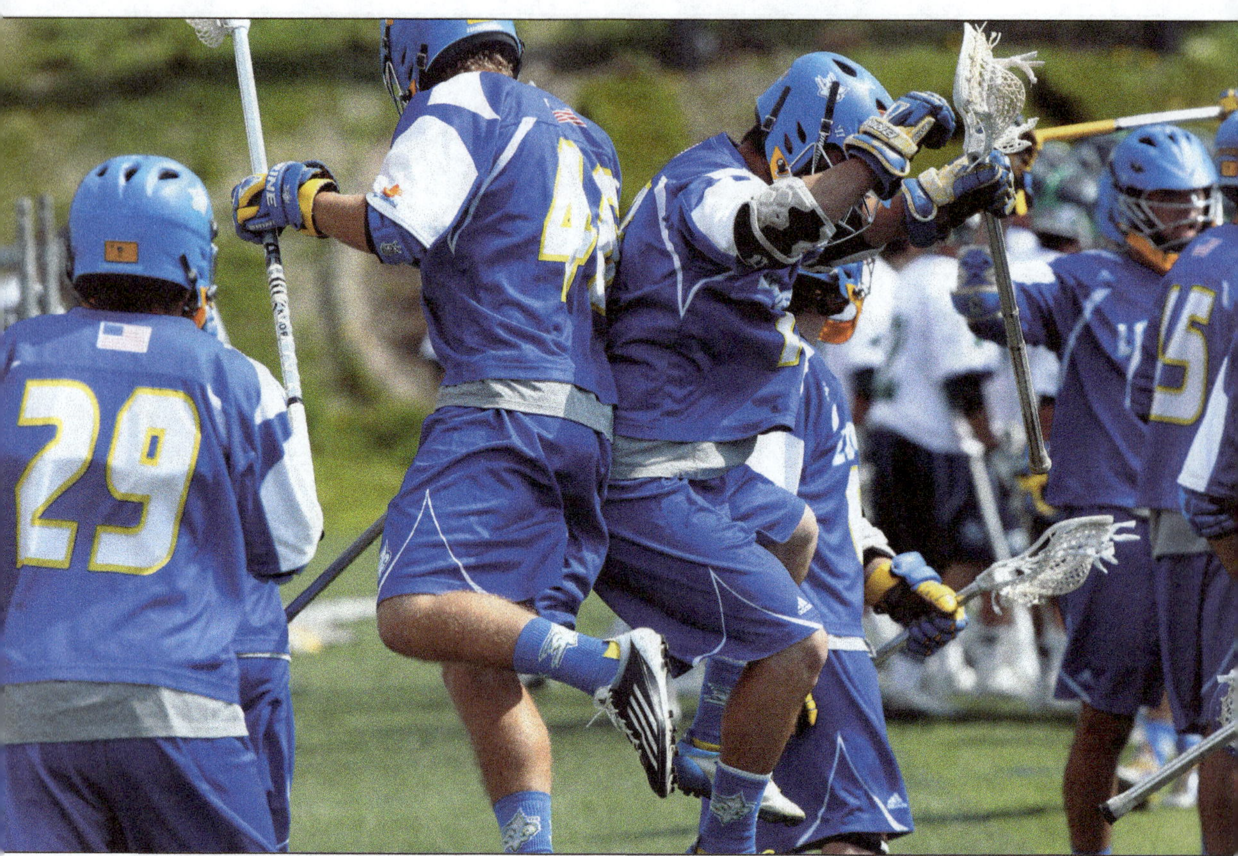

The Saints never trailed in the fourth quarter and held a lead for over 12 minutes, including a two-goal advantage when Rich and Reid Reinholdt put Limestone ahead 17-15 with five minutes to play. The Blue & Gold celebration was short lived, however, as the Lakers bounced back with the game-tying goal in the final seconds to force overtime, where they eventually scored and advanced to spoil Limestone's plans.

Five

Celebrating 25 Years and Beyond

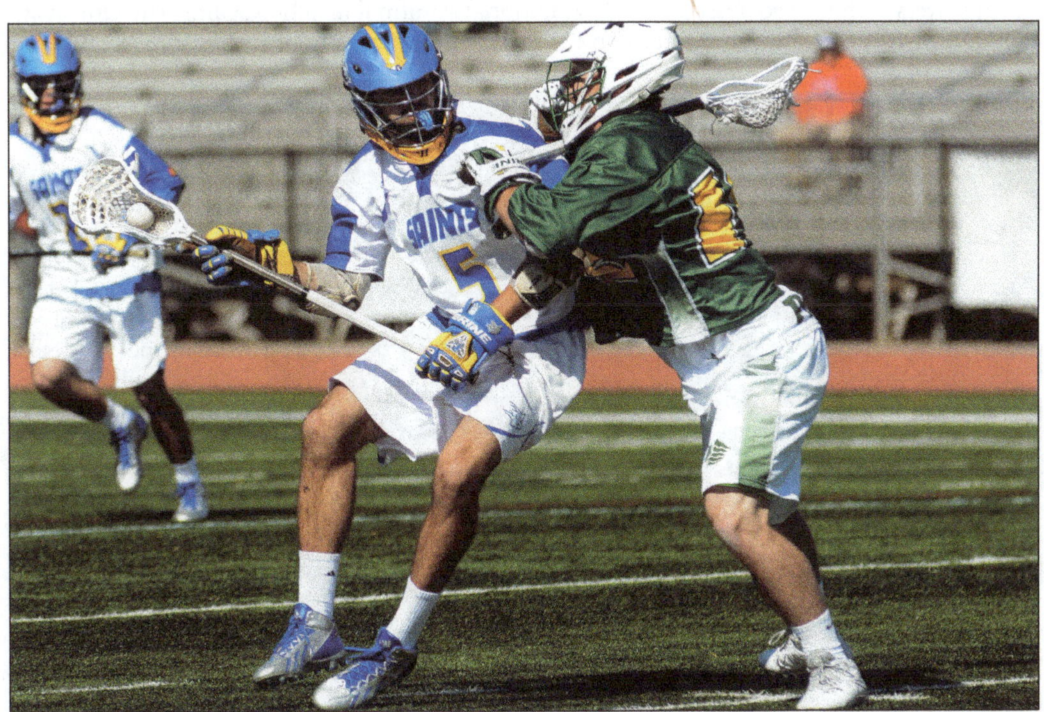

Michael Miranda gets physical with a St. Leo College player during a game played in nearby Spartanburg, South Carolina, early in the 2014 season. Due to construction on campus and the addition of turf to Limestone's home playing surface, the Saints were forced to play home games away from home for a portion of the spring. (Courtesy of Stacey Wylie.)

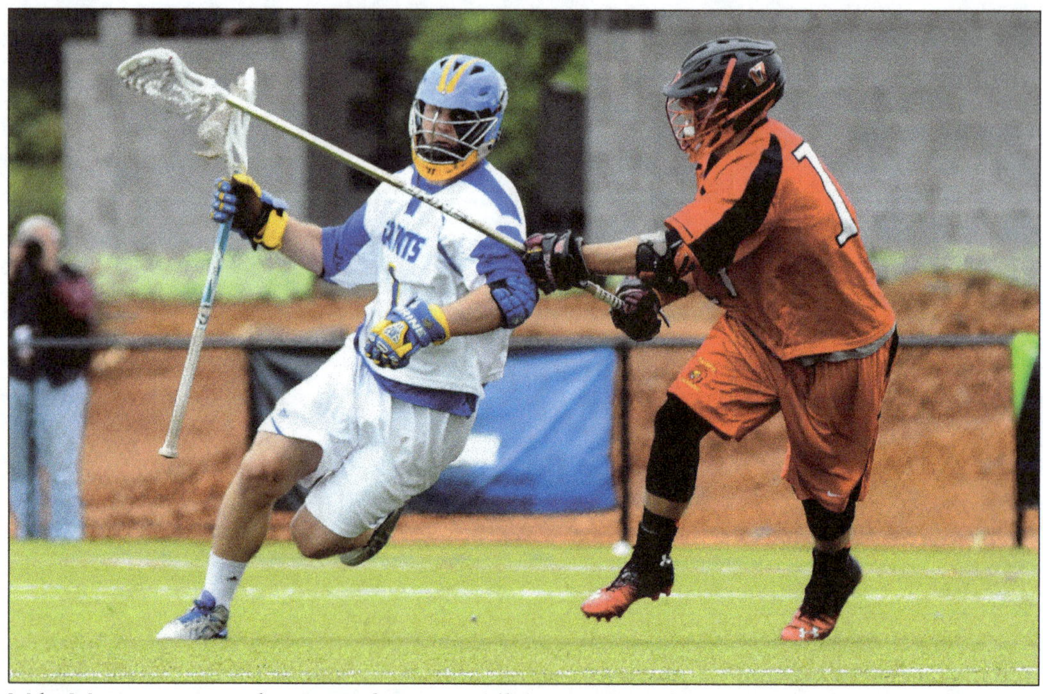

Mike Messenger was a three-time first-team All-American and a catalyst for the 2014 offense. He led all players with four goals in this NCAA national semifinal matchup against the University of Tampa Spartans as the Saints forged on to the national championship game against LIU Post. (Courtesy of Stacey Wylie.)

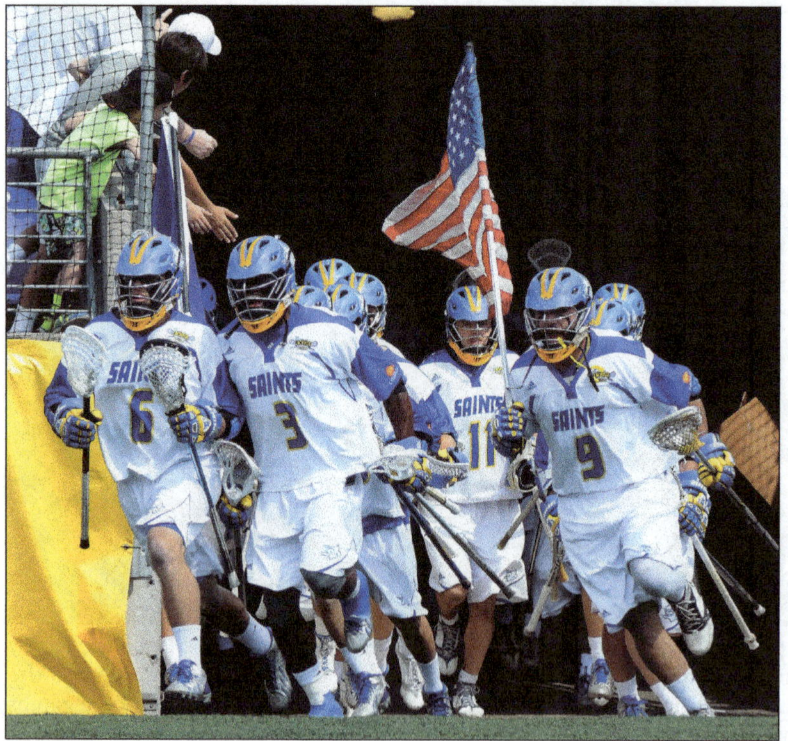

Joshua Williamson (No. 6), Jamar Peete (No. 3), and Glen Trovato (No. 9), all seniors, lead Limestone out of the tunnel at M&T Bank Stadium in Baltimore for the 2014 NCAA Division II national championship game. The No. 2 nationally ranked Saints doubled up No. 7 LIU Post by a 12-6 final tally to bring Limestone College lacrosse its third national title and first in 12 years. (Courtesy of Stacey Wylie.)

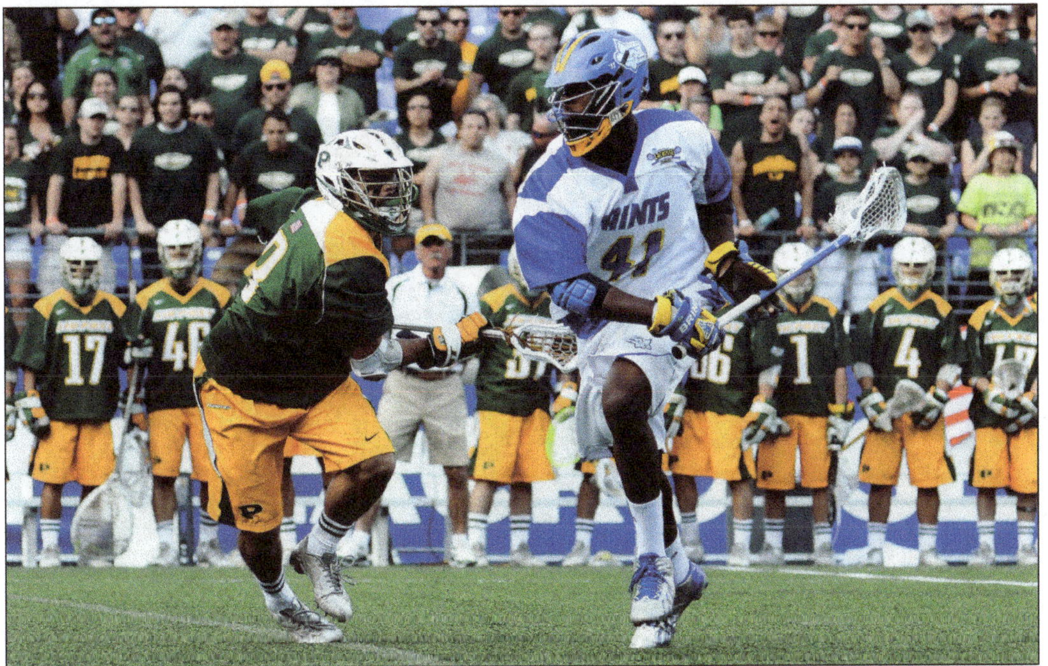

Before becoming an assistant coach for the Saints, Calyl Robinson proved his worth on the field as a member of the 2014 national championship team. Shown here in the title fight with LIU Post, Robinson notched a goal in the 12-6 victory. (Courtesy of Stacey Wylie.)

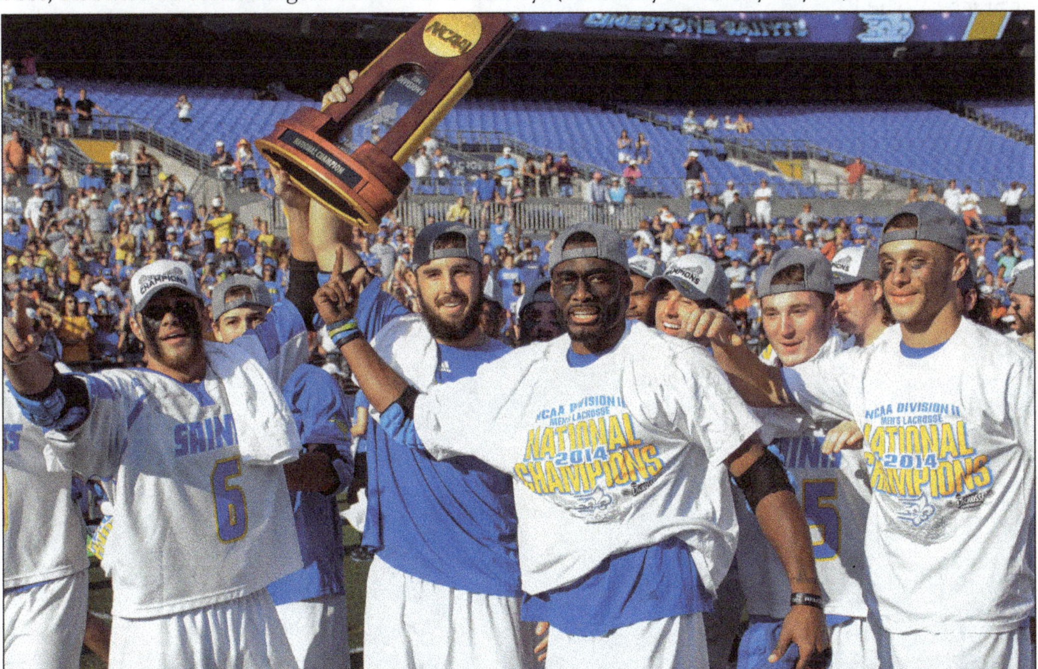

Members of the 2014 national championship team hoist the coveted NCAA trophy after knocking off LIU Post 12-6. Joshua Williams (far left) scored two goals in the win, but it was sophomore Vinny Ricci (not pictured) who fired in four scores and was named the game's Most Outstanding Player. (Courtesy of Stacey Wylie.)

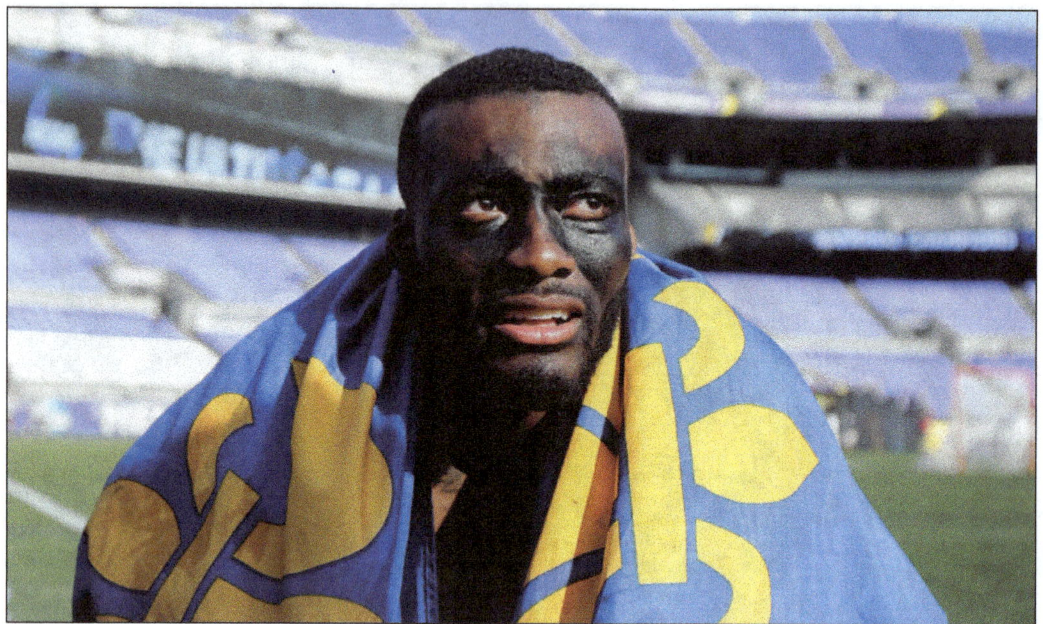

Adorned with a blue and gold Limestone College flag as a cape, Jamar Peete revels in his team's 2014 national championship season inside Baltimore's M&T Bank Stadium as many fans had already found the exits. Although this game marked the end of Peete's lacrosse career, he returned to Limestone in the fall as a member of the Saints' inaugural football team. (Courtesy of Stacey Wylie.)

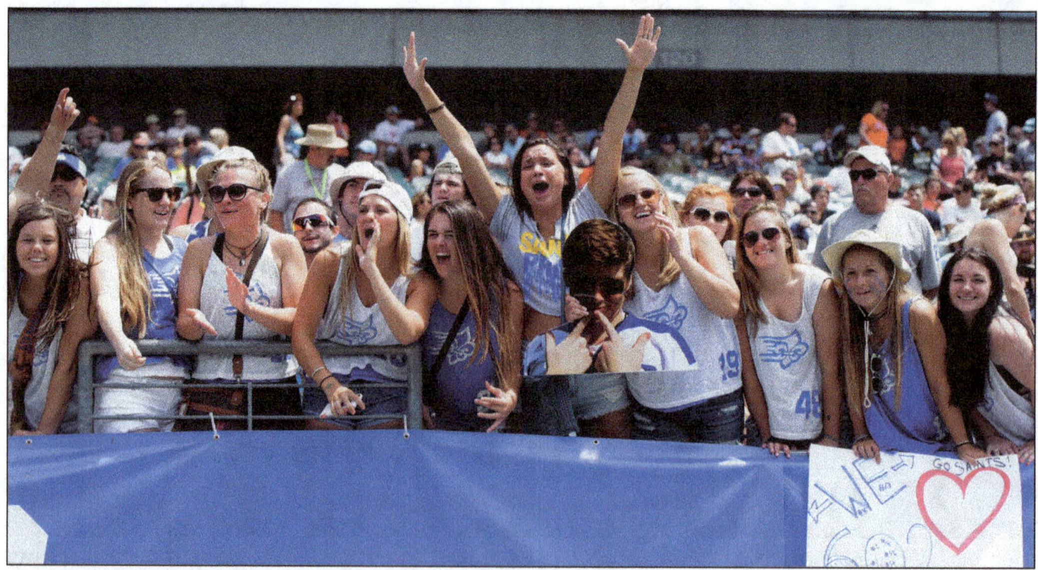

Devoted followers and close friends of the team, members of the Limestone College women's lacrosse team are seen here cheering on the Saints during the 2015 NCAA Division II national championship game at Lincoln Financial Field in Philadelphia. (Courtesy of Stacey Wylie.)

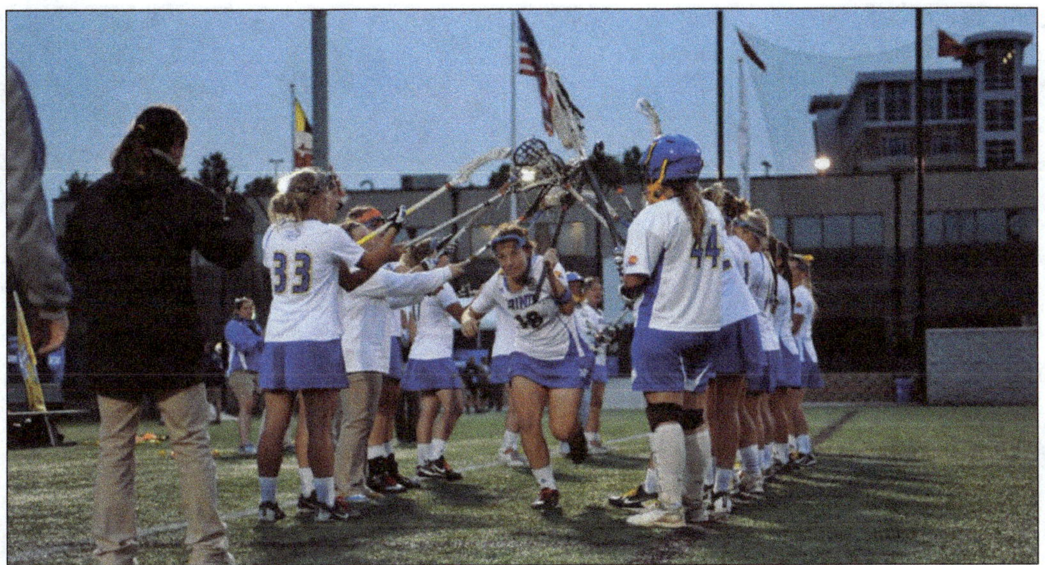

Led by Scott Tucker, the winningest active women's coach in NCAA Division II, the Limestone College women's lacrosse program has remained one of the nation's most successful. The men's and women's programs have supported each other tremendously and combine to make a remarkable duo. (Courtesy of Ernest Meyers.)

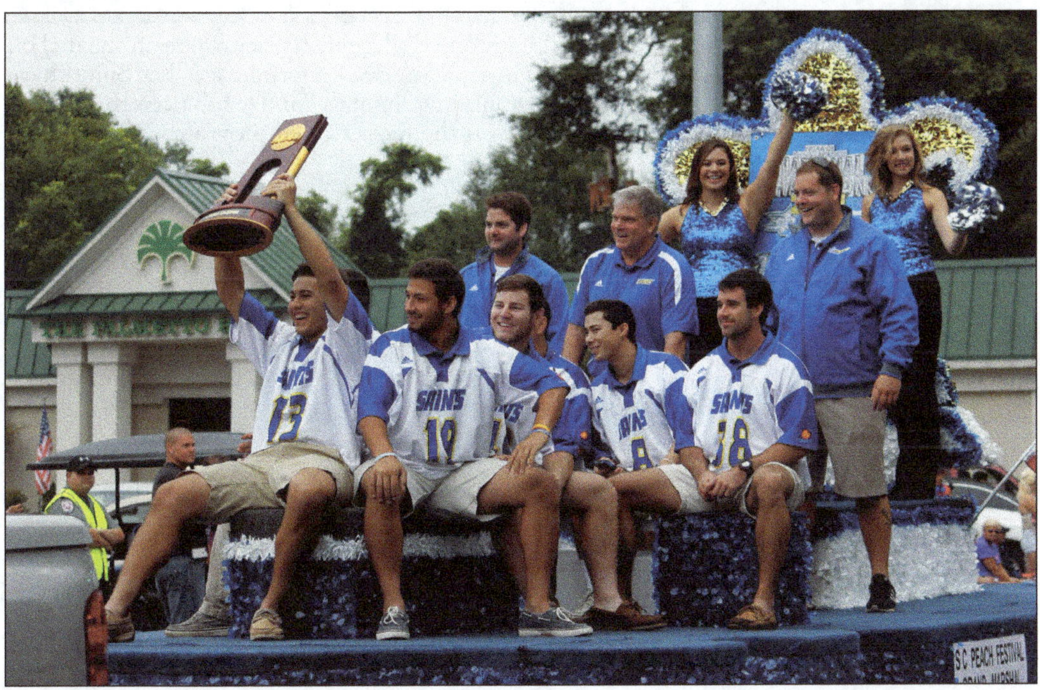

Players and coaches ride a float with members of the Limestone College spirit squad in the 2014 South Carolina Peach Festival parade. The team brought along the 2014 national championship trophy to show off to the crowd of onlookers as the float made its way through downtown Gaffney. (Courtesy of Joshua Darling.)

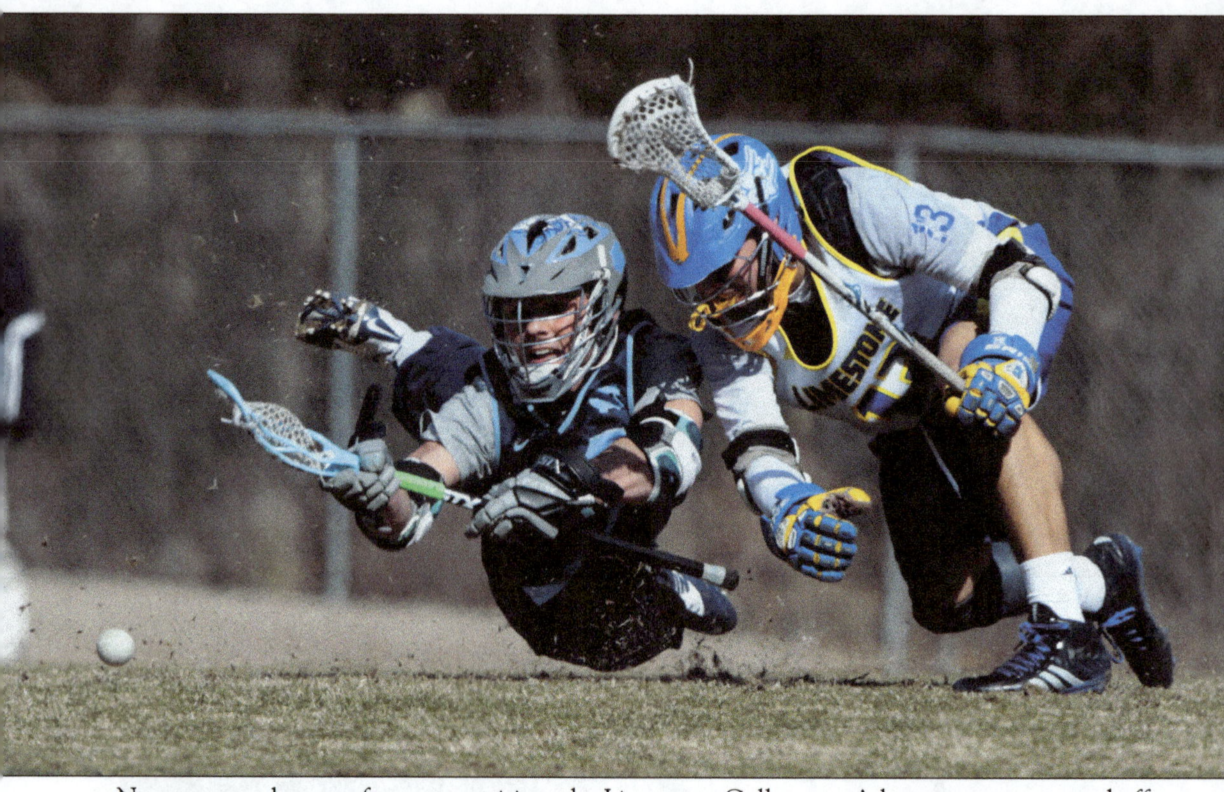

Never one to shy away from competition, the Limestone College men's lacrosse team squared off with the University of North Carolina Tar Heels in a 2015 preseason scrimmage. The Saints have faced off against several of the top Division I programs in scrimmages and exhibitions throughout the years and often prove to be a handful for even the most storied programs. (Courtesy of Reagan Lunn.)

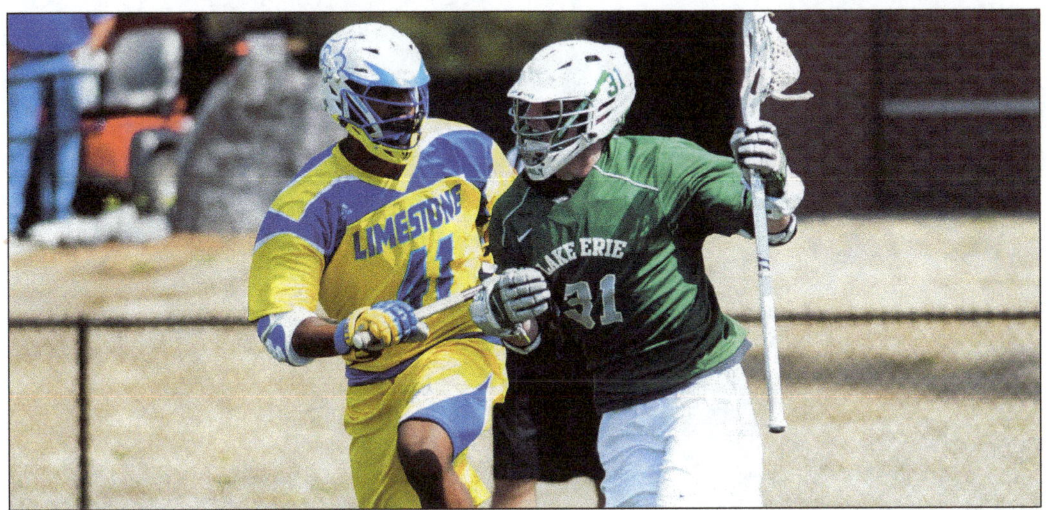

Limestone's yellow throwback uniforms made a brief appearance in 2015 but were quickly abandoned. They were worn during Limestone's only loss that season, a 14-12 setback to the No. 4-ranked Lake Erie College. The Saints would later avenge that loss with a 16-6 win over the Storm in the NCAA Division II semifinals. (Courtesy of Stacey Wylie.)

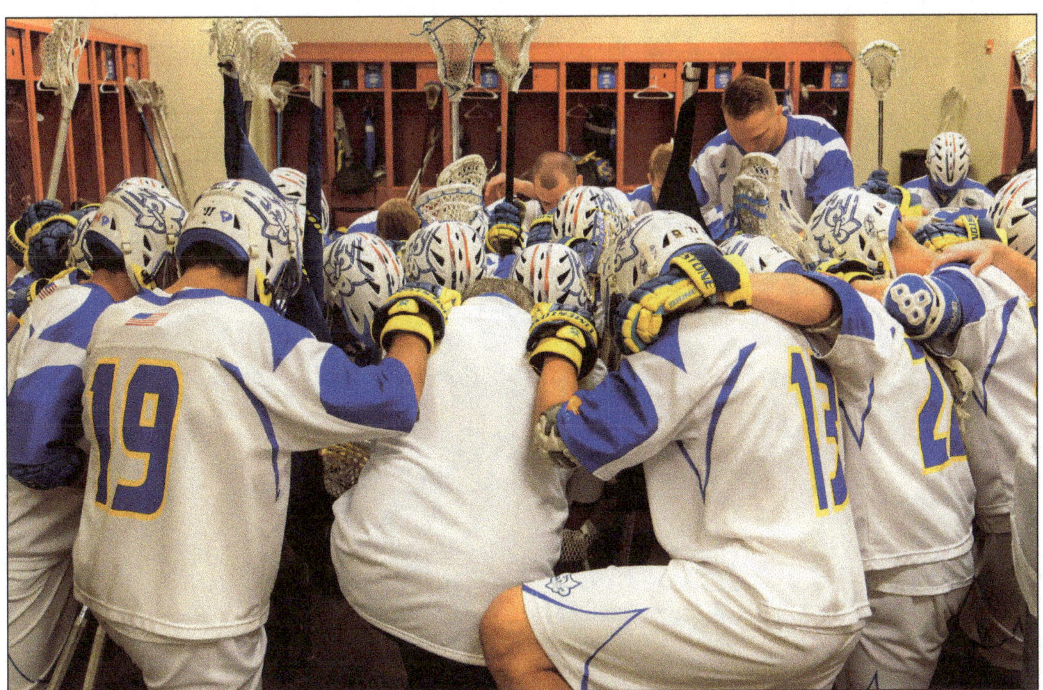

The Saints gather in the locker room before the 2015 national championship game for a moment of prayer and final words of encouragement before taking the field against Le Moyne College. (Courtesy of Stacey Wylie.)

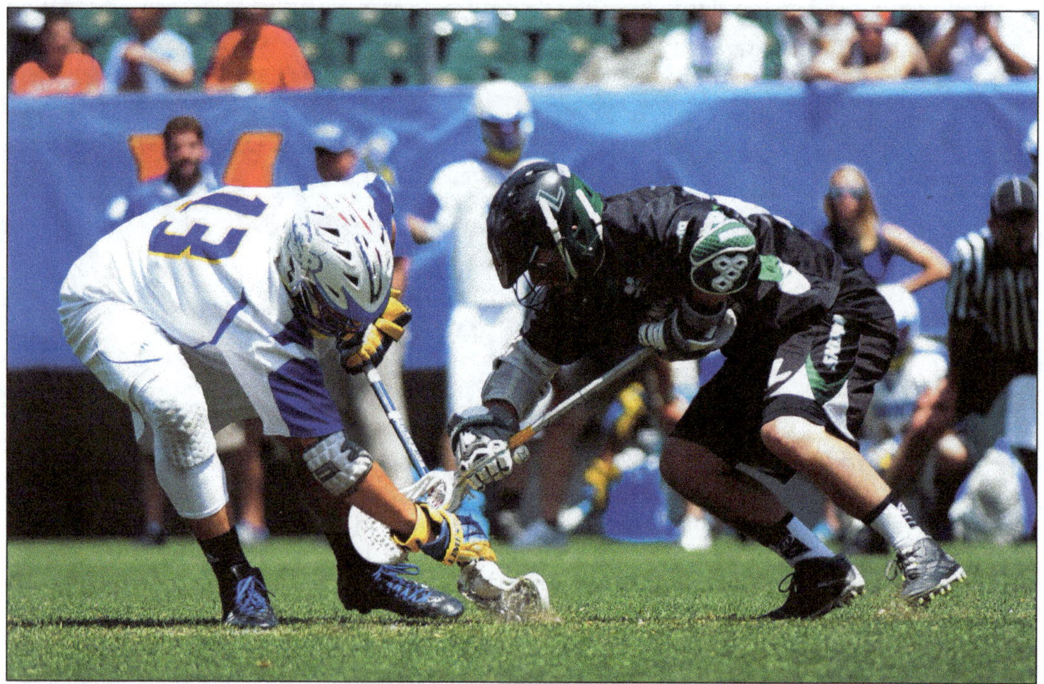

Limestone's Kevin Reisman (No. 13), the 2015 Lt. Raymond J. Enners award winner as the nation's top player, faces off against Le Moyne College to get the title game underway. (Courtesy of Stacey Wylie.)

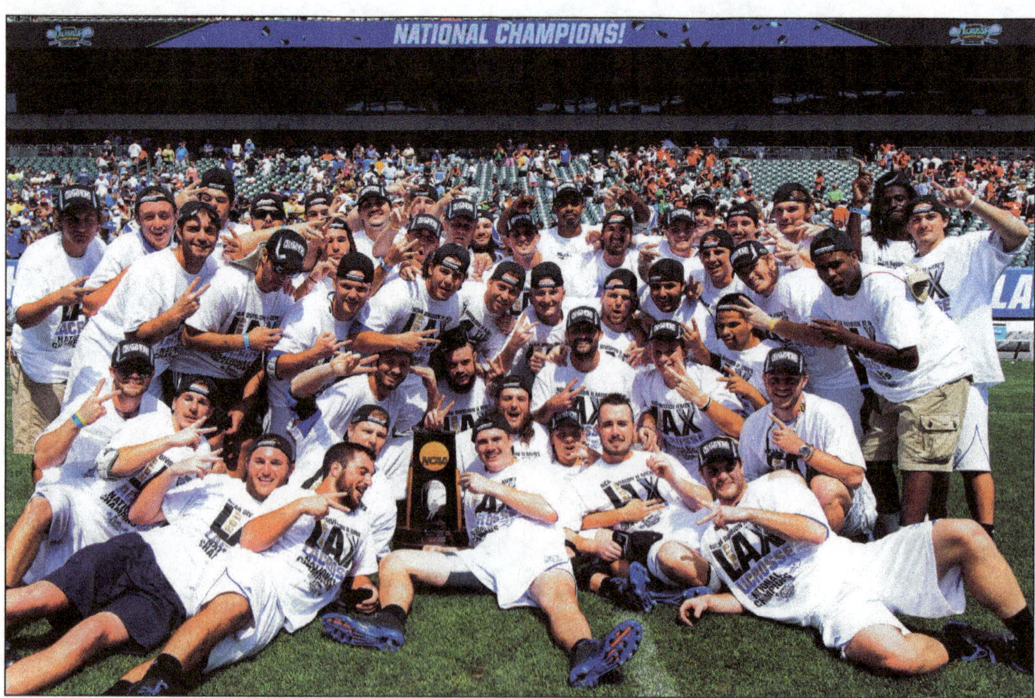

When the clock read all zeros, the Limestone Saints had wrapped up the program's fourth Division II title with a 9-6 heavyweight victory over the Dolphins. (Courtesy of Stacey Wylie.)

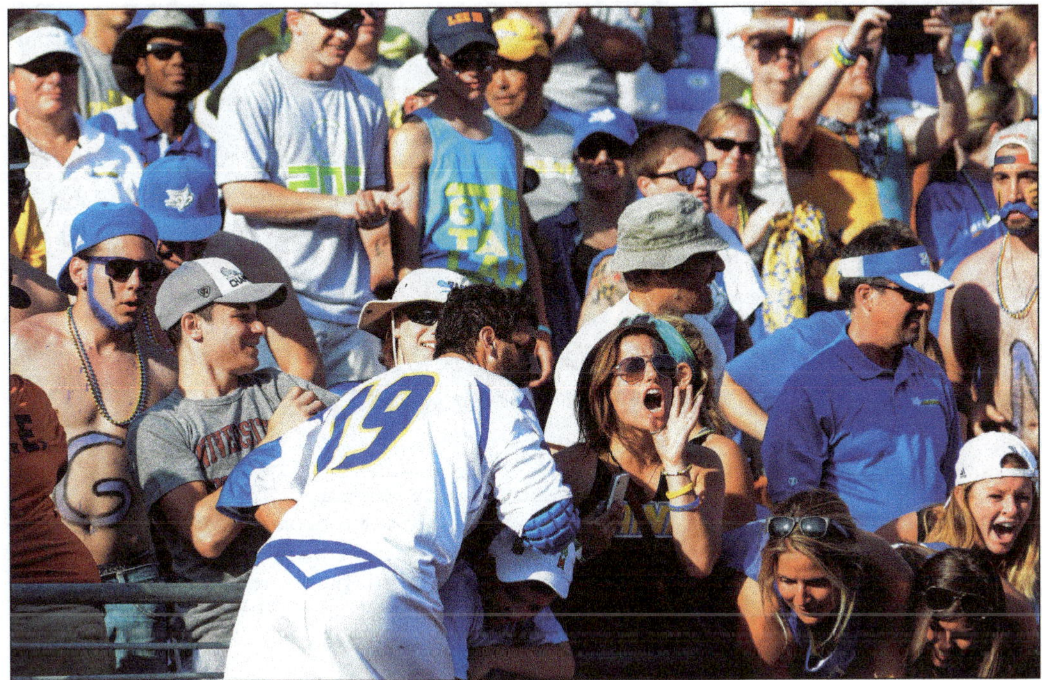

Anthony Quiles celebrates with fans at Philadelphia's Lincoln Financial Field after Limestone's 2015 title win over Le Moyne. One of a small number of South Carolina high school lacrosse players to see playing time for the Blue & Gold, Quiles has starred in three national championship games. (Courtesy of Stacey Wylie.)

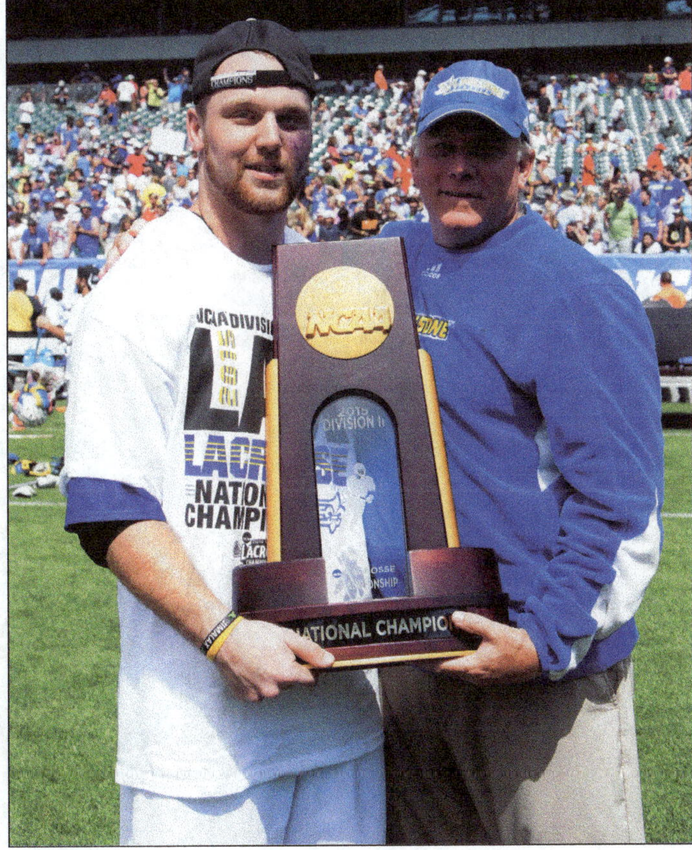

Mike Messenger (left), named the Most Outstanding Player at the 2015 national championship game, stands alongside head coach J.B. Clarke with the NCAA trophy. (Courtesy of Stacey Wylie.)

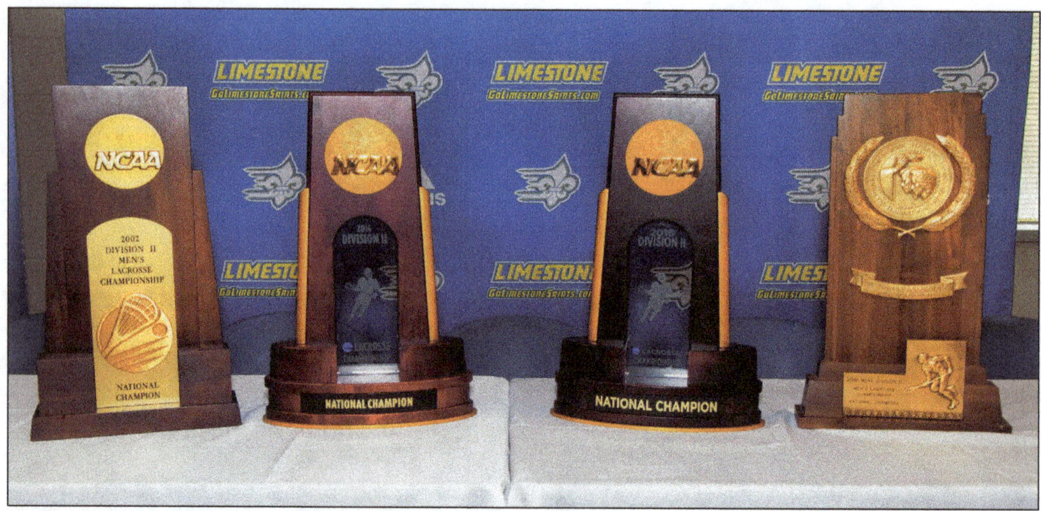

Limestone's four NCAA Division II national championship trophies were assembled for the first time in May 2015 when the school held a celebratory press conference on campus shortly after the Saints' 9-6 title victory over Le Moyne College. Today, this hardware is displayed alongside several other key Blue & Gold accomplishments in the Bob Campbell Field House, home to Limestone's outdoor sport programs. (Courtesy of Stacey Wylie.)

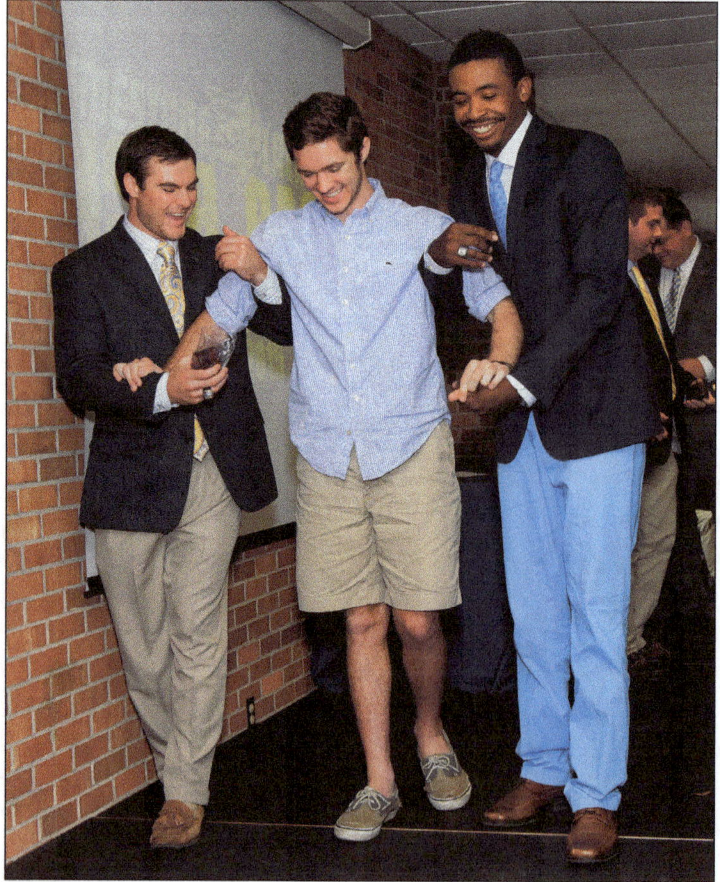

Chris Dill (left) and Calyl Robinson (right) assist Jack Enright in walking across stage to accept his honorary 2015 national championship ring. After suffering an injury during a high school lacrosse game and being given low odds to improve, Enright was "adopted" by the Saints and has continuously showed tremendous improvements on his road to recovery. (Courtesy of Stacey Wylie.)

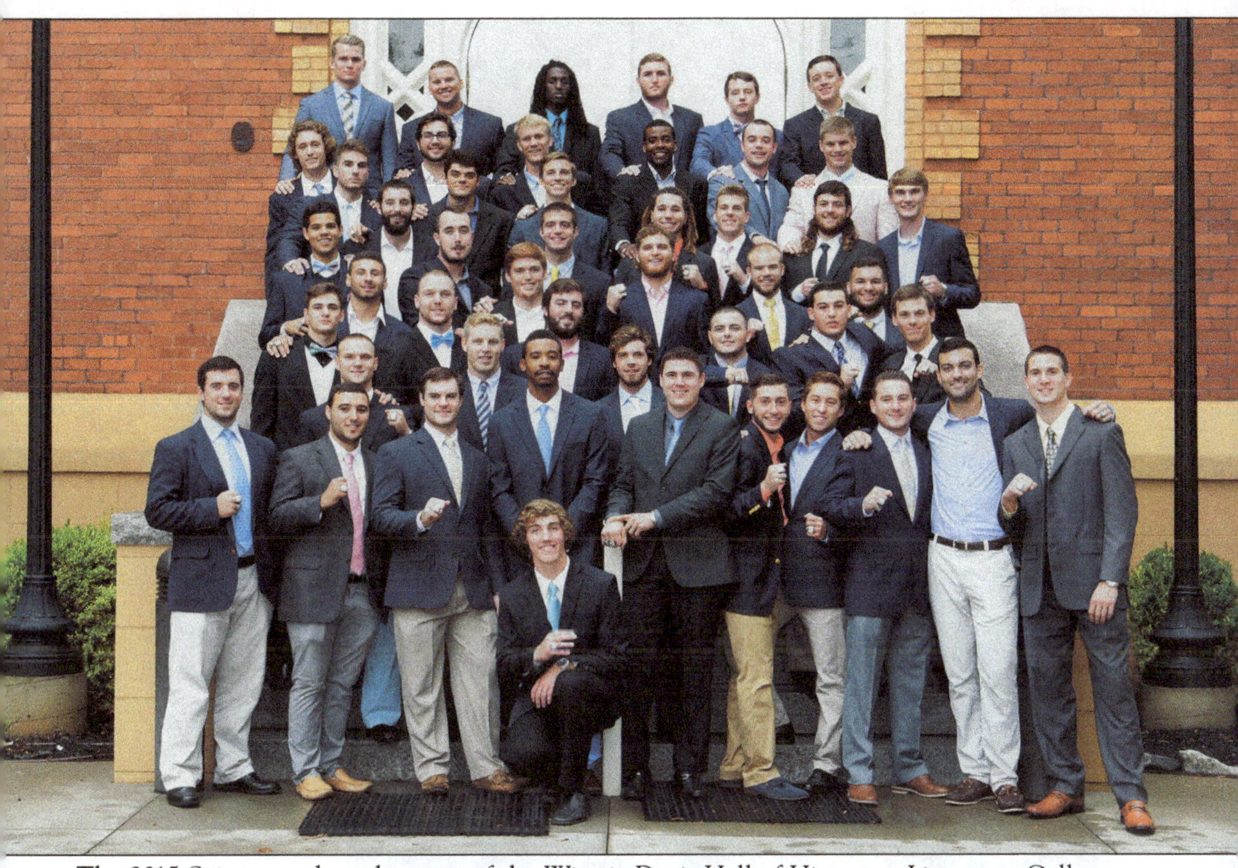

The 2015 Saints stand on the steps of the Winnie Davis Hall of History at Limestone College after receiving their NCAA national championship rings. (Courtesy of Stacey Wylie.)

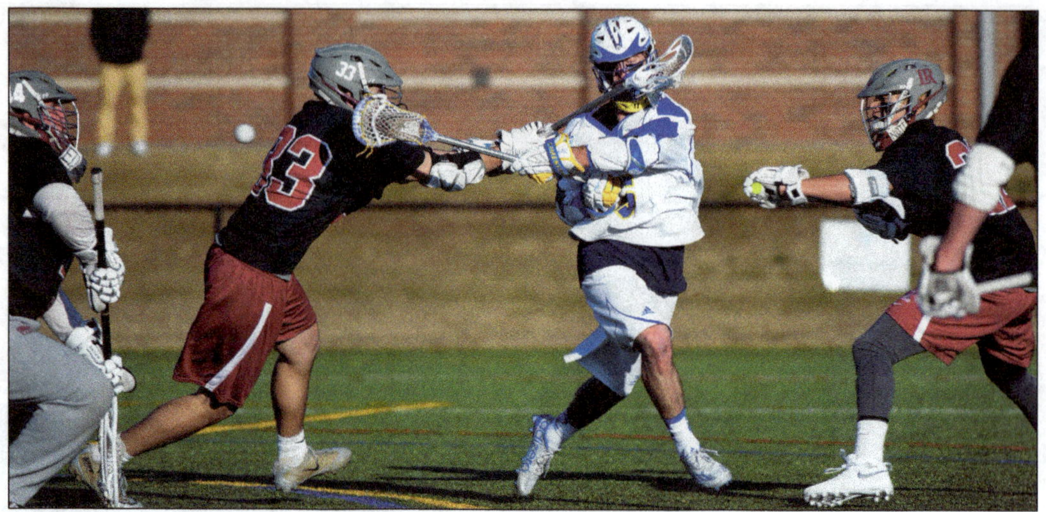

The home slate in 2016 opened up with the Lenoir-Rhyne Bears coming to Saints Field. Three different Saints scored four goals in a double-digit win in front of a packed house. (Courtesy of Stacey Wylie.)

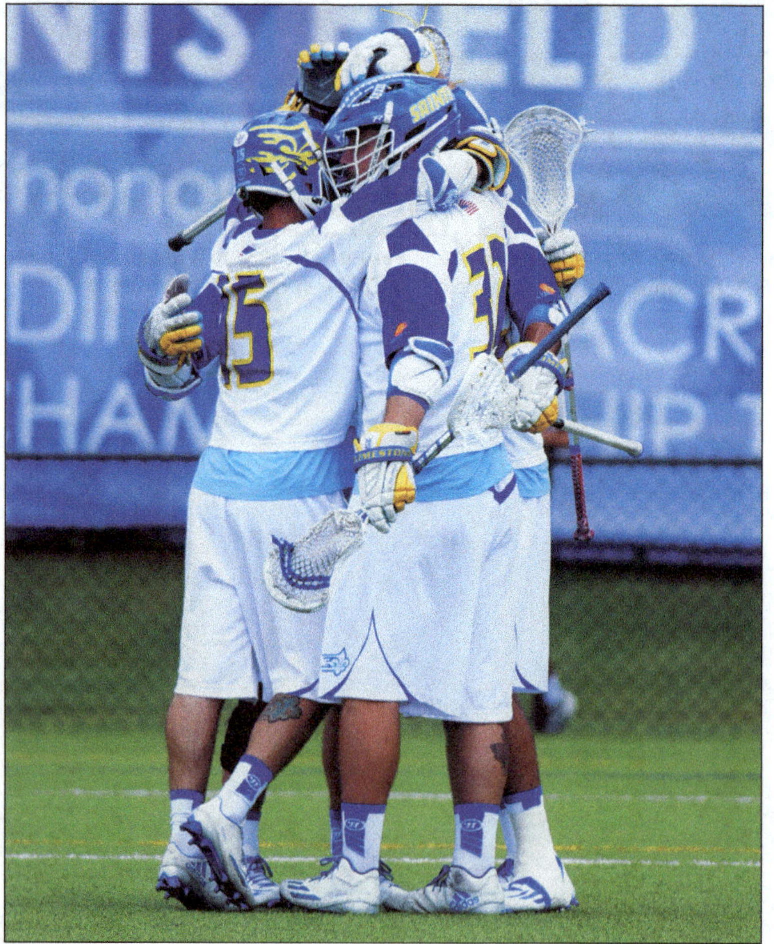

In a monstrous early season test in the spring of 2016, the top-ranked Saints collided with a highly touted University of Tampa team. The game did not live up to the hype, however, as Limestone put up goals early and often en route to a huge 25-7 win. (Courtesy of Stacey Wylie.)

Limestone went up 9-1 on the No. 4-ranked Spartans after one quarter and went on to a 25-7 victory, one of the most lopsided wins against a top-five opponent in NCAA Division II history. (Courtesy of Stacey Wylie.)

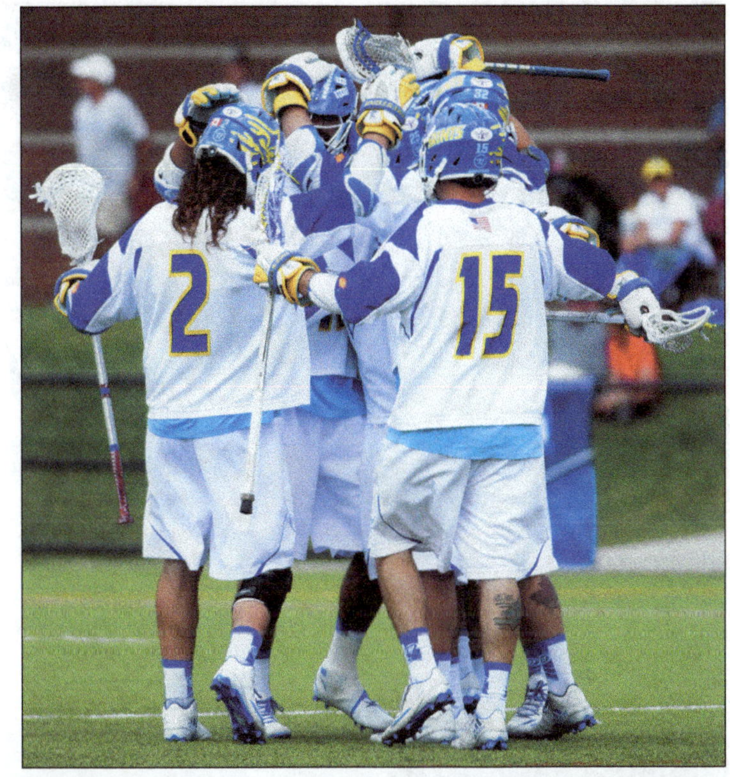

Led out by longtime friend of the program Officer Dave Richardson, Limestone enters Lincoln Financial Field in Philadelphia as the team prepares to do battle in its fourth national title game in five seasons. Since 2000, the Blue & Gold have appeared in 10 NCAA Division II national championship games, more than any other program. (Courtesy of Stacey Wylie.)

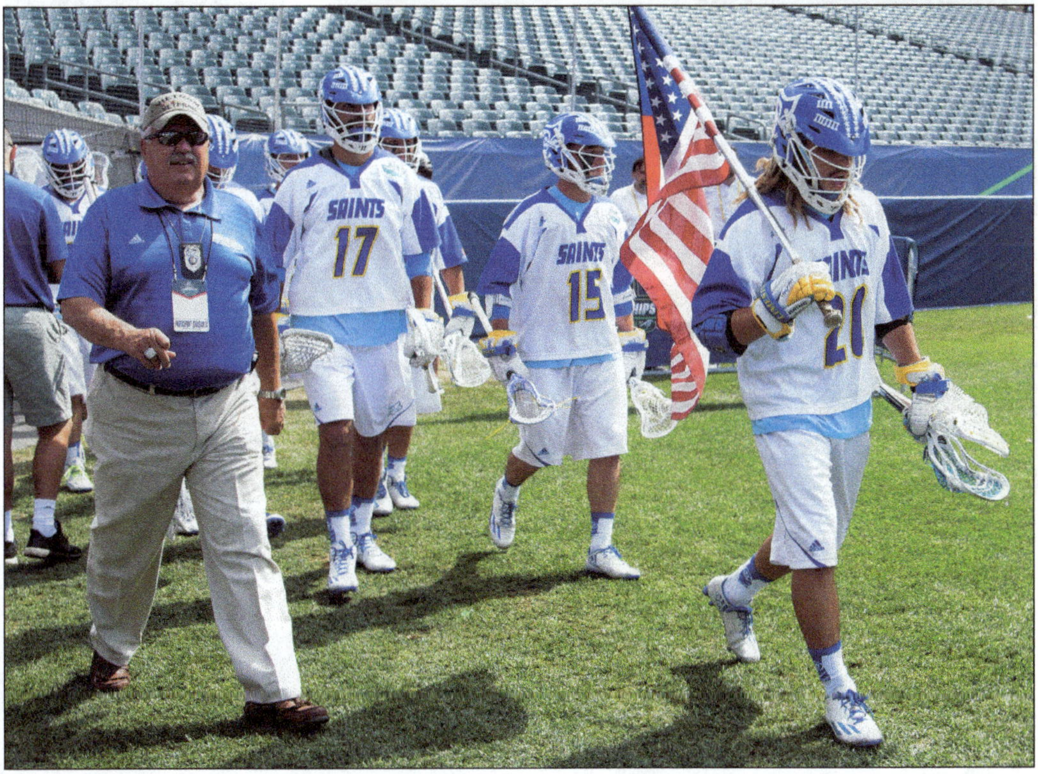

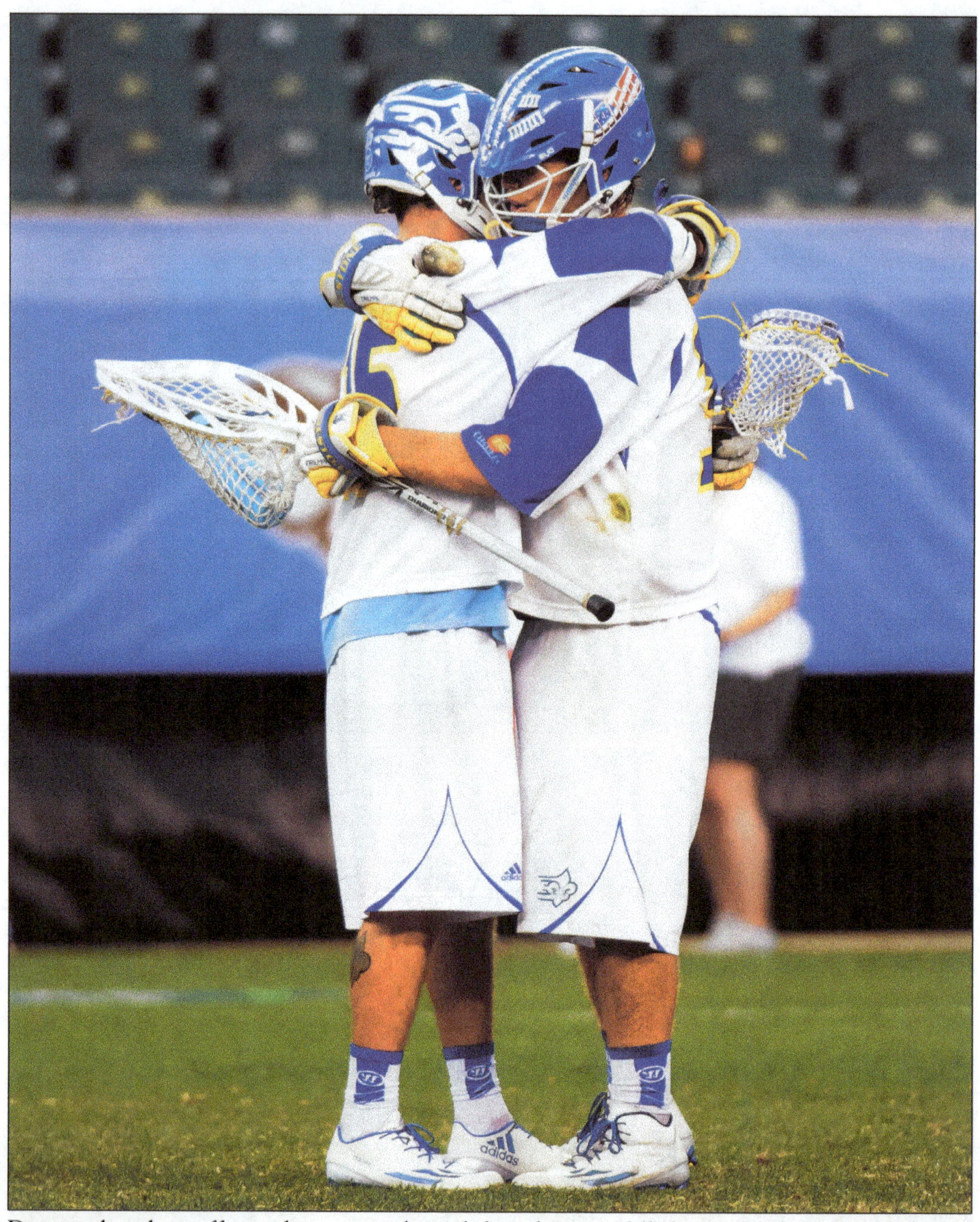

Despite their best efforts, the previously undefeated Saints fell short of a third national title. However, the 2016 senior class finished with a 76-5 overall record, including two NCAA Division II national championships. (Courtesy of Stacey Wylie.)

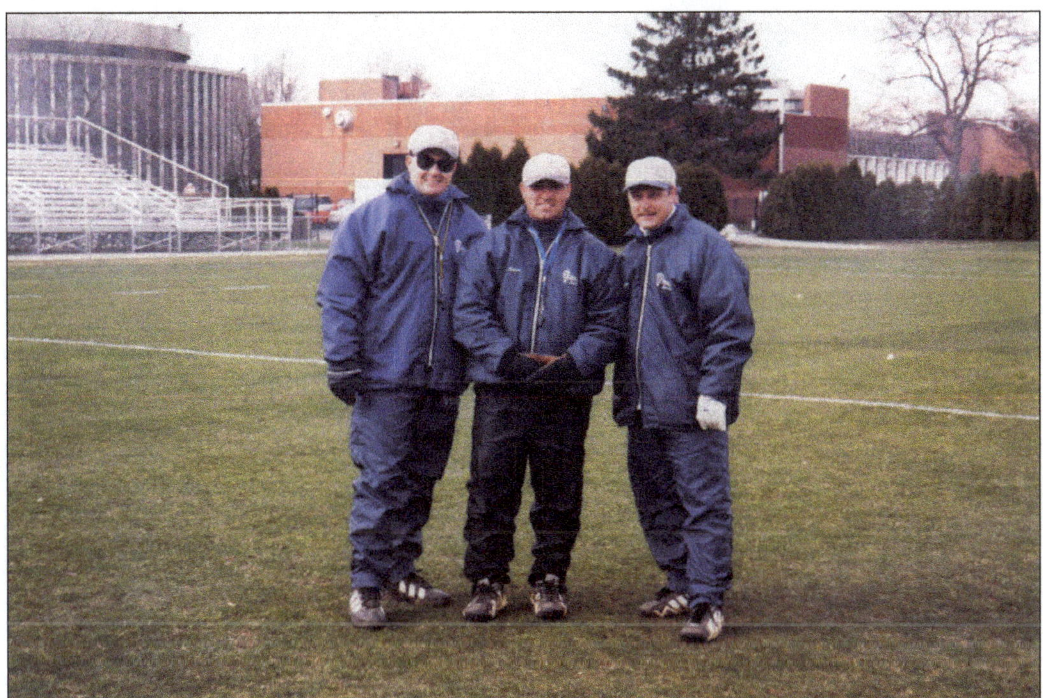

Pictured here from left to right, Mike Cerino, Mike Sessa, and Chris Phenicie each played a part in building the Limestone College men's lacrosse program since its inception.

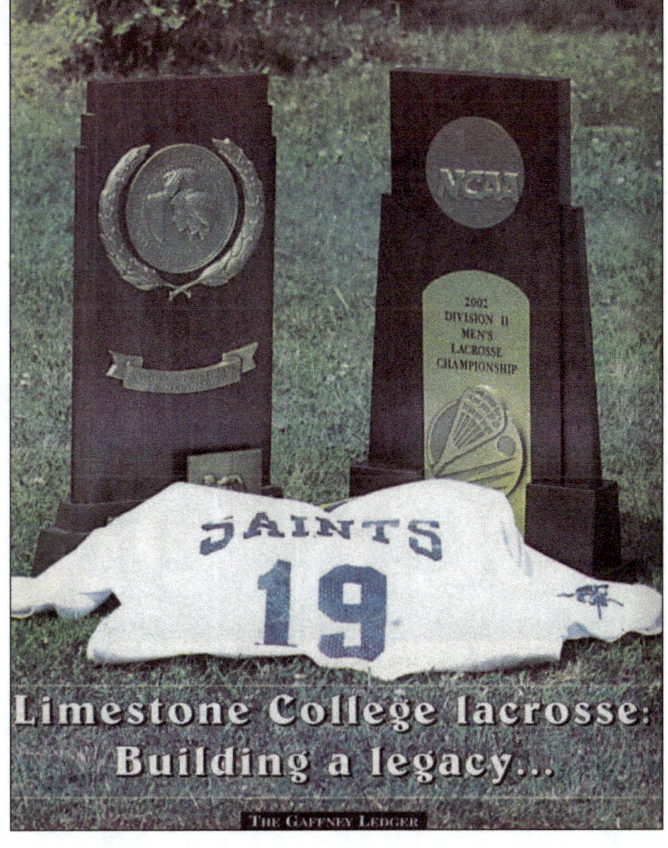

The "Limestone Legacy" has indeed been built throughout the history of the program, as this season preview edition of *The Gaffney Ledger* alludes to. One of the most prolific names in the sport, the Saints have established themselves as a dominant power throughout the country.

www.ingramcontent.com/pod-product-compliance
Lightning Source LLC
LaVergne TN
LVHW081339110826
845153LV00009B/208
* 9 7 8 1 5 4 0 2 1 4 2 7 0 *